D0983545

AUTHORITY AND REBELLION

The Case for Orthodoxy in the Catholic Church

AUTHORITY
AND
REBELLION

THE CASE FOR ORTHODOXY IN THE
CATHOLIC CHURCH

◆

CHARLES E. RICE

◆

GARDEN CITY, NEW YORK

DOUBLEDAY & COMPANY, INC.

1971

Nihil Obstat: Thomas Carroll, S.T.D., Censor
Deputatus Imprimatur: ✠ Leo A. Pursley, D.D.,
LL.D., Bishop of Fort Wayne-South Bend Octo-
ber 19, 1970

Grateful acknowledgment is made to the following for the use of their material,
which is reprinted with their permission:

Barron's for quotes from an editorial September 11, 1967 issue; Chicago Sun
Times for quotes from March 3, 1970 issue, reprinted with permission: Chicago
Tribune for material from issues January 1, 1967, July 19, 1969, November 7,
1969, and June 2, 1970, and an editorial February 2, 1970, which is reprinted
courtesy of the Chicago Tribune; Church League of America, 422 N. Prospect
Street, Wheaton, Illinois 60187 for quotes from May 1969 issue of News &
Views; The Critic, 180 N. Wabash Avenue, Chicago, Illinois 60601 for quotes
from December 1966–January 1967 and December 1967–January 1968 issues;
Crossroads, Holy Cross College for quotes from October 1969, April 1970 issues;
Doubleday & Company for excerpts from The Idea of a University by John
Henry Cardinal Newman; The Ram, Fordham University for quotes from April
11, 1968 issues; Fordham University Press for excerpts from Margaret Clitherow
(1556?–1586) by Mary Claridge (New York, 1966); Belknap Press of Harvard
University Press for permission to quote from Miller & Wright, eds., Ecumenical
Dialogue at Harvard; Houston Tribune for quotes from October 30, 1969 and
December 11, 1969 issues; Long Island Catholic for quotes from December 29,
1966 and June 12, 1969 issues; L'Osservatore Romano, English Edition, Vatican
City for various quotations; The Medical-Moral Newsletter, September 1968,
for quotes by Dr. Frank Ayd; Germain Grisez for material from the article
"Academic Freedom and Catholic Faith," as reprinted from the November 1967
issue of the Bulletin, journal of the National Catholic Educational Association,
Suite 350, One Dupont Circle, Washington, D.C. 20036; The National Catholic
Reporter for quotes from May 29, 1968 and August 21, 1968 issues; New
York Times © 1965/66/67/68/69/70 by the New York Times Company, re-
printed by permission; Doubleday & Company for quotes from Catholic Educa-
tion Faces Its Future by the Reverend Neil G. McCluskey, S.J.; Our Sunday
Visitor for quotes from July 24, 1966, April 12, 1970, April 19, 1970, June 7,
1970, July 26, 1970 issues; South Bend Tribune for quotes from July 31, 1969,
October 17, 1969, December 11, 1969, May 10, 1970 issues; The Catholic
Standard and Times for quotes from October 10, 1968 issue; The Tablet for
quotes from January 9, 1964 issue; Triumph, 927 15th Street N.W., Washington,
D.C. 20005, for excerpts from September 1969, March 1970, and May 1970
issues; Twin Circle for quotes from September 7, 1970 issue; The Wanderer for
various quotations; Dr. Rhoda Lorand and Mrs. A. G. Weiner for permission
to quote from a letter from Dr. Lorand to Mrs. Weiner; The Philadelphia Inquirer for quotes from October 11, 1969 issue; University of Notre Dame Press
for quotes from The Catholic University, A Modern Appraisal by the Reverend
Neil G. McCluskey, S.J., ed.; Christian Book Club of America for quotes from
Lord of the World by Robert Hugh Benson; Look Magazine for excerpts from
"Bensalem" by Isabella Taves, which is reprinted by permission of the editors
from the May 19, 1970 issue of Look Magazine, copyright 1970 by Cowles
Communication, Inc.

I am grateful, for their comments and criticisms of the manuscript, to the Reverend Raymond J. H. Kennedy, S.J., the Reverend John C. Ford, S.J., and the Reverend Thomas Carroll, S.T.D.; to L. Brent Bozell, Professor Germain Grisez, and Sister Maria Martin, I.H.M., for their comments on the concept and organization of the book; to Miss Elizabeth Bartelme for her editorial assistance; to my mother, Mrs. Mary C. Rice, for her suggestions on the manuscript and, indispensably, to my wife, Mary, for her patience and general assistance.

Also, I acknowledge my indebtedness to Mrs. Catherine Wilmering, Mrs. John Ellsworth, Mrs. Michael Suchy, and Mrs. Agnes Ciaffone for their help in typing the manuscript; to Mrs. John Murphy for her aid in typing the manuscript and in handling the general processing of the manuscript; and to Mrs. Bette Groves, Mrs. Vincent Ginestre, and Miss Amanda Gunn for their clerical assistance.

To Mary and our children,
John Laurence, Mary Frances,
Anne Patricia, Joseph Patrick,
Charles Peter, Jeanne Elizabeth,
Theresa Helen, and Kathleen Bernadette

CONTENTS

CONTENTS

I.

DISORDER IN THE RANKS

Five years ago he was a mild-mannered, clean-shaven young priest who made headlines by publicly asking Pope Paul VI to dismiss the then 78-year-old James Francis Cardinal McIntyre as archbishop of Los Angeles.

Today, still mild-mannered, he's a bearded mountain dweller in brown corduroys, pink shirt and clodhopper work shoes, married to a divorcee with four children. The couple expect their own child in October.

Five years ago he was Rev. William H. DuBay. Today he says, "Call me Bill."[1]

Father DuBay, or Bill, supports himself by appearing on the college lecture circuit and by managing a drive-in theater. His only regret is "that I didn't leave a lot earlier. I don't go to Mass. I don't consider myself a believer any more. I'm more of an atheist than anything right now. Or at least an agnostic."

Mr. DuBay's original complaint was that Cardinal McIntyre "has failed to exercise moral leadership among the white Catholics of this diocese on racial discrimination," and "has conducted a vicious program of intimidation and repression against priests, seminarians and the laity who have tried to reach the consciences of white Catholics in his archdiocese." His opposition ultimately resulted in his suspension from the priesthood. One of his projects before his suspension was the American Federation of Priests, which he founded as a labor union. "We priests must beware of the danger of company unionism," he declared.[2]

The Church will survive the defection of Father DuBay. He will pass into obscurity like others over the centuries who have rebelled to leave the Church and the priesthood. We may regard his case as pathetic and he surely has a claim on our charity and prayers. It is unfortunately true, however, that each case of this sort inflicts a wound on the Church. And each defecting shepherd can lead members of his flock astray as he talks his way further into the mist. Nor is this potential for confusion limited to priests who have left the Church. Father DuBay frankly severed his ties. Others, equally aberrant in doctrine or discipline, have declined to do so.

On July 3, 1969, J. P. Shannon, describing himself as a "salesman," took out a marriage license in Auburn, New York, with a thrice-married Protestant divorcee.[3] Mr. Shannon was, of course, Bishop James P. Shannon, who had resigned a short time before as Auxiliary Bishop of the Archdiocese of St. Paul-Minneapolis on account of his disagreement with Pope Paul's encyclical on birth control. Bishop Shannon, in the words of the New York *Times*, "was regarded as a leading force for reform among the Catholic bishops." Between the time of his resignation and his marriage, many Catholic newspapers and journals, several bishops, professors at Catholic colleges, the National Federation of Priests' Councils, and the National Association of Laymen urged that the bishop retain a leadership position in the American hierarchy. Bishop Shannon, however, protested that he could not in conscience continue to serve as a bishop.

The defection of Bishop Shannon is but one among many, although he is the only bishop in the United States to leave the fold. It ought not to be assumed, however, that the crisis is solely one of leadership. It is true that the disloyalty has germinated primarily among the clergy and religious. But the laity, too, are alienated in significant numbers from the Church and from her teaching authority. When Pope Paul issued *Humanae Vitae*, his encyclical on contraception, many lay organizations demurred. The Los Angeles Association of Laymen, for instance, met and resolved: "We simply reject Pope Paul's ban on birth control. No decision—even of the Pope—can change the fact that birth control is not bad." But, having rejected the Papal edict, the members just as strongly insisted on their right to stay in the Church: "We will not leave the Church; we will not be thrown out. We are Catholics," they avowed, "and nothing but our conscience's decision can alter that."[4]

What are we to learn from these cases? To say that respect for authority is declining in the Church, as everywhere, is to offer nothing new. But, in terms of the relation between clergy and laity, it is also a crisis of confidence. The leading architects of the disorder have been those, bishops, priests, and religious, to whom the laity are entitled to look for guidance. Numerically the rebellious voices are those of a distinct minority. But their influence is amplified out of proportion by the Catholic and secular press alike.

In some cases, clerics who dispute the Pope or bishops on points of doctrine or discipline, seem to be masking a more basic erosion of their own belief. Often, when a Father DuBay proclaims himself a champion of freedom against the repressive hierarchy, his posturing is a prelude to his exit from the Church itself. More frequently, as in Bishop Shannon's case, the spoken grievance is a disagreement with *Humanae Vitae* or some other teaching of the Church. The real difficulty, however, appears to be a simple loss of faith. Or, more precisely, it is perhaps a loss of simple faith. Father DuBay candidly declared himself out of the Church, as did Father Charles Davis, the noted English theologian, now married and a teacher at the University of Edmonton in Canada.[5] But Bishop Shannon, on the other hand, said, "I do not intend to leave the Catholic Church."[6] As one priest commented on the Shannon affair:

> The former Bishop made no effort to get married in the Church. He did not even bother to avoid excommunication by not getting "married" before a minister of another denomination. His faith seems to have died completely.
> With all of his education in the Church, with all the honors and responsibilities he had heaped upon him, how can he live in a state of mortal sin by cohabiting with someone to whom he so obviously is not married? Pray for him and his repentance.[7]

Whether their challenge arises from a lack of faith or some other cause, the recalcitrants have engendered a polarization in the Church, importing into it an oversimplified division between liberal and conservative. This division has only a limited application to the Church and is more appropriate to the political sphere.

There are Catholic liberals and Catholic conservatives, as can be seen from any election campaign or public controversy. But this is not the same as a liberal Catholic or a conservative Catholic. You and I may disagree about the grape strike or the antiballistic missile system without compromising our Catholicity. But when doctrine is at issue, only one view is permissible to the extent that the question has been defined by the Church. Here it would be preferable to speak of orthodox and unorthodox rather than conservative and liberal. The latter terms are sometimes useful in an informal, shorthand way to describe a person's attitude toward the Church. But, to avoid confusion, this designation should be used sparingly and not in any way which would imply that contradictory positions can be legitimate on matters of dogma. For if one denies, for example, the reality of the Resurrection, he is not merely articulating a tolerably liberal view. He is unorthodox and a heretic. Similar considerations apply to the authentic, though not infallibly defined, teachings of the Church, as will be discussed in Chapter IV. In either case, the implication that contrary views on basic issues are as acceptable in the Church as they are in civil society, contributes to an improper division of Catholics into parties within the Church. As John Cardinal Wright observed, "we have a solemn obligation to put an end to this polarization."[8] But this condition will continue as long as the notion is tolerated that the teaching authority of the Pope, and of the bishops in communion with him, can be contested on an equal level by laymen, theologians, and even dissident bishops. This is not to say that there is no room for discussion or that everything on which the Pope or bishops utter the slightest word is settled forever. Far from it. But there are matters on which the proper authority has voiced the authentic teaching or discipline of the Church and thus of Christ. Contraception is only one example. On these points the Catholic owes a generous and orthodox adherence to the will of Christ as proclaimed by His Church. Indeed, the Catholic ought to go beyond that and should be ready always to give the teaching Church the clear benefit of the doubt even when the wisdom of its course is not clear to him. Nor should he confuse the voice of the teaching Church with the speculations of theologians. The layman owes his allegiance to the authentic teaching authority, to the Pope supremely and to the bishops when they speak in communion with him. To the theologian he owes due respect as a scholar but not allegiance as a teacher. For theologians are not by their calling vested with the teaching authority of the Church.

"The fundamental temptation of modern man," said Jean Cardinal Daniélou, is the belief "that man does not fully become man unless he is able to do without God, just as the child becomes an adult only when he is able to do without his parents and be responsible for himself."[9] It is the mission of the Church to show man that he can be emancipated only through God rather than without Him. Her course has been charted by the Second Vatican Council and the Holy Father. But the Church is weakened by abdication and rebellion in her ranks, particularly on the intermediate level. Thus hampered, the Church has not effectively countered the atheism and existentialism that grip the world. "The essential problem today," observed Cardinal Daniélou, "lies not in the forces that we have to confront from without. The danger is from within. The danger lies in allowing our faith, the institution, and interiority to become decomposed. The danger lies in disputes that would question the important articles of faith, from the virginal conception to the bodily resurrection of Christ. It lies in the basic issue of the ecclesial institution, of the authority and infallibility of the Sovereign Pontiff, of the value of the sacrament as constituting the vital milieu in which Christian experience grows. And when Christians, and even ecclesiastics, smile somewhat disdainfully when we speak of the Profession of Faith of Paul VI, this would scandalize us were it not a proof of infantilism. Where is the framework of the instruction we must give children, if not in Paul VI's profession of faith?"[10]

The disparagement of Pope Paul's *Credo* is symbolic of the underlying erosion of faith. It cannot be the purpose of this book to analyze the crisis of faith, as others have done so well.[11] Instead we shall focus here on a more limited issue—the failure of obedience and the general disregard for authority in the Church. Obedience follows upon faith. But if respect for authority can be restored on specific matters such as birth control and the liturgy, that restoration in turn may help to enliven the more basic faith itself. And if respect for authority is not restored in the Church, it will hardly be restored elsewhere. With the Church paralyzed by recalcitrance in her ranks, men will look to her in vain for the firm guidance she ought to provide. This guidance is particularly needed today. Recent studies confirm that religious apathy is on the rise generally in American society and within the churches as well.[12] The Gallup Poll in 1970 found that three out of every four Americans believe religion is losing its influence on American life. This is a new high.[13] The change in the public's view has been accompanied by a decline in church-going. Church attendance by adults declined steadily from 1958 through 1969. The fall-off was nearly twice as great among Catholics as among Protestants. The Catholic decline was from seventy-four percent adult attendance in 1958 to sixty-three percent in 1969. The Protestant drop was from forty-three percent in 1958 to thirty-seven percent in 1969. Among all religions, the greatest decrease was among young adults aged twenty-one through twenty-nine.[14]

The 1970 Official Catholic Directory reports that the number of Catholics in the United States fell in 1969 for the first time since 1900. The directory reported 47,872,089 Catholics in this country at the end of 1969. This is a numerical decrease of 1149 from the end of 1968 and a proportional decrease in the percentage of Catholics in the nation's population. Catholics are now 23.5 percent of the total population of 203,616,268. At the end of 1969, there were 37,272 diocesan priests, a decrease of 182 from the 1968 total; 21,920 priests of religous orders, a loss of 246; 11,623 religious brothers, a decline of 132; and 160,931 nuns, a loss of 6236. There were 28,819 seminarians, at all levels, or 5171 fewer than the year before.

The most significant statistic, perhaps, is that converts decreased from 102,865 to 92,670, a decline of ten percent. Infant baptisms fell by 8314 to 1,086,858, while marriages rose more than 11,000 to a total of 417,271 during the year. There were 292 Catholic colleges and universities, or five fewer than the previous year. Enrollment in them decreased by 4853 students to 430,863. There were 1265 diocesan and parochial high schools, a drop of 69; pupils in them declined from 693,270 to 667,408. There were 817 private Catholic high schools, or thirty fewer, with 34,747 fewer students for a total of 387,234. Parochial and institutional elementary schools declined by 449 to 9601, and their enrollment dropped by 247,598 to 3,598,-096. There were 346 private elementary schools, or ten fewer than before, with 67,280 pupils, or 4945 fewer. The decline in full-time pupils in the 12,029 Catholic elementary and high schools was 6.2 percent in one year and 10.2 percent over the preceding two years. Released-time high school students receiving confraternity instruction fell by 93,824 to 1,368,817, while elementary pupils on released time rose by 86,237 to 4,081,929. This last increase probably reflects the drop in enrollment in full-time Catholic elementary schools formerly attended by those confraternity pupils. As one paper commented, the official Catholic Directory, which has almost seventeen hundred pages and weighs more than six pounds, is almost the only thing in American Catholicism that remained as big as the year before.[15]

Bishop Fulton J. Sheen described this drop in Catholic population as "the Good Lord cleaning house . . . the Lord is reducing quantity for quality . . . those that are leaving the Church, none are leaving to become more holy."[16] There is some truth in what he says, but we cannot dismiss these figures out of hand. Statistics can be misleading, but the numerical decline indicates that the liberal or permissive approach to Catholicism does not work even by its own criteria. In the past decade the religion has been made easier, the liturgy, particularly in its English translation, has been drained of its beauty and the clear lines of duty and belief have been obscured by misleading clerics and nuns. Yet the process has not made religion more relevant. If anything, it has made it irrelevant, certainly to those who have left the Church. Who can say that children are better instructed in the Faith today, that confessions are more numerous, that Mass is better attended even by the young for whose captivation an escalating series of changes are made, that Catholic colleges are more Catholic or even more educational, or that the truths of the Faith are more effectively applied in personal and social life? Something is wrong, and it is not with the Pope. Significantly, the Catholic Church in Holland, generally conceded to be the most radical in its flight from orthodoxy, has been experiencing a similar numerical decline in members, clergy, and religious.[17]

It is fair to ascribe this decline of the Church at least in part to the diffidence of her members and some of her leaders. This is especially true of the Church in America. For one thing, she has followed a misdirected notion of pluralism. Patterned upon certain ideas of Father John Courtney Murray, this notion has inhibited the Church from contesting the secularization of American society in some important respects. Also, the energies that ought to be devoted to transforming the world and attracting others to the Church have been siphoned off in fruitless challenges to the internal authority of the Church in a misdirected notion of renewal. It was this tendency, evident in America no less than in other places, that Pope Paul VI discussed at his general audience of October 22, 1969. After exhorting his listeners to "trust the Church," he said:

> Perhaps that magic word *"aggiornamento"* enticed some to shoot beyond the target. An honest and proper but hasty desire for revision has turned into corrosive self-criticism, even into self-mutilation; it has made some lose their sense and taste for Christian militancy and Catholic apostolate. It has been said that the "structures" of the official Church must be changed, much more than the deteriorated ideas and decadent way of living of our century must be changed.[18]

During the Second Vatican Council, the divisions within the Church became clear, aided and abetted by reporters for both Catholic and secular media, who presented the Council, in the words of one Protestant theologian, as a "sort of ecclesiastical horse opera—with good guys and bad buys, heroes and villains, dopes and sparklers, a 'Gunsmoke' in St. Peter's."[19] It is understandable when

Time, Newsweek, the New York *Times* and like journals misrepresent the Church and magnify her troubles.[20] But it is sad when the *National Catholic Reporter, Commonweal, America, The Long Island Catholic,* and some other organs of the Catholic press do virtually the same thing. Applying a false objectivity, they present the views of the Pope side by side with the latest opinion of a lay or clerical theologian as if both were equal and entitled to equal weight. Donald Zirkel, the editor of *The Brooklyn Tablet,* stated the rationale for this sort of thing: "One of the things the Council said is that the Holy Spirit can speak through anyone in the Church. The Pope and bishops don't have any trouble getting their message across. But what about the guy at the bottom?"[21] There is reason to hope, however, that the Catholic press may yet be held to a proper accountability. John Cardinal Carberry, Archbishop of St. Louis, has imposed a limited censorship on his diocesan journal, *The St. Louis Review.* Perhaps other bishops will similarly take charge to prevent their people from being misled.[22]

Since the Vatican Council, rebellious elements within the Church have misrepresented it, advancing what they call "the spirit of Vatican II," as interpreted by themselves. They have spread what John Cardinal Heenan of England called a "cloud of mythology obscuring the real personality of the late Pope John XXIII."[23] These false concepts of renewal have been carried to a damaging extreme. It was a Protestant theologian, Dr. Martin E. Marty, who observed that some critics agitating for renewal of the Catholic Church are more in need of personal therapy than revamping the structure of the institutional church.[24] This is not to minimize the need for authentic renewal according to the precepts of Vatican II. But some who clamor loudly for their own brand of renewal are incipient apostates, heretics, or schismatics. We are not bound to follow them and we need not accept their implicit pretensions that their vocation or avocation, as theologians endow them with the teaching authority of the Church.

Not every issue in the Church is one of doctrinal orthodoxy. One who favors a Mass by the Rolling Stones, in preference to Gregorian Chant, or one who argues for a married clergy, is not on that account a heretic. The points on which doctrinal orthodoxy can be tested are rather few. There are some among the dissidents who have crossed that line and have denied the truth of Church doctrine on the Resurrection, the virgin birth of Our Lord, and other matters. But there are other objectors who are not beyond the line of orthodoxy, as infallibly defined by the Church. Some refuse to accept pronouncements, such as that on contraception, which, though not necessarily infallible, are still the authentic teaching of the Church. Others include liturgical faddists and restive elements within the clergy. They are not heretics. Yet, although we freely presume good faith, they can be as dangerous as the outright heretic who rejects a defined dogma or the formal schismatic who openly denies the authority of the Pope. Even though they remain technically within the pale, the dissidents undermine by their example the habit of obedience among the laity. This habit of obedience is important to the serenity and progress of the Church. While they are not heretics or schismatics, those for whom carping criticism is a routine response to the teachings and suggestions of the Church are guilty of a disservice which is nonetheless real because it does not rise to the level of outright heresy.

The members of the Church are entitled to look to their Bishops for a defense against those who would undermine the Church in doctrine or discipline. But in a number of cases, defense has not been forthcoming. Cardinal Newman wrote that during the Arian heresy in the fourth century, "the Divine tradition committed to the infallible Church was proclaimed and maintained far more by the faithful than by the Episcopate."[25] So it is not unheard of that bishops sometimes will fail to perform their duty. However, we cannot generalize and we must assume, at least in most cases, that the reluctance of bishops to excercise their authority is probably due to their judgment that, in prudence, the error should be tolerated for the time being to avoid worse upheavals. And such a judgment is entitled to our assent. In other cases, however, the inaction of the bishops may fairly be ascribed to weakness, confusion, or perhaps even sympathy with the dissidents. Hopefully the near future will see a more effective enforcement of orthodoxy and discipline. But whatever the bishops do, for each Catholic a choice is inescapable. He will accept the authority of the Church or he will not. The issue is indivisible. There can be no selective shopping around among the doctrines and authentic teachings of the Church. There is a clear duty to obey, a duty which follows from the basic decision to believe. But the times require more than a blind adherence. It is incumbent on the Catholic, therefore, to know why he believes and why he obeys.

In this book we will approach these problems through an examination of specific issues. Underlying these, however, is the general concept of authority in the Church. The approach to this concept provides a definite contrast between legitimate and illegitimate views within the Church. The crisis of authority can be fairly blamed on the dissidents who challenge that authority. But the rest of us are not free from blame. For the problem never would have reached crisis proportions but for our failure to defend and promote that authority. We have failed to convince others of what authority is and why it is essential. Submission to Church authority is not a confining concept but rather it is liberating. Authority defines the bounds within which dissent and experiment can be tolerated and encouraged. At the same time, the existence of that authority provides assurance that within those bounds one does not cut himself off from the Church and from Christ. Essential here is the notion that individual conscience is not infallible and is not supreme. The Catholic has a duty to form his conscience according to the authentic teaching of the Church. And this duty should be freely accepted and generously fulfilled. The Catholic mind should develop an instinctive repulsion toward anything savoring of heresy, schism, or apostasy.

The issue of authority is focused today on sexual questions, such as celibacy and contraception. These issues provide the occasion for a challenge to Papal authority. But that is not their only importance. They are crucial in themselves. Take contraception, for example. We miss the point if we ignore the substance of the rebels' case and consider their stand as if it concerned only the problem of obedience. Rather they contest the Pope on fundamental questions of the meaning of marriage and life itself. Those issues must be understood. Similarly, our acceptance of *Humanae Vitae* should not rest merely on its status as an authentic teaching of the Church, although that status alone is sufficient to warrant obedience. Rather, the Pope speaks soundly here in terms of philosophy and psychology.

The revolt against *Humanae Vitae* reflects a general disinclination among some who would describe themselves as liberals to accept what they consider externally imposed sexual and moral restrictions. The rejection of clerical celibacy is a parallel phenomenon stemming from similar roots. On a related point, this antipathy to objective restrictions on sexual conduct contributes at least in part to the prevailing undervaluation in some quarters of the virtues of purity and modesty. Instead, the tendency is to regard matters of sex in a naturalistic way. The introduction of imprudently detailed sex education into Catholic schools reflects this shift in attitude. The

decline in official Church opposition to indecent films and literature may also be attributed in part to a weakening of the certitude
that there are objective criteria in sexual matters. The related philosophy of situation ethics had made great headway in the Church,
particularly in the Catholic schools. And it has done so because
some clergy and some laity have refused to heed the clear prohibitions of the Church and have timidly acquiesced in the presentation,
by some teachers and clerics, of the situational approach as if it
were consistent with the teaching of the Church.

The liturgy is an area where the virtue of obedience has been
sadly lacking on a level below the dogmatic. The Latin language is
not the issue. Nor are guitars or bongo drums. These features are
incidental. The liturgy is not rendered ineffective merely because it
fails to "turn you on" on any given occasion. On the other hand,
innovations in the liturgy are helpful to many and should not be
criticized as long as they are conducted along authorized and
reasonable lines. What we can criticize, however, is the tendency
toward vagrant experimentation with the liturgy. In defiance of the
express command of the teaching Church, unauthorized liturgies are
sometimes employed which are self-centered in their content,
transient in their durability, and destructive in their effect. At the
other extreme, there are those who are so attached to the old way
that they reject the new rite of the Mass and the Pope's authority
with it. A balanced approach is essential here. While the regulation
of the liturgy is clearly within the disciplinary authority of the Pope,
it is not a doctrinal matter. Therefore, while obeying his directives,
one might still respectfully petition the Pope to consider modifications and improvements in the rites. But the acceptance of his
authority, whether we agree or not, is doubly important here because
the liturgy pervades the life of the Church and rebellion here has a
visibility and potential for scandal not usually present in other situations.

Another issue where disregard of authority has serious consequences
is that of ecumenism. Here it is important to distinguish the true
concept as expounded by Vatican II and the Popes from the false
tendency to ignore differences in the pursuit of a surface display of
unity. The question of ecumenism is related to the liturgy, too, in
that the impetus for change in both areas has come from a desire to
resolve differences with other religions and to remove from our
Catholic rites and profession those things which are needlessly
offensive to members of other faiths.

If the ecumenical spirit inclines some to a watering down of the content of the faith, a corresponding diffidence is evident in the matter of Church-State relations. Here we are concerned with the posture of the Church and society toward each other. All will agree that we should not impose our religious views on others. But then some imply that we should not advance certain views on public issues when they merely happen to coincide with the teaching of the Church. The support given by certain priests and other Catholics to the repeal of laws prohibiting abortion illustrates this tendency. The question of public aid to Church-related schools is relevant here, too. Some Catholics uncritically seek forms of aid which inevitably compromise the independence of their schools while spurning devices, such as the tuition tax credit, which offer financial relief without a substantial threat to the autonomy of the aided schools.

When we consider Catholic schools, however, we should ponder not only the bricks and mortar, but more importantly the content of the instruction. The decline in the number and enrollment of Catholic elementary and secondary schools has been caused not merely by financial pressures, but also because many of those schools are not performing the function for which they exist. Novel and erroneous theological theories are pressed upon the pupils while they are deprived of the authentic catechism instruction which is essential to prepare them for lives as knowledgeable Catholic adults. Corresponding issues are raised on the higher levels of education. In a number of Catholic colleges, defiance of the Church's teaching finds a privileged forum in the classroom. Those who should correct the situation are too often acquiescent. Their failure of will stems in part from their own confusion and in part from the general acceptance of a concept of academic freedom which confers a nearly absolute license in the performance of the teaching function.

Not only in education, but in other quarters of Catholic life, serious errors of doctrine and discipline have gained currency. We must be careful not to exaggerate this problem and not to impute error to those who entertain varying opinions on issues where diversity is legitimate. Nevertheless, the doctrinal deviations are substantial. They provide occasions for challenges to the authority of the Church and they mar the unity that should be hers. Also, the denial of one article of faith involves an implicit rejection of the infallibility upon which all doctrines depend. To a lesser extent, the same can be said of denials of authentic, but not infallibly proclaimed, teachings. The issues, therefore, are not merely academic. On July 24, 1966, the

Sacred Congregation for the Doctrine of the Faith sent a letter, signed by its secretary, Alfredo Cardinal Ottaviani, to the bishops of the world alerting them to certain prevalent doctrinal abuses and exhorting them to safeguard the true doctrine. If anything, these errors are more urgently present today than they were in 1966. It will be useful, therefore, to set them out at length, as summarized in the Congregation's letter:

1. *Revelation and Scripture.* First of all is the attack on Sacred Revelation itself: There are those who treat Sacred Scripture without consulting tradition and who restrict the extent and force of inspiration and inerrancy as well as holding incorrect opinions regarding the value of historical texts.

2. *Magisterium.* The ordinary magisterium (teaching authority) of the Church, especially of the Roman Pontiff, is sometimes so neglected and downgraded that it is nearly relegated to the realm of conjectures.

3. *Relativism.* Some virtually deny absolute, firm and immutable objective truth and subject everything to a certain relativism, and this indeed with that counterfeit reasoning according to which all truth inevitably follows the rhythm of conscience and history.

4. *Divinity of Christ.* The adorable Person of Our Lord Jesus Christ Himself is attacked when in the consideration of Christology those concepts of nature and person are held which can scarcely be reconciled with dogmatic definitions. There is creeping abroad a Christological humanism that would reduce Christ to the condition of a mere man who only gradually becomes aware. Miracles and the Resurrection itself are given lip service, but in reality are reduced to the merely natural order.

5. *Holy Eucharist.* Likewise in theological discussion of the Sacraments certain elements are either ignored or not given sufficient attention, especially in matters dealing with the Most Holy Eucharist. Concerning the Real Presence of Christ under the species of bread and wine, there are those who argue from an exaggerated symbolism, preferring to speak as if the bread and wine are not converted through transubstantiation into the Body and Blood of our Lord Jesus Christ, but merely undergo a certain transfer of signification. There are also those who hold that the concept of an "agape" (love feast) is more proper when speaking of the Mass than the idea of a sacrifice.

6. *Penance.* Some prefer to explain the Sacrament of Penance as a means of reconciliation with the Church, not giving suf-

ficient recognition to reconciliation with God Himself, Who is offended. They hold that the personal confession of sins is not necessary for the celebration of this Sacrament, but take pains to show only its social function in reconciling (the sinner) with the Church.

7. *Original Sin.* There are those who either downgrade the doctrine of the Council of Trent on Original Sin or so explain it that the original guilt of Adam and the transmission of his sin are at least obscured.

8. *Situation Ethics.* Errors of equal import are circulating in the realm of moral theology. Not a few even dare to reject the objective order of morality; others do not accept natural law, but hold rather to the legitimacy of what is called "situation ethics." Dangerous opinions are being spread concerning morality and responsibility in matters of sex and marriage.

9. *Ecumenism.* To all these must be added a note on ecumenism. The Holy See indeed praises those who in the spirit of the Council's decree on Ecumenism foster undertakings designated to promote charity (between us and) the separated brethren and to attract them to the unity of the Church. But it is lamentable that there are those, who, interpreting the conciliar decree in their own way, press for a kind of ecumenical activity which is offensive to truth regarding the unity of the Faith and of the Church, fostering a dangerous irenicism and indifferentism which is indeed altogether alien to the Council's intention. (Headnotes added)[26]

The abuses in the Church are considerable. But this is an optimistic book. "We have the right to be optimistic," said Cardinal Daniélou, "but to the extent that this optimism will be a fighting optimism. The future will not be given us by itself, but if we know how to contribute our share to it, we have no reason to believe that it will not be along the lines of a humanism in which God will have His rightful place and which will be able to raise up an authentically human civilization."[27] If we dwell here on the things that are wrong it is only to indicate the magnitude of the crisis. But if we overemphasize the negative, we can lose sight of the positive and the good which predominate in the Church. There is reason to believe that a sound and constructive reaction is germinating among the Catholic people and their leaders. The aim of this book is to offer suggestions in this direction on certain issues, including especially a plea that the teaching Church be accorded the obedience and respect that are her due. Perhaps these suggestions will be useful to those who do accept the Church's authority but are at a loss to explain why. But this book is also an appeal to dissidents to reconsider their position. It is not my intention to read anyone out of the Church or to imply that anyone should declare himself out. Exclusion from the Church is a matter for ecclesiastical and not private determination. But it is my purpose here to offer some considerations on authority with the hope that they will be helpful in promoting a stronger adherence by all of us to the authority of His Church and therefore to Christ.

II

THE ANTI-LIFE SOCIETY

Before we examine the crisis of obedience in the Church, it will be useful to note the rise in America and elsewhere of a morally permissive attitude that generates a hostility toward innocent life. The legalization of abortion is the most striking manifestation of this. But we are concerned in this book with this tendency because the Church is uniquely suited to reverse it and because the erosion of authority in the Church has impeded its effort in this direction. In short, the Church's response to the anti-life trend is a measure of her own vitality. In this context, then, we ought to note a few characteristics of what we can fairly describe as the anti-life society.

Abortion

Norman St. John-Stevas, a Catholic member of the British Parliament opposed to abortion, recently claimed that live aborted children had been bought by English doctors for experimental purposes. The children were allegedly purchased so that they could be used in medical research. St. John-Stevas described the asserted trade as "the most horrible that has ever taken place in Britain." There is no doubt that aborted babies, both alive and dead, are used extensively for medical experimentation and research.[1] But what is new in the British controversy is the allegation that the children were sold for that purpose. It is curious that this monetary element should arouse such controversy, for a more basic question is whether live children, who are incapable of consent, should be experimented upon. And, of course, the critical issue is whether innocent children should be killed by abortion at all.

Experimentation on live aborted babies is reminiscent of the vivisection controversies that used to erupt every so often. Helpless dogs and cats were involved then. But now the victims are helpless infants. If we find this shocking, it still ought not to be surprising. For a society that will legitimize abortion is a society that has already lost its reverence for innocent life. As an abortion mentality takes hold and finds expression in practice, a greater callousness toward life is generated. The British controversy reminds us of Nazi Germany, where many Jews and others were subjected to medical experiments, including freezing, malaria tests, mustard gas and starvation diet experiments. Or its callousness brings to mind the frequent descriptions in recent months of babies aborted alive, in New York and elsewhere, and cast aside to die without significant effort to save them. In an abortion room the dignity of life is not highly regarded. One widely circulated photograph shows the fully formed body of an aborted child lying in the bottom of a surgical bucket on a bed of gauze pads soaked in his own blood.[2]

But whether the child is older or younger is irrelevant. From conception he is a living, growing person and his abortion is murder.

Abortion, of course, is evil. The abortion movement rests upon the principle that underlay the Nazi extermination of the Jews. It is the principle that an innocent human being can be killed if his existence is inconvenient or uncomfortable to others or if those others consider him unfit to live.

The unborn child is in fact a human being from the moment of his conception. This could easily be demonstrated at length. It is so clearly a scientific fact that we teach it as such in our schools. As the fifth grade sex education text in the New York City school system flatly says, "Human life begins when the sperm cells of the father and the egg cells of the mother unite." When the child in the womb weighs only one thirtieth of an ounce he has every internal organ he will ever have as an adult. On the eighteenth day after his conception his heart starts beating. At eighteen weeks he can suck his thumb, scratch himself, and even cry, although he makes no sound because there is no air in the womb. He can feel pain. Even if one somehow does not believe that the child in the womb is a living human being, he ought at least to give him the benefit of the doubt.

If an innocent human being can be killed because he is too young, that is, he has not lived nine months from his conception, there is no reason in principle why he cannot be killed because he is too retarded. Or too old. Or too black. Or too politically undesirable. The philosophy is Nazi Germany's. And this nation is adopting it.

Abortion, however, is not an isolated evil. Rather, no society will legitimize abortion unless that society is first corrupted. The corruption involves the rejection of absolute standards in favor of the new morality with its flexible standard of permissiveness-with-affection. It involves irresponsibility in sexual matters and the separation of the unitive and procreative functions of the sexual act. Society's interest, in turn, becomes not the promotion of virtue and the strengthening of the family, but merely the prevention of the socially inconvenient consequences of vice, such as babies. In a society where internal moral restraints are abandoned, order and peace are unattainable unless externally imposed. The state, therefore, must step in to enforce them. But since absolute standards are rejected, they bind neither state nor citizen. There are no unyielding rights which the state may not invade in pursuit of its social purpose. Nor is the state bound by any objective limits in its choice of social purposes or in its pursuit of them. Euthanasia is one example. The ultimate test of legitimacy becomes power, whether exercised by the majority at the polls or by a ruling clique. Predictably, that power will be exercised against the very right of innocent people to live.

This description is generalized. But it is not necessarily overdrawn, as witness the trend in the United States. As birth control mores took hold in this country, contraception became a way of life. Abortion soon followed. As of the summer of 1970 at least sixteen states allowed abortion where it is not necessary to preserve the life of the mother. In New York the child can be killed up to twenty-four weeks after conception and the only significant requirement is that the killing be done by a licensed physician in a certified medical facility. Hawaii is almost as liberal and laws in some other states are so worded as to be virtually warrants for abortion on request. Laws forbidding abortion have been invalidated by the courts in some other states on the grounds that they are too vague or they violate the mother's right to privacy. In New York City alone 69,000 babies were slain during the first six months under the new abortion law.[3] Half of these murdered babies were brought to New York by their mothers from out of state for that purpose. The 69,000 figure, moreover, is a gross understatement, since it does not include abortions performed illegally or in doctors' offices. Hawaii requires that the mother be a resident of that state for ninety days before the killing. Yet legal abortions have averaged thirteen a day in that comparatively small state since the law went into effect.[4]

Not surprisingly, influential voices are now raised in favor of euthanasia. A recent vote by the members of the Colorado Nursing Association disclosed 173 in favor of euthanasia in some cases, with 109 against it and 55 abstaining. Significantly, this vote was held after a debate on the issue. Before the debate only one third favored euthanasia, yet after hearing the arguments, a majority supported it.[5] A seventy-member panel of health experts, convened by the American Assembly and including the presidents of the American Association of Medical Colleges, the Blue Cross Association, and Johns Hopkins Hospital in Baltimore, issued a three-thousand-word report in May 1970, calling for euthanasia "to avoid the unwelcome prolongation of life" among fatally ill patients.[6] Of course, if we allow an incurably ill person to be killed on his own request, it follows that we should accord the same right to the incurably ill patient who is so badly off that he is physically incapable of asking to be killed. And what then about the patient who is capable of asking for death but does not do so, but would if he knew what was good for him?

As might be expected, the American Assembly panel also urged repeal of all anti-abortion laws and laws against homosexual acts between consenting adults. This is not the place for a detailed analysis of homosexuality. It should be noted merely that the rising acceptability of homosexuality is, like abortion and contraception, an incident of the moral relaxation with which we are concerned. It is also indicative of the rapidity with which the family is yielding its place as the foundation of society.

The Copulation Explosion

The acceptance of abortion is the hallmark of the anti-life society. But the relaxation of objective moral standards goes beyond abortion and permeates the entire society. One reliable indicator of this relaxation is the rising venereal disease rate, particularly among the young. A New York *Times* survey of thirty major American cities concluded that "Gonorrhea, a disease once thought under control, is rampaging through the country, crossing socio-economic lines, making inroads into suburbia and afflicting an overwhelming proportion of youngsters."[7] With more than one and a half million new cases each year, the survey concluded that "venereal disease is the nation's most common communicable disease, except for the common cold." An "alarming" increase in cases of venereal disease was reported by New

York City Health Commissioner Mary C. McLaughlin in February 1970. In 1946, when the use of antibiotics was just beginning, there were 24,000 reported cases in New York City. The figure was reduced to 10,482 in 1956, but since then it has risen steadily to 37,000 in 1968 and 36,727 in 1969.[8] A national survey of private physicians, moreover, disclosed that, although they treat about eighty percent of the cases of venereal disease, they report only one case in nine to public health officials.[9] One out of every ten persons aged fifteen to twenty-four in San Francisco had venereal disease in 1970.[10] The fifteen to nineteen age group has a reported rate of gonorrhea and infectious syphilis more than double that of any other age group.[11] Significantly, too, illegitimate births in this country have tripled in number in the past twenty-five years. Forty percent of the unwed mothers are fifteen to nineteen years of age.[12] When Dr. James S. McKenzie-Pollock, medical director of the American Social Health Association, announced that, between July 1, 1969, and June 30, 1970, the rate of infectious syphilis in this country showed a record increase of 8.5 percent, he generally attributed the rise to "the increase in sex." "There's not only more sex, especially among the young people," he said, "but more indiscriminate sex."[13] "This increase," in the rate of syphilis, "is so dramatic," Dr. McKenzie-Pollock concluded, "that national emergency action is needed."

Indecency

One element contributing to the rise of promiscuity is the withdrawal by society of some legal supports it traditionally provided for family values. Perhaps the clearest example is in the area of pornography. Dr. Nicholas G. Frignito, Medical Director and Chief Psychiatrist of the County Court in Philadelphia, believes that "the most singular factor inducing the adolescent to sexual activities is pornography." Recent trends lend credence to this remark. Whether it can be proven that pornography causes sexual experimentation is irrelevant to the point at issue. We do not need a survey to conclude that a society in which all restraints on pornography are eliminated as a matter of principle is a society which will not be conducive to a healthy family situation:

Two bearded Danes sawed a bit of lingerie in half tonight, and the world's first sex and pornography trade fair opened for business.

With topless sales girls promoting items aimed at various sexual appetites, big crowds of Danes and foreign tourists thronged the converted sports stadium. They saw the most ambitious display ever attempted by Denmark's booming pornographic industry.

Fifty-four companies—including some Swedish ones—participated in the so-called Sex 69 Exposition, using closed-circuit television and movies with sexual themes that left nothing to the imagination.[14]

This was how the Associated Press described "Sex 69," the pornography trade show which opened in Copenhagen in October 1969. Denmark and Sweden have become models of what is widely called the contraceptive society and the pornography fair is an appropriate symbol of it. But a poignant note can be found in the comment of an emancipated Danish housewife, who said, on arriving with her husband, "The failure of the fair is that we had to leave the children at home."[15] Incidentally, the four-day pornography show, "Sex for the Millions," held in Odense, Denmark, in March 1970, featured an erotic variety show including an act of sexual intercouse on stage. Admission to the performance cost $16.50.[16] It is interesting to note that, in Denmark, the registered maternal births to mothers under eighteen are four times what they were in 1940. In Sweden, one in three brides is pregnant on her wedding day.

We have not gone quite as far in this country as the Scandinavians. But although there have been no pornography trade shows in Yankee Stadium, we do tolerate similar performances in some films and live theater. And the situation is not improving. "Pornography laws for the United States," reported the New York *Times*, "that would be nearly as liberal as Denmark's" are among the recommendations of the President's Commission on Obscenity and Pornography.[17] The pornography commission's report was rejected by the President and the Congress. But its recommendations reflect a permissive view that is widespread in the courts, in the schools, and in public life. Also, there is a discernible relaxation in conduct in this country as well, regardless of whether it is a result of the pornography explosion, or merely coincidental with it. The federal government's National Center for Health Statistics reported in 1970 that one third of all first-born children in the United States from 1964 through 1966 were conceived out of wedlock. Forty-two percent of the married women under twenty had been wed less than eight months when their first baby was born. There is also an interesting connection between income and pregnancy, at the time of marriage. More than thirty-seven percent of women in families earning less than $3000 a year went to the altar pregnant, as compared with slightly more than eight percent from families with income exceeding $10,000.[18]

The toleration of pornography is one of the incidental characteristics of the anti-life society. This is perhaps because pornography itself is based on the separation of the unitive and procreative functions of sex which characterizes the anti-life society. Only a depraved or indifferent society would raise pornography to a level of acceptability. In turn the prevalence of obscene material contributes to the worsening of the weakness which led to its toleration in the first place. The crucial point on pornography, however, is its inherent tendency to bring family values into contempt. It is this factor that particularly concerns the Church.

Society has a legitimate interest in promoting the stability of the family and in encouraging proper attitudes toward marriage and family life. Society has a corresponding right to discourage adultery, promiscuity, and whatever would bring marriage and the family into disrepute. It is in this light that we should consider the right and duty of society to restrain the dissemination of pornography. The debate on this matter frequently rests on an assumption that society can regulate the distribution of obscene material only to the extent that such material can be shown to cause its readers or viewers to commit sexual crimes or other antisocial acts. This assumption, however, is mistaken because it restricts society and the state to a merely negative role. On the contrary, as Thomas Aquinas emphasized, "The purpose of human law is to lead men to virtue, not suddenly, but gradually."[19] Of course the state should not undertake to forbid every vice or actively prescribe every virtue. The experience of Prohibition teaches us that imprudent use of the law can bring the law into disrepute and discourage the practice of virtue. The state, however, has the positive duty to promote the stability of the family as well as the negative duty to prevent sex crimes. In this context, the right of the state to control pornography, with due allowance for the important, though not absolute, liberties of privacy and expression, is clear.

The danger of pornography is especially urgent in view of the impact on children and others of mass media, including television, movies, radio, and books and magazines. "Ours is an age when laws are flouted and traditions are abandoned," said the Reverend Dr. Ernest R. Palen, of New York. "We are seeking freedom through license and abandonment of the good and the pure and the beautiful." Dr. Palen was particularly critical of newspaper advertisements promoting motion pictures and other entertainments. "They are so close to the obscene and the pornographic," he declared, "that anyone reading them must be convinced that we are a sex-crazed people. We have drained sex of its God-given purity and filled the vacuum with obscenities and impurities that shout out the depravity of man. I sometimes wonder if our teenagers need education in sex as much as they need education in purity and chastity."[20]

A standard liberal solution for this problem is to reject legal restrictions, except perhaps where children are concerned, and curb pornography by laughing at it. The objection is made that forbidding pornography only enhances its attractiveness. If we ignore it, the argument goes, people will soon get accustomed to it and will pay no attention to it. Many, if not most, adults may be able to laugh at pornography or ignore it. But the trouble is that every year there are new persons growing into the reading and viewing public. Before those new readers and viewers reach a stage of immunity to pornography, if they ever do, some of them are liable to be hurt. Also, when the law treats pornography as acceptable, whether for adults only or for children as well, it implicitly disparages those family values to which the portrayal as well as the act of promiscuity is inherently opposed.

Another unrealistic suggestion is that we should restrict the dissemination of pornography to children but that there should be no restraints where adults are concerned. However, when obscene material is freely available to adults, it is impossible to prevent its incidental availability and distribution to children. Pornography, moreover, is simply unsuitable for distribution to people of any age, young or adult. In its nature it is hostile to the family values which it ought to be the concern of society to promote.

A more serious objection to the restriction of pornography is that it would violate that freedom of speech which is essential to free, constitutional government. Freedom, however, is not license and a balance must be sought to reconcile the protection of society with the freedom of the individual. Unfortunately, the Supreme Court of the United States has seriously limited the power of federal, state, and local governments to curb the dissemination of obscene films and literature.[21] A discussion of the legal details would be beyond the scope of this work. But it should be noted that one little-known feature of the problem is the tendency of judges in federal and state appellate courts to assume for themselves the power to judge whether a particular work is or is not obscene. Judges are ill qualified to decide questions of this sort, which should be left to juries to determine. For juries are especially well suited to articulate the community standards in this area and to ensure a proper balance between the rights of defendants and the rights of the state. Bills have been introduced in Congress[22] to provide that, once the jury has been properly instructed by the trial court judge on the meaning of the applicable law, the jury's decision as to whether or not a particular item is obscene within the meaning of that law should be respected. These bills are worthy of enactment and they should be supported, not least of all by Catholics and by the bishops as a national body.

Pope Paul VI has repeatedly called for reforms in public media and entertainment. Calling on Christians to "recognize your dignity," the Pope warned against "the gravest and most insidious danger" to that dignity:

It is the threat of an aggressive and epidemic eroticism expressing itself in unbridled, revolting, public and publicized ways. We find in this sad phenomenon the theory which opens the road to license disguised as liberty, to aberrations of the instincts, described as liberation from conventional scruples. (Cf. Freud, Marcuse, etc.)

Eroticism in promiscuity, pornographic representations of various kinds, then drugs. The senses are extolled, then brutalized. They find abject expressions in ways which God's Word has cursed. Such eroticism is now assailing even the healthiest and most reserved circles, the family, the school, recreations.[23]

The Pope deplored the lowering of legal barriers to indecency and noted that "a sense of the inevitable seems to deter good and responsible people from rightful and effective action against all this." When a proper militance is called for, Catholics are often paralyzed. With this tendency in mind, the Pope summoned Catholics to rise from their slumber:

Dearly beloved children! Do not lose your awareness of sin, which is your ability to judge between good and evil. Do not let your sense of liberty, of Christian, civilized responsibility be put to sleep. Do not think that some inferiority complex lies behind frank and dignified defense of decency in the press, in shows, in social life and habits. Do not think that knowledge of evil is something that has to be acquired through personal experience. Do not call purity and self-control ignorance and weakness. Do not imagine that love and happiness will escape you if you seek them along the calm and broad ways of authentic Christian Life.[24]

It is the purpose of this chapter to note some features of contemporary society, not to catalogue the Church's responses to it. Nevertheless, it can be said here that major elements in the American Church seem afflicted by that "inferiority complex" of which the Pope speaks. Indeed, parents are exhorted in some Catholic schools and in some quarters of the Catholic press to introduce their children to "reality" and "adult art" so that they will develop mature tastes.[25] Pope Paul, as might be expected, has a different view. "Do not think that you must acquire a knowledge of evil through personal experience," he has said.[26] The late Father Francis Connell, C.SS.R., who was long the outstanding Catholic moral theologian in America, once expressed his strong disagreement with the notion that children should be deliberately introduced to salacious literature:

> I cannot see what particular value is to be found in that type of literature that is filled with vile and filthy language, if not downright obscenity. Yet there are educators today who believe that this type of writing is beneficial to our boys and girls, especially in the high school grades.
>
> Some defend this kind of literature on the score that our boys and girls are bound to encounter in later life situations and characters such as these books describe, and they can be better prepared to meet them if they are familiarized with them in their early years. Others claim that salacious books can possess great literary value that outweighs their objectionable features. But neither argument has any solidity.[27]

Speaking of his own youth, Father Connell said, "We were aided to appreciate the great classics of literature, both prose and poetry, and I do not believe that we were deprived of true culture because we did not have any of the smutty books that are so common today." On the one hand, it is said that isolation of Catholic youth from sensual books and films deprives them of contact with reality. But on the other hand, can it not be said that the lessening of formal Catholic opposition is a contributing factor in the degeneration of the arts? It is not unreasonable to say so. Indeed there is an air of unreality in the tendency of spiritual leaders to find value in some modern productions. Malcolm Muggeridge, a Protestant and former editor of *Punch*, made this point well:

> There is no need to be mesmerized by the motley procession of writers, critics, crazed clerics and other miscellaneous intelligentsia prepared at the drop of a hat to pronounce the latest outpourings of substandard smut an essential contribution to contemporary letters. The simple fact is that in all this unsavory output there is practically nothing of any lasting value or true artistic significance. Posterity, I am convinced, assuming they interest themselves in the matter at all, will be astonished to the point of incredulity that writers like Henry Miller and William Burroughs should ever have been taken seriously, and will split their sides over the thought of an Anglican Bishop's finding in poor D. H. Lawrence's sick perverse sexual ravings an edifying exposition of the Christian Sacrament of marriage.[28]

Another incidental measure of the decline in moral attitudes is the radical change recently evident in standards of dress. When Our Lady appeared to the three children at Fatima in 1917, she told them that her Son was much offended by immodest fashions. More than half a century later, Pope Paul denounced immoral fashions and publications in an address commemorating Saint Maria Goretti: "Innocence and purity are virtues that one is almost afraid to mention nowadays. We think there is need to mention them, however, for the honor of the title of 'Christian,' to guard human dignity, for the sake of social customs, for the sincerity of love, for the honesty and happiness of the family and the moral strength of the young. We know, for example, how immodesty in dress is required by the dictates of fashion, how the provocative, even pornographic illustrations of certain papers, some shows and advertisements are deliberately intended to excite the basest passions and profane life; and this not only in external matters but in the most sacred ties, in the psychological field, in our hearts, so that they are no longer the fount of pure feelings, but of vicious and inhuman fantasies and thoughts, and so sometimes the cause of terrible crimes."[29] Pope Paul here echoed the earlier sentiment of Pope Pius XII: "That sense of modesty, which in its spontaneous abhorrence from the impure is akin to the sense of religion, is made of little account in these days. But you, mothers, will take care that they do not lose it through indecency in dress or self-adornment, through unbecoming familiarities or immoral spectacles."[30] One wonders whether Pius XII, or his successors, would be edified in this respect by a visit to some of our Catholic high schools or colleges today. There is a danger of overplaying this incidental issue of fashion. Nobody wants to go back to high button shoes. But in some respects matters have gone to extremes in recent years and the bishops in this country do not seem greatly disturbed over it.

Contraception

What should be remembered, however, is that the erosion of morality is not simply a function of indecency or immodesty. Rather, the problem arises from the prevailing attitude toward life itself and its origins. The root issue here is contraception. Recent years have seen the institutionalization of contraception as an accepted part of American life, regardless of religious objections and physical dangers. In February 1970 two sociologists affiliated with the Office of Population Research reported that sixty-four percent of Catholic wives interviewed acknowledged the use of birth control measures disapproved by the Church. The authors concluded that the Papal ban had had no effect on the use of contraceptives by the fifty-six-hundred wives involved in their national sample.[31] With increasing frequency, American hospitals are converting beds from maternity to nonmaternity uses. "And a noticeable number of affluent, young marrieds," according to Newsweek, "are also taking the pledge" to have no children, "openly declaring that they prefer an unfettered, mobile, pleasure-centered life to the responsibilities of parenthood."[32] Recent studies indicate that American women, regardless of their religious, racial, or economic backgrounds, are approaching a total acceptance of birth control.[33]

The popularity of artificial birth control keeps growing despite the mounting evidence that the pill and some other methods of contraception are simply unsafe. Nor is this merely an abstraction. When Mrs. Stella Humphries, twenty-nine and the mother of four, suffered a pulmonary embolism and died in Worcester, England, the pathologist in the case testified, "I have no hesitation whatsoever in saying that this young woman died from the effects of taking what is, in my opinion, a very dangerous medicament which is called the pill."[34] Recent studies and the Senate subcommittee hearings

chaired by Senator Gaylord Nelson of Wisconsin demonstrate clearly
that the pill is significantly dangerous for some women.[35] The Food
and Drug Administration has issued warnings explaining the hazards
of the pill to the eight and one-half million American women who
use it.[36] And those dangers are substantial. Also, more than one
million American women are obtaining birth control pills illegally
without a prescription, according to Dr. Charles C. Edwards, head
of the Food and Drug Administration.[37]

It would be a mistake, however, to condemn the pill solely or even
primarily because it is dangerous to the user. For one thing, safer,
though less effective, methods of contraception are available. But
more importantly, even if the contraceptive pill were entirely safe
to the user, the objections to its use would be just as strong as they
are now. For the pill and other contraceptives are primarily to be
attacked as symbols of the irresponsibility and self-indulgence that
characterize the anti-life society. It is irresponsible to seize the pleasures without assuming the potential responsibilities, to insist on sexual
intercourse while willfully preventing even the possibility that the
intercourse might bring to fruition the new life which it is designed
to create as fully as it is designed to foster mutual love and support.
The two purposes, the generation of children and the expression of
marital love, as explained by Pope Paul in *Humanae Vitae*, are in-
extricably intertwined. When they are separated, it may be with the
best of intentions. But with the purposes of the act willfully separated, the exercise of the sexual act for an isolated unitive purpose
ultimately loses even its capacity to unite. As Pope Paul said in his
interview with Jean Guitton, "often love is no more than the juxtaposition of two solitudes."[38] The act soon degenerates into an
exercise in selfishness. For the parties in contraception have with-
held from each other their ultimate resource. They have deliberately
prevented a total mutual donation of self. The result is perversion.
The marital act is reduced to an exercise in mutual masturbation.

Beyond this, when the practice of contraception is generalized,
the result is a spread of promiscuity, a lowering of moral standards,
and, incidentally, a perversion of the woman's role. "Damn the pill,"
recently said Baroness Edith Summerskill, Britain's best-known feminist. "The pill seems to control the future of so many people today
because for some reason young girls feel that you have to be 'with
it.' Being 'with it' means that you have to have premarital sexual
intercourse. It seems that to be a virgin today is somehow to have
missed the boat. Yet the male is as old-fashioned as ever. A recent

survey in Britain showed that the vast majority still want the girl they marry to be a virgin."[39] The baroness also criticized the pill on medical grounds: "Every husband, if he loves his wife, would stop her from taking the pill until it is proved 100 percent safe." Incidentally, one task assigned the Human Life Foundation, established in 1968 by the Catholic Bishops of the United States, is to promote research to improve the rhythm method, the alternative to artificial contraception, as a more effective way of spacing births.[40]

Dr. Lennard Ejerfeldt, the editor of *Kit*, the publication of the Catholic Information Service in Stockholm, Sweden, has noted the parallel in the rise of both contraception and promiscuity. "When the marital act has been radically separated from the chance of propagation, it is time to separate sexual life from marriage. The risk of a similar development among the Catholics probably has been an important motive of the Pope."[41] He continued:

> The sexual liberation that was supposed to give woman equality to man, has resulted in a formerly unknown exploiting of woman as a sexual object in commercial advertising and pornography.
>
> Another aspect of the same development, is the general disregard and devaluation of chastity and sexual abstinence characterizing our milieu.[42]

One of the sharpest commentaries on the inherent evil of contraception comes from Mahatma Gandhi. This may surprise some, since it seems to be an article of the contraceptionist creed that the swarming millions of India provide an argument for world-wide and even compulsory birth control. While he favored the limitation of births, Gandhi approved only the method of self-control. He put his finger rightly on the tendency of contraception to foster immorality. "Artificial methods," he said, "make a man and woman reckless. . . . It is wrong and immoral to seek to escape the consequences of one's acts."[43] In a similar vein, he observed that "artificial methods . . . are harmful . . . because they increase the appetite which grows with every feed. The mind that is so tuned as to regard indulgence, not only lawful but even desirable, will simply feed itself on indulgence and will at last become so weak as to lose all strength of will.[44]

"Self-control," he believed, "is the surest and the only method of regulating birth rate. Birth control by contraceptives is race suicide."[45] Gandhi rejected the argument that overpopulation justifies contraception. He was also concerned about the effect on general morals of a separation of the sexual act from its procreative function:

> It is futile to hope that the use of contraceptives will be restricted to the mere regulation of progeny. There is hope for a decent life only so long as the sexual act is definitely related to the conception of precious life. This rules out perverted sexuality and to a lesser degree promiscuity. Divorce of sexual act from its natural consequence must lead to hideous promiscuity and condonation if not endorsement of natural vice.[46]

Finally, echoing a point Pope Paul was to make two decades later in *Humanae Vitae*, Gandhi attacked contraception as an assault on the dignity of women: "Contraceptives are an insult to womanhood. The difference between a prostitute and a woman using contraceptives is only that the former sells her body to several men, the latter sells it to one man."[47] Mahatma Gandhi is telling the truth and so is Pope Paul. Nevertheless, the world pays little attention.

Coercion

The anti-life society, however, goes beyond the prevention of birth. Rather, its hostility to life is manifested pre-eminently in abortion. Nor should this be surprising. Of course, contraception, which is the prevention of life, differs from the taking of life by abortion. But contraception is one of those truly determinative issues. One can accept contraception only if he accepts the irresponsibility inherent in taking the pleasures of the sexual act while deliberately preventing even the possibility of assuming the responsibilities of procreation. A similar irresponsibility is involved in the refusal of the mother to assume responsibility for the child with whom she is pregnant and who is totally dependent on her for continued life. The evil underlying both contraception and abortion is the separation of the unitive and procreative functions of the sexual act. It is not surprising, then, that some advocates of contraception are not content with espousing a relaxation on contraception alone. In some cases they move beyond birth control to condone euthanasia, abortion, and other incidents of the anti-life society. The Reverend Charles E. Curran is one such. He now believes that Catholic moral theologians "should explore the possibility of interfering to hasten the dying process." In cases of "assisted abortion," where "the best available medical knowledge indicates that the woman cannot bring the living child to term," Father Curran wonders why should the doctor "sit back and wait for nature to take its course when by interfering now he can avoid great harm to the mother?"[48]

Abortion, unlike contraception, involves the taking of existing life. But the advocates of both rely upon a situation ethic that tends to blur the distinction. Having broken the moral barrier against artificial birth control, the Catholic contraceptionist is susceptible to arguments condoning abortion, euthanasia, and other evils in at least some circumstances. Also, if he decides that these things can be justified, he has no enduring principle on which to deny to the state the power to induce, and even to coerce, its citizens to practice them.

Government coercion in this area is a present reality. In 1966 the Roman Catholic bishops of this country warned against the inherent tendency of government-sponsored birth control programs to degenerate into coercion of the recipients. The bishops were particularly concerned about government programs which offer information on family planning to welfare recipients. The recipient's decision to accept or reject the birth control advice was ostensibly "voluntary." But the reality was far different, as the bishops pointed out:

> Far from merely seeking to provide information in response to requests from the needy, government activities increasingly seek aggressively to persuade and even coerce the underprivileged to practice birth control.
> In this, government far exceeds its proper role. The citizen's right to decide without pressure is now threatened. Intimate details of personal, marital and family life are suddenly becoming the province of government officials in programs of assistance to the poor.
> We decry this overreaching by government and assert again the inviolability of the right of human privacy.[49]

It is claimed on the contrary, that government should merely make contraceptive material and information, or abortion information, available to the citizen so that he can freely choose. However, government neutrality is illusory here. For the very basis of the government program is that contraception, or abortion as the case may be, is a good thing. Else why would government take pains to promote its availability? This is especially true among poor people, whose acceptance of birth control is a desired object of public policy today. When the welfare case worker, who can approve or reject welfare claims, suggests ever so indirectly that it would be a good idea for the client to consider contraception, the implicit intrusion on freedom of choice is clear. This is even more evident where, in states where abortion is legally available, the case worker suggests that the pregnant welfare recipient consider killing her child by an abortion. We may fairly surmise that if the beliefs of other religions were the targets of such government seduction the protests, properly, would resound through the corridors of Washington. Catholics, on the other hand, seem to have waived their rights in pursuit of pluralism and ecumenism. In any event, it is incumbent on Catholics and the bishops to resist governmental intrusion in this area.

If the government were to promote the family and discourage promiscuity, as it ought, it would punish abortion and discourage contraception. For obvious reasons, government cannot punish the use, as distinguished from the sale, of contraceptives. The Supreme Court of the United States has held that such punishment, as applied to married persons, violates the constitutional right of privacy.[50] But a carefully drawn statute regulating in a reasonable manner the sale of contraceptives or the promotion of contraceptive information should be considered a valid exercise of the state's power to promote the family and discourage promiscuity. Beyond that, government should cease to regard contraception as a desirable or indifferent thing. It should not promote contraception and should refuse to provide contraceptive material or information even when asked for it.

There are indications, however, that government is moving beyond implicit coercion and promotion of "family planning" in which the decision to have children is theoretically retained by the husband and wife. Rather, we are tending toward an acceptance of "population control" as a legitimate end of government, including the coercive mechanisms involved in the concept of control. And since the methods of birth control include abortion as well as contraception and sterilization it becomes clear that we now confront an assertion by government of the power to kill, as a matter of public policy, those innocent persons whom it deems to be surplus, unfit, or simply unwanted.

Researchers are developing a pill that can be taken the "morning after" intercourse. This would operate as an abortificient since it would destroy the life of the child after it had begun at the moment of fertilization. Also in the works are capsules that can be inserted under the skin to prevent conception for periods up to six months and more and contraceptives that can be mixed in public water supplies, with the antidote to be given to selected persons who are deemed worthy to bear children. The potential use of these methods for government compulsion of birth control is obvious. Nor is this an unreal suggestion.

Dr. Paul Ehrlich of Stanford University says that, if voluntary programs do not reduce the population growth, the nation should consider "the addition of a temporary sterilant to staple food, or to the water supply," with limited distribution of antidote chemicals, perhaps by lottery.[51] Professor Walter E. Howard, of the University of California, argues that "some form of compulsory control of birth rates is now essential." He proposes that "if a woman or a couple exceeds the limit set by society they must be dealt with by law compelling them to be sterilized or to have an abortion or by some other repayment to Society." Alan Barth, a senior editorial writer for the Washington *Post*, believes the government should establish "reasonable conditions" for granting a license for parenthood. One of the conditions, he suggests, should be "financial responsibility."[52]

Government officials, too, have been active in advocating coercion in this area. Robert Finch, secretary of Health, Education and Welfare, suggested in February 1970 that parents should limit their families to two children and that government might have to offer "disincentives" to that end.[53] In 1970 the Health, Education and Welfare Department budgeted $140 million for birth control devices, mainly for the poor and racial minorities. This is twice as much as the government has ever spent before on artificial birth control.[54] According to Senator Henry Jackson (D. Wash.), "It will no longer suffice just to make birth control information available to those who want it." Rather, "We are going to have to recognize limitations on our right to have as many children as we want."[55] When Senator Robert Packwood (R. Ore.) introduced his bill to increase government and family planning activities and to allow a maximum of three children per family for federal income tax exemptions, he coupled it with a bill to allow abortion on demand in the District of Columbia. He said the proposals were an effort to "control, restrain and plan the population in this country" so as to ease the strain on the environment.[56] More recently, Senator Packwood has introduced a bill to allow abortion on demand throughout the United States.[57] Needless to say, when the government combines abortion on demand with financial penalties on families having more than three children, then, as to a mother with three children who conceives another child, government is clearly coercing her to kill the child she is carrying. Incidentally, Dr. Roger O. Egeberg, President Nixon's top advisor on medical policies, declared in February 1970 that "we've got to face abortion as the backup of many methods of contraception which aren't perfect."[58]

There is added to this problem the factor of racism. For the concentration by the federal government on the promotion of birth control among minority groups raises an inference that this is the main purpose of the program. Indeed, it is increasingly clear that this is the case. Significantly, Marvin Davies, Florida field secretary for the National Association for the Advancement of Colored People, attacked the Nixon Administration's birth control programs, saying, "I do not think the President's plan is in the best interests of the black people. Our women need to produce more babies, not less. Our problems are mainly economic ones, and until we comprise 30 to 35% of the population, we won't be able to really affect the power structure in this country."[59] Cesar Chavez, the leader of the California grape strike, has protested government-sponsored birth control programs which aim to "exterminate all the poor and all the non-white peoples of the world." He charged that "some people believe that you can get rid of poverty by getting rid of the poor."[60] Forcible population control would serve the purpose of slowing down the rapid birth rate among minority groups, thereby alleviating a threat to the dominance of the white upper and middle classes. It would also, in the eyes of some, solve the costly welfare problem by implicitly preventing the birth of children to welfare mothers. It is an interesting comment on the prevailing public morality that the answer to welfare illegitimacy is seen as the prevention of children rather than the discouragement of promiscuity. There are laws in some states which would permit the fine and imprisonment of fathers who fail to contribute, to the extent their means allow, to the support of their children whether legitimate or illegitimate. A general application of criminal sanctions to irresponsible fathers would be a symbolic and effective first step in establishing the principle that society's interest is the promotion of the family and the discouragement of promiscuity.

The degeneracy of public policy in this area reinforces Pope Paul's argument that contraception has an inevitably corrupting effect on persons who practice it and societies which tolerate it. It is worth recalling John Cardinal Wright's comment that the Pope "resisted the compulsions of the statistics, the economic determinism and the political absolutism of an age of computers and conformism destructive of the person. He has defended life and love against political controls and the selfishness ultimately destructive of both. With Apostolic integrity he has braved the sneers of the cynical and the honest dissent of those who do not share his faith concerning the divine origins and eternal purposes of life and of love."[61]

It would be merely academic to discuss authority in the Church without relation to the crucial immediate task of that Church. That is, particularly in the United States, to provide the leadership to reverse these dehumanizing tendencies and to affirm the dignity of life itself. The Church is impeded in that work by the rebellion in her ranks, a rebellion for which *Humanae Vitae* was the occasion but not the cause. In his encyclical on birth control, Pope Paul also stated clearly the principles upon which a Catholic approach to the anti-life society should be based. It is appropriate, therefore, that we next examine *Humanae Vitae*, which Cardinal Wright has truly called "prophetic in the root sense of the word."

III.

HUMANAE VITAE

If there is no room for Charlie in the Catholic University of America, there is no room for the Catholic University in America.[1]

Charlie is the Reverend Charles E. Curran. He was then, in April 1967, assistant professor of moral theology at the Catholic University of America. The above legend was on a large sign carried by two habited nuns as they picketed on the school grounds. Charlie had been notified that he would not be rehired for the coming year, apparently, as the New York *Times* put it, on account of "his liberal views on doctrinal matters, particularly those on birth control." His threatened dismissal had triggered a strike by the faculty and students. Characteristically for Catholic University, the strike was settled by reinstating Father Curran who continues his crusade for, among other things, a more liberal attitude toward contraception in the Church.

The Controversy

Five or so years previously, liberal elements in the Catholic press had begun to generate a controversy over the Church's unyielding prohibition against contraception. In an interesting article, more than a year before the encyclical, John Leo traced the "interlocking directorate" of "The Catholic Establishment" of which he himself is a part.[2] He emphasized the role of the "Establishment" in generating the entire birth control controversy:

It is the Establishment that decides what Catholics will discuss, not just in Establishment journals, but—after a time lag—in nearly all Catholic journals and discussion groups from coast to coast. The birth control discussion in the United

States, for instance, was entirely an Establishment production. After the stage was set by (1) the Council, (2) the changing of the guard among the world's moral theologians (none of them American, at that time), and (3) the publication of Dr. John Rock's book, *The Time Has Come*, the Establishment moved. *Jubilee, Cross Currents* and *Commonweal* broke the ground in 1963, and hammered away for most of 1964, as did the new *National Catholic Reporter*, until the issue took hold. Louis Dupre's two articles in *Cross Currents* and *Commonweal* were shaped into a book by fellow Establishment member David McManus of Helicon. Daniel Callahan, Father Gregory Baum, James O'Gara and Michael Novak wrote editorials, articles, and letters. Macmillan published *The Experience of Marriage*. Rosemary Ruether, who broke the ice in *Jubilee* late in 1963, rewrote the article for the *Saturday Evening Post* and later turned up in an Establishment anthology, *What Modern Catholics Think About Birth Control*. The book, which contained fifteen essays, eleven of them by the Establishment, sold well over 100,000 copies. Justus George Lawler, as Editor of Herder and Herder, published an important anthology, *Contraception and Holiness*, edited by Establishment favorite Archbishop Roberts and featuring such leading Establishmentarians as Leslie Dewart and Fr. Gregory Baum. . . . By late 1964 it was clear that the Establishment had won. The issue could not be swept under the rug.

The most prominent theory underlying the demand for a relaxation of the Church's ban was that the birth control pill is different and that the prohibition should be restricted to the more usual mechanical means of birth control. In 1963 Pope John XXIII appointed a small commission to study the subject. Pope Paul continued this commission and enlarged it in June 1964. The members of this Pontifical Commission for the Study of Problems of Family, Population and Birth included clergy and laity, bishops, theologians, married couples, and experts in medicine, psychology, and demography from all continents and twenty nations. This commission met in 1965 and submitted reports to the Pope. After the Second Vatican Council adjourned in 1965, the Pope reorganized the commission so that sixteen cardinals, archbishops, and bishops were its only full members retained only a limited membership as advisors and were therefore not entitled to vote. In June 1966 the "final report" of the commission was submitted to the Pope. Four months later, the Pope indicated his disapproval of certain conclusions by stating, "These conclusions cannot be considered definitive, by reason of the fact that they contain grave implications as to other questions, by no means few or unimportant . . . both at the doctrinal level and at the pastoral and social level. . . . This fact . . . imposes on Our responsibility a supplementary study. . . ."[3]

The apparent majority of the commission urged that methods of birth regulation be left to the consciences of spouses so long as unselfishness was avoided and the dignity of the marital act preserved. It was this opinion which Pope Paul rejected when he issued *Humanae Vitae*. The encyclical affirmed instead the validity of the rhythm method as the only method of birth control authorized for Catholics and it outlawed, without specific mention, the use of birth control pills, intrauterine loops, diaphragms, condoms, creams or jellies, and other artificial or mechanical means. While the majority in that commission was not as clear-cut as some commentaries would lead us to believe, the Pope took pains in the encyclical itself to forestall objections on this score. As he pointed out, the commission was merely advisory, with the ultimate power of decision retained by the Pope:

> The conclusions at which the commission arrived could not, nevertheless, be considered by us as definitive, nor dispense us from a personal examination of this serious question; and this also because, within the commission itself, no full concordance of judgments concerning the moral norms to be proposed had been reached, and above all because certain criteria of solutions had emerged which departed from the moral teaching on marriage proposed with constant firmness by the teaching authority of the Church.

The Decision

On July 29, 1968, the Pope issued *Humanae Vitae*. The reactions were immediate, the most vocal being negative. Jesuit Father Norris Clark rebuked the Pope at a Fordham symposium, "We can't hear you. We demand that you do not speak to us in this way."[4] As British Cardinal John C. Heenan remarked later about *Humanae Vitae*, "Many excellent Catholics said, 'We will not listen to the Pope.'"[5] Apart from the curiosity of describing as "excellent Catholics" those who refuse to listen to an authentic teaching of the

Pope, the cardinal aptly described the attitude of many who frankly turned the Pontiff off when he spoke on this issue. The dissent to the encyclical was widespread, sometimes angry and always abundantly publicized. However, before looking at the dissent, and the less well-publicized voices of assent, it would be useful to examine *Humanae Vitae* itself and see what the Pope actually said and did.

The Pope began by affirming the authority of the Church to interpret the natural moral law as well as "the law of the Gospel." It has been intimated in some quarters that the authority of the Church itself, and hence of the Pope, should not extend to the determination of precise applications of the natural moral law. Pope Paul noted that this natural law "is also an expression of the will of God, the faithful fulfillment of which is equally necessary for salvation," along with the law of the Gospel. In performing this responsibility to define the natural law, he said, the Church has always provided "a coherent teaching concerning both the nature of marriage and the correct use of conjugal rights and the duties of husband and wife."

It is unfortunate that, in the storm over *Humanae Vitae*, so little has been said about the positive message of the encyclical. It contains a powerful and perceptive analysis of conjugal love and of marriage. Throughout the encyclical, Pope Paul is calling his hearers, not to a sterile observance of a merely negative rule, but to a challenge to serve God and each other in marriage by a love transcending selfishness and attuned to the will of God. It is in light of this proper concept of marriage that contraception is not only impermissible but abhorrent.

Pope Paul rejected the argument that the rightness of an act of contraception should be determined in the context of the entire marriage. This argument would deny that the morality of contraception can be judged by viewing each act of intercourse in isolation. This was described by Pope Paul as the "principle of totality," that "the intention of a less abundant but more rationalized fecundity might transform a materially sterilizing intervention into a licit and wise control of birth . . . , that finality of procreation pertains to the ensemble of conjugal life rather than to its single acts. . . ." If the general tenor of the marriage is in keeping with God's law, this argument maintains, the separate acts of contraception must be considered as an integral part of the entire marriage. Under this theory, therefore, those acts of contraception could be sanctified by association with other acts of intercourse performed without contraception and by constituting a part of the entire marriage relationship.

The Pope, however, rejected this argument and he declared: "To justify conjugal acts made intentionally unfecund, one cannot invoke as valid reasons the lesser evil, or the fact that such acts would constitute a whole together with the fecund acts already performed or to follow later, and hence would share in one and the same moral goodness. In truth, if it is sometimes licit to tolerate a lesser evil in order to avoid a greater evil or to promote a greater good, it is not licit, even for the gravest reasons, to do evil so that good may follow therefrom that is, to make into the object of a positive act of the will something which is intrinsically disordered, and hence unworthy of the human person, even when the intention is to safeguard or promote individual, family, or social well-being. Consequently it is an error to think that a conjugal act which is deliberately made infecund and so is intrinsically dishonest could be made honest and right by the ensemble of a fecund conjugal life." The correct principle is that "each and every marriage act (quilibet matrimonii usus) must remain open to the transmission of life."

The Pontiff reiterated the Church's condemnation of abortion and direct sterilization. After condemning sterilization, he reinforced the ban on contraception by language broad enough to cover the pill and any other refinements now in view: "Similarly excluded is every action which, either in anticipation of the conjugal act, or in its accomplishment, or in the development of its natural consequences, proposes, whether as an end or as a means, to render procreation impossible."[6]

This basic teaching of *Humanae Vitae* was not an innovation. Rather it was a development of principles enunciated by earlier Popes, including especially Pius XI and Pius XII. It was the work of Pope Paul to apply those principles to the pill and other recent refinements of contraceptive technique. Jesuit Father Joseph F. Costanzo summarized the progressive application of these principles to the developing techniques: "The all-comprehensive statement of (Pius XI's encyclical) *Casti Connubii*, 'any use whatsoever of matrimony,' which condemned at least coital contraception, and which Pope Pius XII explicated to include post-coital defeat of the 'natural consequences' of conjugal relations, now is elaborated to comprehend precoital preventive contraception, 'in anticipation of the conjugal act.' "[7]

The rhythm method of spacing births, that is, relying upon "the natural rhythms immanent in the generative functions, for the use of marriage in the infecund periods only, and in this way to regulate birth without offending the moral principles which have been recalled earlier," was approved in the encyclical. The difference between rhythm and contraception was explained by Pope Paul as follows:

The Church is coherent with herself when she considers recourse to the infecund periods to be licit, while at the same time condemning, as being always illicit, the use of means directly contrary to fecundation, even if such use is inspired by reasons which may appear honest and serious. In reality, there are essential differences between the two cases; in the former, the married couple make legitimate use of a natural disposition; in the latter, they impede the development of natural processes. It is true that, in the one and the other case, the married couple are concordant in the positive will of avoiding children for plausible reasons, seeking the certainty that the offspring will not arrive; but it is also true that only in the former case are they able to renounce the use of marriage in the fecund periods when, for just motives, procreation is not desirable, while making use of it during infecund periods to manifest their affection and to safeguard their mutual fidelity. By so doing, they give proof of a truly and integrally honest love.

The Pontiff next alluded to the dangerous consequences of "methods of artificial birth control." "A road would thus be opened up toward conjugal infidelity and the general lowering of morality. Not much experience is needed in order to know human weakness, and to understand that men—especially the young, who are so vulnerable on this point—have need of encouragement to be faithful to the moral law so that they must not be offered some easy means of eluding its observance."

This is the age of liberated women. Feminist groups are actively advancing women's rights, as they conceive them. The National Organization of Women, for example, objects to the use of feminine names for hurricanes. This is exploitation, the ladies think. These groups are uniformly opposed to the Catholic teaching on birth control, principally because they regard it as an infringement of their dignity and rights as women. Yet one of the striking points in the encyclical is Pope Paul's insistence that it is contraception,

not its prohibition, which poses a threat to the dignity of womanhood. He fears that in a contraceptive society women would come
to be regarded as mere objects of enjoyment instead of as persons:

> It is also feared that the man, growing used to the employ-
> ment of anti-conceptive practices, may finally lose respect for
> the woman, and, no longer caring for her physical and psycho-
> logical equilibrium, may come to the point of considering her
> as a mere instrument of selfish enjoyment, and no longer as
> his respected and beloved companion.

The Pontiff next warned that a legitimization of contraception
within marriage would provide a pretext for governments to urge it,
and even compel it, as a matter of public policy. He urged man
"not to abdicate from his own responsibility in order to rely on
technical means" and affirmed the Church's determination to defend "the dignity of man and wife."

Humanae Vitae rejected any concept that would regard the be-
getting of children as the sole end of marital intercourse. Rather, the
Pope explained that there is an "inseparable connection, willed by
God and unable to be broken by man on his own initiative, between the two meanings of the conjugal act: the unitive meaning
and the procreative meaning. Indeed, by its intimate structure, the
conjugal act, while most closely uniting husband and wife, capaci-
tates them for the generation of new lives, according to laws in-
scribed in the very being of man and of woman. By safeguarding
both these essential aspects, the unitive and the procreative, the
conjugal act preserves in its fullness the sense of true mutual love
and its ordination toward man's most high calling to parenthood.
We believe that the men of our day are particularly capable of
seizing the deeply reasonable and human character of this fundamental principle."

The final part of the encyclical consists of pastoral directives. The
Pope urged husbands and wives to strive for "perfect self-mastery."
He asked educators to promote the virtue of chastity and he deplored the hostile attitude toward this virtue which permeates "the
modern media of social communications." The Pontiff then turned
to public authorities and, quoting Pope John XXIII's encyclical
Mater et Magistra, warned them against any attempts to reduce
population pressures by any solution " 'which does violence to man's
essential dignity' and is based only on 'an utterly materialistic conception of man himself and of his life.' " Instead, he urged, in re-

liance on his own encyclical, *Populorum Progressio*, that more efficient and equitable means be sought to increase production and
distribution of the goods of this world. He then exhorted "men of
science" to work toward perfecting the rhythm system of regulating
births. The encyclical concluded with pastoral exhortations to husbands and wives, doctors and medical personnel, priests and bishops.
The Pope said the "first task" of priests "is to expound the Church's
teaching on marriage without ambiguity." He exhorted them to
"teach married couples the indispensable way of prayer; prepare
them to have recourse often and with faith to the sacraments of the
Eucharist and of Penance, without ever allowing themselves to be
discouraged by their own weakness."

The Reaction

Reaction to the encyclical was polarized. The attitude of many
critics was typified by the later remark of Norman St. John-Stevas,
a Conservative member of the British Parliament and a leading
English Catholic: "Papal authority can never be the same again."[8]
A group of American Catholic laymen who had attended the
1967 meeting of the World Congress of the Laity spoke out shortly
after the encyclical was issued to reaffirm their support for a resolution of the Congress which placed responsibility for birth control
upon the spouses and which advocated "leaving the choice of
means to the conscience of parents in conformity with their Christian faith and in consultation with trained medical and scientific
advisors."[9] The encyclical was making the Church's teaching authority "kind of ridiculous," said one Dutch Dominican and he urged
Catholics to "just go ahead and do what they think is right." Jesuit
Father Robert Johann was prompt to separate himself from less
well-educated Catholics: "One hopeful sign," he said, "is that educated Catholics are not going to pay any attention to this statement. If they did we'd be back in the Dark Ages."[10] Non-Catholic
voices, too, were raised in opposition. On the very day of the encyclical, Hugh Moore, chairman of the Association for Voluntary
Sterilization, observed: "The statement attributed to Pope Paul today reasserting the Catholic outdated position on birth control
could result in the death of millions of people by starvation in the
years ahead."[11] It is difficult to see how such statements contribute
to a sober consideration of the problem. The American Association

for the Advancement of Science found its December 1968 meeting beset by the birth control issue. Jeffrey J. W. Baker, a biologist from the University of Puerto Rico, obtained the signatures of twenty-six-hundred scientists protesting *Humanae Vitae* and charging Pope Paul with promoting war and poverty and with sanctioning "the deaths of countless numbers of human beings with his misguided and immoral encyclical."[12]

In a performance that should set a track record for committee deliberations, eighty-seven self-described Roman Catholic theologians issued a statement within twenty-four hours of the release of the encyclical in which they criticized the "ecclesiology implied and the methodology used by Paul VI in the writing and promulgation of the document." The statement scored *Humanae Vitae* on other grounds which are basically reducible to the fact that the Pope had the poor judgment to reject the advice of the majority of his birth control commission and the conclusions of such theologians as the signers of the statement. Finally, these experts drew upon the thorough and prayerful analysis they had given to the 7500-word encyclical, in the twenty-four hours since its issuance, to proclaim "that spouses may responsibly decide according to their conscience that artificial contraception in some circumstances is permissible and indeed necessary to preserve and foster the values and sacredness of marriage."[13] The spokesman for the eighty-seven was Father Charles E. Curran, the reinstated professor of moral theology at Catholic University. By August 1, 1968, 172 American theologians had signed the statement, and the number more than tripled in succeeding weeks.[14]

One observer made this pointed comment on the statement of the eighty-seven theologians:

It is interesting to note the leader of the dissenting theologians, the Rev. Charles E. Curran, is vice president of the Theological Society of America. His position is in sharp contrast with that of the society's president, Msgr. Joseph Vaughan of St. Joseph Seminary, Dunwoodie, N.Y. who hailed the encyclical, saying it "eliminates the confusion over just what the Church is teaching at this moment." Msgr. Vaughan's more orthodox remarks have not, of course, gained the publicity given the dissenters. That would hardly be consistent with the secular media's flair for sensation.

Msgr. Vaughan informs us that there are twelve hundred members of the Theological Society. There may be as many as four thousand Catholic teachers of theology around the Country. The number eighty-seven, as compared with twelve hundred membership and the four thousand teachers, pales a bit. I'm sure the Holy Father has consulted with far more than eighty-seven theologians in this matter, with many of them of far greater stature. . . .[15]

At a panel at Fordham University, the day after the encyclical, the Reverend John G. Milhaven, S.J., said, "I cannot accept this teaching as true, nor do most of my colleagues, nor do most Catholics under the age of 45—and many over that age, too."[16] The New York *Times* reported that "his statement was greeted with loud applause from an audience that contained about 300 nuns and priests." It soon developed, however, that one thrust of the opponents would be to express their respect for the Pope, but to reduce his opinion to merely one among many to be considered in forming an opinion on the issue. In their early statement on the encyclical, for example, the Dutch bishops said the encyclical was only one of "many factors that determine the individual conscience in regard to the conjugal act." Among the other factors, the Dutch bishops listed "mutual love, relations in the family and social circumstances."[17]

The criticism of his encyclical has not gone unnoticed by Pope Paul himself. On several occasions he has deplored the "corrosive criticism" leveled against the encyclical and the institutions of the Church. In one significant statement, the Pontiff drew attention to the tendency of some critics to assume for themselves a certitude which they deny to the teaching Church. Many troubles, he said, "arise from individuals who are in error and take a collective form. This is the source of those indeterminate currents of spirituality or activity which polarize around one person as interpreter, or around one single formula or one school or even one magazine. Often the promoter is a priest or a religious who is responsible for such fervent groups. From time to time they attempt to attribute to themselves special vocations or even charismatic gifts."[18] These critics, the Pope implied, avow their rejection of the structures and institutions of the Church. Yet they inevitably erect for themselves tight little ghettos far more arbitrary and closed than they claim the Church to be:

There is a summons today to religious liberty, to autonomy of conscience, to maturity of the contemporary Christian. There is recourse to a spirit of criticism that is often intractable and superficial, and very close to free examination. It unwillingly tolerates the magisterium of the Church and frequently contests the limits of that magisterium. It wishes to pass outside the lines of organized Catholic forces, which it considers to be a closed ghetto, yet it does not notice that it is forming other ghettos still more closed and arbitrary, where only the initiates are acceptable and esteemed. The proponents of these ideas find superiors and their brothers a nuisance and they empathize more readily with outsiders and adversaries. There is not infrequently a lack of doctrinal integrity and of real fraternal and social charity. They form an understanding of the Church which is all their own, devoid of the usual obligations towards community and unaccompanied by any canonical norms. They propose, instead, their own norms, perhaps good and austere, but cut off from the context of the Church and therefore virtually adrift.[19]

Quite lost in the turmoil that followed the encyclical were the voices of assent. The secular and Catholic press focused on the dissenters, largely ignoring, for example, the fifty-three members of the Jesuit community at Fordham University who issued the following statement one week after the encyclical:

We the undersigned members of the Fordham University Jesuit Community, wish to disassociate ourselves from views that have been expressed in certain quarters of this University concerning the recent encyclical of Pope Paul VI, *Humanae Vitae*, on marriage and birth control. Statements have been made that question or deny the binding character of Papal teaching and assert that individual Catholics may decide for themselves whether they will accept the norms for married life laid down in this encyclical. We wish to make it clear that no statements of this kind represent the collective viewpoint of the Jesuits at Fordham.

Our own position is fully in accord with the following passage from Chapter 3 of the Second Vatican Council's *Dogmatic Constitution on the Church*:

"In matters of faith and morals, the Bishops speak in the name of Christ, and the faithful are to accept their teaching and adhere to it with a religious assent of soul. This religious submission of will and of mind must be shown in a special way to the authentic teaching authority of the Roman Pontiff, even when he is not speaking ex cathedra. That is it must be shown in such a way that his supreme magisterium is acknowledged with reverence, the judgments made by him are sincerely adhered to, according to his manifest mind and will."

The Catholic bishops of the world responded in varying accents to the encyclical. Some of the statements, including particularly the French and the Dutch, were clouded in ambiguity in their efforts to resolve the claims of conscience and the authority of the Holy Father. One of the most forthright stands, however, was taken by the bishops of the United States in their pastoral letter of November 1968, "Human Life in Our Day." The key passage drew the critical distinctions without compromise:

We feel bound to remind Catholic married couples, when they are subjected to the pressures which prompt the Holy Father's concern, that however circumstances may reduce moral guilt, no one following the teaching of the Church can deny the objective evil of artificial contraception itself. With pastoral solicitude we urge those who have resorted to artificial contraception never to lose heart but to continue to take full advantage of the strength which comes from the Sacrament of Penance and the grace, healing, and peace in the Eucharist. May we all be mindful of the invitation of Jesus: "The man who comes to me I will never turn away" (Jn. 6:37). Humility, awareness of our pilgrim state, a willingness and determination to grow in the likeness of the Risen Christ will help to restore direction of purpose and spiritual stability.

The New York *Times* headlined the story, "Catholic Bishops Temper Curbs on Birth Control," and led off with this misstatement:

The nation's Roman Catholic Bishops declared today that artificial birth control was an "objective evil," but that Catholics who could not in conscience follow the church's teaching should not feel cut off from holy communion.[20]

What the bishops did, of course, was to urge Catholics "to continue to take full advantage of the strength which comes from the Sacrament of Penance and the grace, healing, and peace in the Eucharist." They did not say that the practice of contraception is no impediment to the reception of Holy Communion. Bishop, now Cardinal, John J. Wright, in presenting the pastoral to the news media, said, "I cannot conceive of circumstances under which a person could use artificial contraception and not think of himself as committing a grave sin." Bishop Wright explained that "those who are practicing artificial contraception are in fact acting against the teaching of the Church. If you are acting against the teaching of the Church, then objectively you are in sin. . . . We have noted that circumstances, including their own conscience, may enter to reduce moral guilt. . . . Those who know themselves to be guilty cannot receive the Eucharist without going to confession."

These are the same principles that apply to determine culpability for any sin, whether it be murder, lying, or contraception. The bishop was then asked directly if married people who practice artificial contraception and "feel no guilt" could receive the Eucharist without going to Confession. He replied: "I have no way of entering into their head; they must weigh this decision as if they stood before God. . . . People have to decide on a hundred different moral questions on whether they are prepared to go to the communion rail. They can have the further problem of asking themselves whether they care to add sacrilege."[21]

In assessing the reporting of the pastoral, Archbishop Alter of Cincinnati said the news media had "gravely misinterpreted" the pastoral, "both in respect to its content and its implications." Cardinal Krol of Philadelphia said he was "completely shocked by the very grave distortions" in the media presentations.

It turned out that the press distortions were partly caused by the premature leak to wire services of a rough draft of the pastoral. One of the major additions in the final draft of the pastoral was that the bishops added their express condemnation, quoted above, of contraception as an "objective evil," and their exhortation to Catholics to seek the remission of such sin through the sacrament of Penance. Another factor apparently was the bishops' presentation of a lengthy pastoral without an approved condensation containing short verbatim excerpts of critical passages. The confusion was in large part a product of haste and a controlling desire to accommodate the deliberations of the Church to the imperative deadline of the six o'clock news.

The Population Explosion

One strenuous criticism of *Humanae Vitae* concerns its alleged neglect of the world-wide population explosion. In the first place, however, the population crisis is largely a myth. The problem has been exaggerated in three respects: First, as to the total number of people in the world; second, as to our capacity to feed them; and third, as to our capacity to solve the pollution and environmental problems attendant upon a growing population.

It would be beyond the scope of this work to examine this issue in detail, but it is worth noting that the population problem is essentially one of maldistribution of people rather than sheer quantity of numbers.

Unfortunately it is difficult to visualize how many people there actually are in the world. Most people would be surprised to know that if you took all the people in the world and gave each one six square feet of ground to stand on, they would all fit into about four fifths of Suffolk County, which covers the eastern half of Long Island, New York, and there would be 168 square miles left over. Or they would all fit into about three fifths of the area of Rhode Island. This is not to suggest that each person should be allocated six square feet to live on. But the erroneous impression is current that the world is far more crowded than it really is. This false impression is heightened by the tendency of some population controllers to make simplistic projections of short-term population trends.

The fact is that in many parts of the world birth rates are declining sharply. This is particularly true of the United States. The fertility rate, that is, the number of babies born per thousand women, aged fifteen to forty-four, reached an all-time low in the United States of 76 in the Depression year of 1936. In 1940, it was 80; by 1950 the postwar baby boom had driven it up to 106; in 1957 it reached 123. But since 1957, the rate has gone down, so that in 1969 it was 85.5, which is not too far above the Depression level. The population of the United States is 205 million. In 1960 it was growing at a rate of 1.8 percent per year but the growth rate has now dropped to 1.0 percent.[22] It is sometimes claimed that a problem of overpopulation is caused by the combination of rising birth rates and falling death rates. But this contention is not borne out by the figures. In the United States there were 4,257,850 people born in 1960, for a rate of 23.7 per thousand population, but by 1968 the number had fallen to 3,470,000 for a rate of 17.4. In the same period deaths rose in this country from 1,711,982 for a rate of 9.5 per thousand population to 1,923,000 for a rate of 9.6.[23]

There is a problem of overconcentration of people in some places throughout the world, including particularly urban areas. But one constructive answer to this is to provide incentives for the voluntary relocation of people. Moreover, this can be done within the framework of a free society. "I would put the heavy payroll tax on all employment in the capital cities and I would give a payroll rebate to employers who went to the new towns," recently said Dr. Colin Clark, the Oxford economist and population expert. This may not be the ultimate answer. But at least the idea is worthy of more intensive consideration than it has received to date. For it is clear that the world is not suffering from an absolute excess of people and that solutions premised on that assumption are simplistic and distract attention from the real problems of economics and social justice.

The second exaggeration of the population crisis concerns the food supply. Many people in the world are starving. But this cannot be fairly blamed on an excess of population or a shortage of food. The new technology in agriculture has made it possible for us to conquer hunger regardless of population growth. The Food and Agriculture Organization of the United Nations, in its 1969 report, noted that the world will face a problem of food surpluses, not shortages, in the near future. The gain in food production, resulting from the new technology used in agriculture, is especially notable in the Far East.

In the "developed regions of the world," according to FAO Director-General A. H. Boerma, by 1969, "excess supplies, not only of cereals, but also of butter and dry skim milk reached proportions that led to serious problems in the commodity markets, and although the general level of output in these countries was unlikely to show any increase in 1969, a further expansion of stocks seemed to be in the offing."[24] Nor is the increase in food production limited to the high-income and developed regions. "An increasing number of developing countries," said Director-General Boerma, "are on the threshold of a real technological break-through in cereal production. Some of them will have exportable surpluses and will need markets for the commodities that they produce efficiently." The FAO report noted especially that "real progress is evident in the widespread increases in output achieved in 1968 in the developing countries of the Far East, the most populous region and the one where the food situation in recent years has been most critical." Significantly, the Nobel Peace Prize for 1970 was awarded to an American agronomist, Dr. Norman E. Borlaug, for his leadership of the Green Revolution—the development through "genetic engineering" of new, highly productive strains of wheat, rice, corn, sorghum, and millet. Dr. Colin Clark commented on these increases in food production:

There is hunger and malnutrition in the world but to nothing like the extent of half or two thirds of the world population. Most of it is to be found in China, where it is due to Communist misgovernment, and in India, where there is enough food to go around, but the lower castes are systematically kept hungry and denied economic opportunities.

Agricultural production has been advancing faster than population, not only in the advanced countries, but in almost every country in the world, to the point where there is considerable anxiety about being able to sell agricultural produce.

These anxieties must now be greatly accentuated by the breeding of IR 8 rice in the Philippines, and the new varieties of short stemmed wheat from Mexico, which have shown themselves capable of being grown in most parts of Asia, and which even the most cautious agricultural scientists certify as capable of giving yields far higher than have been seen in the world before.

The menace of world food shortage (which has been exaggerated in any case) is over, and the world is now faced with the very different problem of a prospective glut of agricultural produce.[25]

One of President Nixon's Council of Economic Advisors, Hendrick S. Houthakker, has described population control as a "simpleminded idea" and a "panacea."[26] In his comments, Mr. Houthakker predicted, "There is little reason to expect overpopulation for the world as a whole in the foreseeable future. Most serious studies of the subject suggest that the food supply can be expanded to accommodate a much larger population than now exists on earth. . . . What is of course more serious is that overpopulation may lead to a degradation of the social and physical environment, but this appears to be more a matter of proper distribution of the population than of total numbers. Much can be done to improve the environment without attempting to influence population trends." While some minerals might become scarce, Mr. Houthakker suggested that "substitution should prevent this from becoming a critical problem."

The third exaggeration of the population crisis is caused by an underestimation of our capacity to solve the pollution problem. Environmental contamination is not something to be lightly regarded. But science has already provided adequate means to control this problem. And the future holds even greater promise. For example, Dr. Glenn Seaborg, chairman of the Atomic Energy Commission, has announced that AEC scientists are optimistic about their efforts to perfect the fusion torch, which would use thermonuclear power to vaporize waste products into electrified particles of their constituent elements. These elements could then be separated and collected into raw materials to be used all over again.[27] Junked automobiles, garbage, sewage, and other wastes could be broken down to their elements and reused. Ultraviolet radiation from the fusion torch, according to Dr. Seaborg, could be used for desalting sea water; bulk heating; food production through algae culture; reviving "dead" lakes and rivers by reducing their excessive organic matter; and for other purposes. Dr. Seaborg estimates that controlled fusion would give us an energy equivalent of five hundred Pacific oceans filled with high-grade fuel oil. As the Chicago *Tribune* editorialized, the scientists working on the fusion torch "have much more respectable credentials than the doomsday prophets who are spreading hysteria about the imminent demise of the human race from pollution."[28]

The solution to the population explosion, to the extent that it exists, lies in a blending of the principles of *Humanae Vitae* with the principles of economic development outlined by Pope Paul in 1967 in his encyclical *Populorum Progressio*.[29]

In truth, however, the drive for contraception is not simply an outgrowth of the conviction that our planet is overcrowded. Rather, it finds favor with those who, in Pope Paul's words, entertain "a secret wish to abolish a difficult law in order to make life easier."[30] "They want an easy Christianity," he said, "in faith and in morality." Or, as Patrick Cardinal O'Boyle summed it up, "nowadays people think regular intercourse is absolutely necessary."[31] When all is said and done, however, contraception can only guarantee its practitioners what Pope Paul called an "old age" of "solitude or boredom, affective or spiritual emptiness, the sadness of a sunset without love."[32] In a 1967 interview Pope Paul said, "The link between love and fecundity is deep, hidden and substantial." When love is "separated from the fruit of love," he said, the result is "egoism," so that "to love can mean to love oneself, and often love is no more than the juxtaposition of two solitudes."[33]

A Certain Teaching

When the intrinsic nature of contraception is considered, it becomes easy to see why the Church has always condemned it. Opponents of *Humanae Vitae* have stressed the fact that the encyclical was not, in its express terms, an infallible pronouncement. It was rather an exercise of the authentic teaching authority of the Pope. But even before *Humanae Vitae*, it was clear that the authentic teaching of the Church forbade the practice of contraception and that Catholics were bound to obey. Two Jesuit theologians, the Reverend John C. Ford, S.J., and the Reverend John J. Lynch, S.J., analyzed it this way five months before the encyclical was issued:

> The morality of contraception is not in a state of practical doubt because no opinion can be practically probable if it contradicts the authoritative teaching of the magisterium. To use the theory of probabilism in such a way that one concedes practical probability to the opinions of private theologians even when they contradict the teaching of the Church goes counter to the very nature of probabilism and to the very nature of the magisterium. . . .
>
> *For the reasons given in this article we believe that up to now (March 1, 1968) the Church has proposed and continues to propose for acceptance and observance her traditional teaching that contraception is intrinsically immoral. Therefore there is as yet no room for probabilism or practical doubt."* (Emphasis in original)[34]

It is important "to distinguish," said Jesuit Father John J. Reed, "the notions of infallibility and certainty. In matters of conduct, a doctrine which is not taught with the plenitude of infallibility may still be taught with certainty, in the sense of moral, practical certitude, so as to exclude any solidly probable opinion to the contrary here and now, i.e., with the effect that at a given time a particular mode of conduct is certainly licit or certainly illicit, without the abstract question of its relation to right order being definitively closed. . . . While such a teaching does not altogether close the question from a speculative point of view, it does normally preclude the possibility of acting in contradiction of the doctrine, relying on the principle of probabilism. . . . Probabilism depends upon the justification that while there is still the possibility of a material violation of law, yet one who acts with reliance on a solidly probable opinion is not exposing himself imprudently to this danger— which is not true when one acts on the basis of a mere possibility or a tenuously probable view. But when the authentic Magisterium of the Church professedly teaches a particular moral doctrine, it will not be easy to say that one who acts in contradiction of it is not exposing himself imprudently to the danger of violating the moral law."[35]

An argument can be legitimately made that the teaching on contraception is in fact infallible, as a product of the consistent worldwide teaching of the Church. According to the Reverend Daniel S. Hamilton of Rockville Centre, New York:

> Rather than saying that the teaching of the Catholic Church on contraception is not a dogma, we should say that it is not necessarily a dogma. Whether or not the present and past teaching constitutes an infallible interpretation of the revealed moral law is something that only the teaching authority of the Church itself is competent to pronounce upon.[36]

Jesuit theologian T. L. Bouscaren maintains that "although the encyclical *Humanae Vitae* is not in itself an 'ex cathedra' pronouncement, the doctrine which it proclaims was already infallible as the constant and universal teaching of the Church's magisterium. And of course it has remained so."[37] In modern times, the teaching was proclaimed, before *Humanae Vitae*, by Pope Pius XI in his encyclical *Casti Connubii* in 1930; by Pius XII in his 1951 address to the midwives and in his 1958 address to the hematologists; by John XXIII in his 1961 encyclical, *Christianity and Social Progress*; in general terms by the Second Vatican Council's *Pastoral Constitution on the Church in the Present-Day World*; by Pope Paul VI in a 1964 address to the cardinals; in his 1966 address to the National Congress of the Italian Women's center and in his 1966 address to the Italian Society of Obstetrics and Gynecology.[38] The earlier affirmations of the teaching were listed by John Noonan:

> The propositions constituting a condemnation of contraception are, it will be seen, recurrent. Since the first clear mention of contraception by a Christian theologian, when a harsh third-century moralist accused a pope of encouraging it, the artic-

ulated judgment has been the same. In the world of the late Empire known to St. Jerome and St. Augustine, in the Ostrogothic Arles of Bishop Caesarius and the Suevian Braga of Bishop Martin, in the Paris of St. Albert and St. Thomas, in the Renaissance Rome of Sixtus V and the Renaissance Milan of St. Charles Borromeo, in the Naples of St. Alphonsus Liguori and the Liège of Charles Billuart, in the Philadelphia of Bishop Kenrick, and in the Bombay of Cardinal Gracias, the teachers of the Church have taught without hesitation or variation that certain acts preventing procreation are gravely sinful. No Catholic theologian has ever taught, "Contraception is a good act."[39]

Professor Noonan, who favors a relaxation of the Church's position, concluded, "The teaching on contraception is clear and apparently fixed forever." Although the teaching is clear, Professor Noonan argued that the teaching should be reconsidered because the "reasons, related doctrine, and environment" underlying it have changed. The encyclical *Humanae Vitae*, however, categorically rejected the idea that any change in circumstances had undermined the constant teaching of the Church against contraception.

"The language" of *Humanae Vitae*, says Father Joseph F. Costanzo, S.J., "is so absolute and exclusionary as to fulfill every rigid requirement for a dogmatic and incontrovertible doctrinal teaching. . . . The technical formality of an ex cathedra definition would not add to the intrinsic validity, that is, its certitude and the obligatory force of *Humanae Vitae*."[40] Father Costanzo rejected the "insinuating argument" that "what is not formally infallible is fallible. It supposes infallibility may not derive from another source than a solemn ex cathedra definition. Church documents and the 'theologians' themselves have traditionally acknowledged an infallibility ex ordinario magisterio. This means more than mere longevity but a continuing active and constant witness of the teaching authority of the Church to the general moral principle that opposes all contraceptive practices, the novelty being only its authoritative application to specific problems as they emerged in time."

Nor is there any escape from obedience to this doctrine in the fact that it was expressed in an encyclical rather than a more formal and infallible pronouncement. The authority of encyclical letters was spelled out by Pius XI and Pius XII. The former said, in *Casti Connubii:*

It is quite foreign to anyone bearing the name of Christian, to trust his own mental powers with such pride as to agree only with those things which he can examine from their inner nature and to imagine that the Church, sent by God to teach and guide all nations, is not conversant with present affairs and circumstances; or even that they must obey only in those matters which she has decreed by solemn definition, as though her other decisions might be presumed to be false or putting forward insufficient motive for truth and honesty.

Quite to the contrary, a characteristic of all true followers of Christ, lettered or unlettered, is to suffer themselves to be guided and led in all things that touch upon faith or morals by the Holy Church of God through its Supreme Pastor the Roman Pontiff, who is himself guided by Jesus Christ Our Lord.

Pius XII made the point, in his 1950 encyclical, *Humani Generis*, that "if the Supreme Pontiffs in their official documents purposely pass judgment on a matter up to that time under dispute, it is obvious that the matter, according to the mind and will of the same Pontiffs, cannot be any longer considered a question open to discussion among theologians."

It is not the intention of this book to attempt to prove that *Humanae Vitae* is an infallible teaching of the Church. For the practical significance of the encyclical is not reduced by freely conceding that its teaching is not technically infallible. Viewed as an authentic Papal teaching, even on a less than infallible level, *Humanae Vitae* clearly is entitled to that "religious submission of will and of mind" required by the Second Vatican Council.[41] However, the implication is widely advanced that, assuming *Humanae Vitae* not to be infallible, it may properly be regarded as simply another opinion entitled to respect but not to obedience and submission. It is relevant, therefore, to note that, far from being a personal opinion of the Pope which may be considered and accepted or rejected at the discretion of the faithful, *Humanae Vitae* is an articulation of a teaching so firmly grounded that there are even serious analysts who regard that teaching as infallible. It is in this context of *Humanae Vitae* as at least an authentic teaching of the Church that we must consider its rejection by many Catholics.

Humanae Vitae did not cause the current disorder in the Church. Rather, that disorder is the product of two dangerous trends within the Church. One involves the rejection of authority. The other arises from a widespread absorption of relativist and secularist principles of theology and philosophy. Although both trends have deeper origins in a loss of faith, they work on each other as cause and effect. It will be appropriate, therefore, to examine next a few characteristics of authority in the Church and then to discuss those underlying errors, their treatment by recent Popes and the extent to which they have affected the thinking of some Catholics. Both trends, the rejection of authority and the acceptance of the new morality, secularism, and a New Modernism, have contributed to a growing spirit among Catholics of compromise with the standards of a secular and sensual society.

IV.

AUTHORITY

Epistles appeared from time to time . . . laying down the principles of the papal claims with as much tranquility as if they were everywhere acknowledged . . . men were urged to remember their immortal souls and the Majesty of God, and to reflect upon the fact that in a few years all would be called to give their account to Him Who was Creator and Ruler of the world, Whose Vicar was John XXIV, P.P., whose name and seal were appended. . . . Here was this silly old man, talking in his sleep, babbling of the Cross, and the inner life and the forgiveness of sins, exactly as his predecessors had talked two thousand years before. Well, it was only one sign more that Rome had lost not only its power, but its common sense as well. It was really time that something should be done.[1]

Writing in 1907, the same year that Pope St. Pius X condemned Modernism, Monsignor Robert Hugh Benson described the triumph of the humanitarian Lord of the World over the penultimate Pope and, for a time, over his successor. These fictional Popes spoke and acted much as the Popes of our own time. And, like them, they were ignored and their claims of authority discounted. In our real world, as in Benson's fictional one, respect for Papal authority has declined proportionately with religion and morality. In Benson's world the ascendancy of the tyrant was preceded by the establishment of "dogmatic secularism," a menace of global war, and a rising threat of civil anarchy—conditions much like our own, except that the vacuum of authority today is more pronounced.

"All over the world there seems to be a breaking down of authority, disrespect for property, and disrespect for law," said Bishop Fulton J. Sheen in 1966. If anything, the situation has deteriorated in the last five years. Man is, in the words of Pope Paul, increasingly "seized by a frenzy, a giddy exaltation, sometimes a madness urging him to overturn everything . . . in the blind belief that a new order . . . the form of which cannot yet be clearly foreseen, is about to occur, inevitably."[2] Though the breakdown of authority is world-wide and penetrates every institution, its effects are most striking in the Catholic Church. For the Church depends, more than civil society, upon the willingness of her members to accept her authority without the compulsion of tangible sanctions.

The revolt against authority in the Church is symptomatic of a deeper crisis of faith. If one really believes that Christ is God and that He founded the Catholic Church to teach on His behalf, he will have little difficulty in accepting the authority of that Church. But though the challenge to authority arises from a deeper source, it will be helpful to outline some characteristics of the authority possessed by the Church. This cannot pretend to be a comprehensive analysis. However, the need for a renewal of obedience cannot be appreciated without noting the basic outlines of that authority to which obedience is so widely refused. Secondly, some understanding of that authority is desirable if, in promoting respect for authority, we are to maintain a due regard for the rights of individual conscience. Also, a wider understanding of some basic elements of Church authority may serve as a catalyst for the needed regeneration of faith which can hardly be sparked by merely general exhortations.

There are three aspects of this authority question which ought to be examined. One involves the procedural issue of who shall decide, whether Pope, bishops, the laity, or all three. The second concerns the substantive content of the subjects upon which the Church's authority is to be exercised. The third relates to the problem of conscience. Who has the authority? In what areas may that authority be exercised? To what extent does a conscientious objection excuse one from obedience?

Who Shall Decide?

When he announced his marriage and exit from the Church, Charles Davis, the English theologian, gave as one reason, that "indeed, I must confess that the workings of papal authority have for me become increasingly disreputable. The lack of concern for truth, with the subordination of truth to authority, and to the preservation of the whole system, pervades the whole institution."[3] Mr. Davis' concentration of fire upon the Pope is not surprising. For in any dispute with Church authority, the ultimate target is the Papacy on account of the nature of the office.

Authority in the Church differs from civil authority most prominently in the fact that "in virtue of his office, that is, as Vicar of Christ and pastor of the whole Church, the Roman Pontiff has full, supreme, and universal power over the Church. And he can always exercise this power freely."[4] In the *Decree on the Bishops' Pastoral Office in the Church*, the Council emphasized that this primacy is vested in the Pope as such, beyond the power of the people to vest it in another:

> In this Church of Christ the Roman Pontiff is the successor of Peter, to whom Christ entrusted the feeding of His sheep and lambs. Hence by divine institution he enjoys supreme, full, immediate, and universal authority over the care of souls.[5]

In this respect, Vatican II added nothing new to what the Church had already taught. The First Vatican Council, which met from 1868 to 1870, defined two dogmas concerning the Papacy. As Pope Paul VI described Vatican I, "The doctrines that were treated in the Council were given dogmatic definition, by solemn and extraordinary acts of the ecclesiastical magisterium, and were thus declared to be truths of the Church's faith."[6] Among the truths defined by Vatican I, two are directly concerned with the Papacy. "One, the pontifical primacy, concerns government of the Church. The other, Papal infallibility, concerns the Church's magisterium. These two dogmas," continued Pope Paul, "were defined by the promulgation of the constitution, *Pastor Aeternus* on July 18th, 1870, after long, fiery and tumultuous debates. The 535 Fathers present approved the constitution unanimously; eighty-three Fathers were absent (cf. U. Betti, La Constituzione dogmatica 'Pastor Aeternus,' Rome 1961). It was a dramatic page in the Church's history, but quite clear and definitive for all that."

The decisions of Vatican I are important in this book, first, because they were dogmatic declarations and therefore definitive and, second, because "The First and Second Council of the Vatican complement each other."[7] *Pastor Aeternus*, which is the First Dogmatic Constitution issued by the Vatican Council, affirmed the Papal sovereignty over the Church in these words:

> (*Canon*) If then any shall say that the Roman Pontiff has the office merely of inspection or direction, and not full and supreme power of jurisdiction over the universal Church, not

only in things which belong to faith and morals, but also in those things which relate to the discipline and government of the Church spread throughout the world; or assert that he possesses merely the principal part, and not all the fullness of this supreme power; or that this power which he enjoys is not ordinary and immediate, both over each and all the Churches and over each and all the pastors of the faithful; let him be anathema.[8]

In the paragraph preceding this passage the Council had declared:

And since, by the divine right of Apostolic primacy, one Roman Pontiff is placed over the universal Church, We further teach and declare that he is the supreme judge of the faithful, and that in all causes the decision of which belongs to the Church recourse may be had to his tribunal, but that none may reopen the judgment of the Apostolic See, than whose authority there is no greater, nor can any lawfully review its judgment. Wherefore they err from the right path of truth who assert that it is lawful to appeal from the judgments of the Roman pontiffs to an ecumenical council, as to an authority higher than that of the Roman Pontiff.

Then the constitution proceeded to define the infallibility of the Pope:

Therefore, faithfully adhering to the tradition received from the beginning of the Christian faith, for the glory of God our Saviour, the exaltation of the Catholic religion, and the salvation of Christian people, with the approval of the sacred council, We teach and define that it is a dogma divinely revealed: that the Roman Pontiff, when he speaks *ex cathedra*, that is, when, in discharge of the office of pastor and teacher of all Christians, by virtue of his supreme Apostolic authority, he defines a doctrine regarding faith or morals to be held by the universal Church, is, by the divine assistance promised to him in Blessed Peter, possessed of that infallibility with which the Divine Redeemer willed that His Church should be endowed in defining doctrine regarding faith or morals; and that, therefore, such definitions of the Roman pontiff are of themselves, and not from the consent of the Church, irreformable.
But if anyone—which may God avert!—presume to contradict this our definition, let him be anathema.

The objection is made by some that when the Pope asserts his infallibility he is lifting himself by his own bootstraps—what he says is infallible is infallible because he says he is infallible. But Papal infallibility was not proclaimed by the Pope alone. Rather it was decreed by the First Vatican Council speaking in unity with the Pope, that is, by the Church speaking as a whole. And Vatican I did not spring this dogma as a surprise. Rather, the infallibility of the Pope had been generally acknowledged informally before, just as the Assumption of the Blessed Mother was believed before it was officially proclaimed in 1950. Nor did Vatican I exceed the authority conferred on the Church by Christ, for the Church is more than a mere agent without any power to determine the scope of his authority. Rather, the general commission by Christ to the Apostles and His promise to be with the Church to the end of the world necessarily included some power in the Church to determine the extent of its jurisdiction on particular issues. This is true especially of the Pope, whose primary place was clearly conferred by Christ. Uncertainty concerning the capacity of the Church to declare her own infallibility and that of the Pope generally results from a failure to keep in mind that the Church is not a merely human organization or agent. She has her own attributes and prerogatives, which are unique. Of course, we are not concerned here only with the power of the Church to teach infallibly, but also with the authentic teaching authority exercised on a less than infallible plane. In both cases, we should accept the assertions of authority issued by the Pope and by the councils speaking in unity with the Pope because the demarcation, for the guidance of the faithful, of the authority conferred on her by Christ is fully in keeping with the unique character of the Church and with her teaching mission.

This unique, nontransferable authority of the Pope is a crucial distinction between authority in the Church and in civil society. It is beyond the rightful power of the cardinals to refuse to fill the Papal office, to dilute its powers, or to transfer to any other office the powers conferred on the Pope by Christ. The faithful, whether clergy or laity, do not have the right possessed in civil society to alter the form of ecclesiastical government in which the Roman Pontiff is supreme. For this supremacy was conferred on Peter and his successors by Christ and it was meant by Him to endure. "Loyalty to the Pope," said Scottish Archbishop Gordon J. Gray recently, "is not a sentimental loyalty, but a loyalty rooted in our Catholic belief that the Holy Father is the vicar of Christ on earth, and that his directives and guidance enjoy a unique authority."

Father Hans Küng, a leading critic of Papal authority, once commented, "The Pope has an exaggerated view of his office. The Papacy, after all has been said, is a human institution and has no origin in the Gospels." On the contrary, the primacy of Peter and of his successors was specifically willed by Christ as a permanent and integral part of the structure of His Church. This primacy was not generated by the needs of any historical period and it could not be discarded by the present or any other generation on the ground that it is unsuited to modern times. Cardinal Daniélou emphasized the origin of Papal authority in these terms:

> As Peter exercised the primacy in that first community of apostles, so, in the collegiality of the bishops, the successor of Peter has always exercised the primacy. This was established personally by Christ and it will endure until the end of the world. . . .
>
> It is then absolutely false from an historical point of view to assert that in the Church this is a phenomenon on a secondary level, the reflection of certain sociological circumstances. It is instead an aspect fundamental to that which Christ willed to establish. He conferred all the riches which are His own on those whom He chose to be the instruments through whom he would have his own gifts transmitted. To contest the existence of this authority in the Church means to contest the very institution willed by Jesus Christ.[9]

It is important to understand the authority of the Pope in relation to the authority of the bishops. The distinction between their powers derives from the dual nature of the powers conferred upon the apostles. Charles Cardinal Journet recently explained this point:

> The power of authoritatively stating the things that have to be believed and done in the Kingdom of God was conferred in a double form: extraordinary powers designed for the purpose of founding the Church during the apostolic age, in the way that builders lay the foundation of a structure that will outlast themselves; secondly, ordinary powers, designed to preserve the church in the post-Apostolic age, that is to say, the foundation in respect of her duration in time, just as the foundation and the rock upon which they rest hold up the whole building.
>
> The Apostles received the extraordinary power in equal meas-

ure, but received the ordinary power in different ways. Inasmuch as they were apostles, they were all equal in regard to constructing the Church, and Peter was therefore "primus inter pares." But inasmuch as one of them was the pastor and the others the sheep, they were not equal in the power which they were later to transmit to their own successors to govern Christ's Church till the end of time. This distinction is of basic importance.[10]

An example of this distinction of powers is found in St. Paul's epistle to the Galatians, where the apostle relates, "But when Cephas came to Antioch, I opposed him to his face, because he was deserving of blame."[11] St. Thomas Aquinas, commenting on this confrontation between Peter and Paul, observes, "To withstand anyone in public exceeds the mode of fraternal correction, and so Paul would not have withstood Peter then, unless he were in some way his equal as regards the defense of the faith."[12] St. Thomas was referring here to the equality of the apostles in their possession of extraordinary powers, as described by Cardinal Journet. Elsewhere, St. Thomas affirms that the "Pope has the plenitude of power in the Church."[13] He quotes approvingly from the Council of Constantinople, held in 869: "In accordance with the Scriptures and the statutes and definitions of the canons, we venerate the most holy bishop of ancient Rome the first and greatest of bishops, and after him the bishop of Constantinople."[14] St. Thomas then quotes an even stronger affirmation of Papal authority from the prayer of Cyril, Bishop of Alexandria: "That we may remain members of our apostolic head, the throne of the Roman Pontiffs, of whom it is our duty to seek what we are to believe and what we are to hold, venerating him, beseeching him above others; for his it is to reprove, to correct, to appoint, to loose, and to bind in place of Him who set up that very throne, and Who gave the fullness of His own to no other, but to him alone, to whom by divine right all bow the head, and the primates of the world are obedient as to our Lord Jesus Christ Himself."[15]

This Papal primacy was described by St. Thomas as necessary for the common good and unity of the Church:

Wherever there are several authorities directed to one purpose, there must needs be one universal authority over the particular authorities, because . . . otherwise there would be no cohesion towards the one object. Hence since the whole Church is one body, it behooves, if this oneness is to be preserved, that there be a governing power in respect of the whole Church, above the episcopal power whereby each particular Church is governed, and this is the power of the Pope. Consequently those who deny this power are called schismatics as causing a division in the unit of the Church.[16]

It is interesting to note that in the same paragraph in which he comments on Paul's rebuke of Peter as an equal, Aquinas comments on the duty of the faithful to reprove even their bishops at times: "But one who is not an equal can reprove privately and respectfully. Hence the apostle in writing to the Colossians[17] tells them to admonish their prelates: 'Say to Archippus: Fulfill thy ministry.' It must be observed, however, that if the faith were endangered, a subject ought to reprove his prelate even publicly. Hence Paul, who was Peter's subject, rebuked him in public, on account of the imminent danger of scandal concerning faith, and, as the gloss of Augustine says on Gal. 2:11, 'Peter gave an example to superiors, that if at any time they should happen to stray from the straight path, they should not disdain to be reproved by their subjects.' "[18]

The primacy of Peter is essential to a proper understanding of the concept of collegiality. The Prefatory note of explanation appended by the Second Vatican Council to the Dogmatic Constitution on the Church emphasized that "there is no distinction between the Roman Pontiff and the bishops taken collectively, but between the Roman Pontiff by himself and the Roman Pontiff together with the bishops. Since the Supreme Pontiff is the head of the College, he alone can perform certain acts which in no wise belong to the bishops, for example, convoking and directing the College, approving the norms of action, etc." In the words of the Dogmatic Constitution itself:

But the college or body of bishops has no authority unless it is simultaneously conceived of in terms of its head, the Roman Pontiff, Peter's successor, and without any lessening of his power of primacy over all, pastors as well as the general faithful. For in virtue of his office, that is, as Vicar of Christ and pastor of the whole Church, the Roman Pontiff has full, supreme and universal power over the Church. And he can always exercise this power freely.

The order of bishops is the successor to the college of the apostles in teaching authority and pastoral rule, or, rather, in the episcopal order the apostolic body continues without a break. Together with its head, the Roman Pontiff, and never without this head, the episcopal order is the subject of supreme and full power over the universal Church. But this power can be exercised only with the consent of the Roman Pontiff. For our Lord made Simon Peter alone the rock and keybearer of the Church (cf. Mt. 16:18–19) and appointed him shepherd of the whole flock (cf. Jn. 21:15ff.).[19]

This Papal primacy is so important that Cardinal Daniélou was led to comment, "If one does not accept that, one is no longer speaking of the Church."[20] These principles were reaffirmed by the synods of bishops held since the Second Vatican Council adjourned in 1965. Although the bishops are being given a greater opportunity and responsibility to work with the Pope and to participate in the governance of the Church, it is still true, as John Cardinal Dearden of Detroit put it, that "the Holy Father is the supreme pastor with complete, full, direct and personal jurisdiction over the entire Church. Therefore, that authority cannot and will not be curtailed."[21]

In his address at the opening of the synod of bishops in 1969, Pope Paul affirmed his support for the concept of collegiality as enunciated by Vatican II, promised to give greater recognition to the prerogatives and powers of the bishops and to promote "a more organic sharing and a more solid co-responsibility in the government of the universal Church." But then, in a passage that led one priest to complain, "He is really throwing the gauntlet in our face," the Pope asserted the pre-eminence of his own office:

But let it be clear, even in this regard, that the government of the Church must not take on the appearances and the norms of temporal regimes, which are today guided by democratic institutions that are sometimes irresponsible and going to excess, or by totalitarian forms that are contrary to the dignity of the man who is subject to them; the government of the Church has an original form of its own, which aims to reflect in its expressions the wisdom and the will of its Divine Founder. And it is in this respect that We must remember Our supreme responsibility, which Christ wished to entrust to Us when He gave Peter the keys of the Kingdom and made him the foundation of the edifice of the Church, committing to him a most delicate charism, that of strengthening his brethren (Lk. 22:32), receiving from him the highest and firmest profession of faith (Mt. 16:17; Jn. 6:68), and asking of him a most singular threefold confession of love intended to find expression in the primary virtue of pastoral charity (Jn. 21:15 et seq.). A responsibility that Tradition and the Councils attribute to Our specific ministry as Vicar of Christ, Head of the Apostolic College, Universal Pastor, and Servant of the servants of God, and which cannot be conditioned on the authority, supreme though it be, of the Episcopal College, which We are the first to wish to honor, defend and promote, but which would not be such, were it to lack Our support.[22]

When we ask, "Who shall decide?" the answer, in view of the foregoing, must be that the jurisdiction of the Pope and of the bishops, teaching in communion with him, is clear.[23]

What Can Be Decided?

There are two types of authority here. One may be described as the teaching authority and the other as the disciplinary authority.

THE TEACHING AUTHORITY

The teaching authority concerns itself with the definition or explanation of a truth of faith or morals. It appeals to our belief. A truth may be infallibly proclaimed as being in accord with revelation, as with the Assumption of the Blessed Virgin. In such a case, the definition of that truth can never be changed. "All are obliged to maintain and to be ruled by this revelation," in the words of Vatican II.[24] Or a truth may be defined or explained pursuant to the authentic teaching authority of the Pope or of the bishops teaching with the Pope. Such a teaching, when it is not infallible, may theoretically be reformed at some future date. This is the case with the ban on artificial birth control, unless, as was discussed in the preceding chapter, that teaching took on a character of infallibility from its unbroken universality throughout the history of the Church. Yet even the noninfallible teachings of the Church demand assent and submission. The Second Vatican Council described this quality as follows:

Bishops, teaching in communion with the Roman Pontiff, are to be respected by all as witnesses to divine and Catholic truth. In matters of faith and morals, the bishops speak in the name of Christ and the faithful are to accept their teaching and adhere to it with a religious assent of soul. This religious submission of will and of mind must be shown in a special way to the authentic teaching authority of the Roman Pontiff, even when he is not speaking ex cathedra. That is, it must be shown in such a way that his supreme magisterium is acknowledged with reverence, the judgments made by him are sincerely adhered to, according to his manifest mind and will. His mind and will in the matter may be known chiefly either from the character of the documents, from his frequent repetition of the same doctrine, or from his manner of speaking.[25]

The "religious submission of will and of mind" that must be shown to authentic teachings of the Holy Father does not involve a merely external observance. Significantly, Pope Paul included in *Humanae Vitae* an admonition to priests to "be the first to give, in the exercise of your ministry, the example of loyal internal and external obedience to the teaching authority of the Church." When Monsignor Ferdinando Lambruschini, the spokesman for the Pope, presented *Humanae Vitae* to the press, he said:

The decision has been given and it is not infallible. But it does not leave the question of the regulation of birth in a state of vague uncertainty. Only definitions strictly so called command the assent of theological faith. But a pronouncement of the authentic Magisterium requires full and loyal assent— internal and not merely external—in proportion to the importance of the authority that issues it (in this case the Supreme Pontiff), and the manner with which he deals (in the present case a matter of the greatest importance, treating as it does the vexed question of the regulation of birth). This decision binds the conscience of all without any ambiguity. In particular, it can and must be said that the authentic pronouncement contained in the Encyclical *Humanae Vitae* excludes the possibility of a contrary opinion, valid on the moral plane, opposed to this teaching and that notwithstanding the number and the authority (hierarchical, scientific and theological) of those who have in recent years maintained that it is possible to have such a probable opinion. The pretext of the presumed doubt in the Church owing to the long silence of the Pope is not consistent, and conflicts with the repeated appeals of the Pope and Council to abide by the previous directives of the Magisterium which were still binding. *All those who have in recent years incautiously taught that it is lawful to use artificial contraception to regulate births and have acted accordingly in their pastoral guidance and in the ministry of the confessional, must now change their attitude and set an example by their full acceptance of the teaching of the Encyclical.*[26] (Emphasis added)

It is true, as one commentator noted, that "internal assent or obedience is, then, entirely compatible with the critical study of the doctrinal point proposed in an encyclical."[27] But the "supreme magisterium" of the Pope must be "acknowledged with reverence."[28] The legitimacy of serious study of a doctrinal point surely does not warrant a public rejection of it or a public disparagement of the Papal authority.

The teaching authority of the Church, then, may be exercised in an infallible or in a less than infallible way. The teachings issued pursuant to that authority are entitled to internal as well as external submission of mind and will in both cases, although noninfallible teachings theoretically can be changed at a future time.

THE DISCIPLINARY AUTHORITY

The disciplinary authority of the Church, however, does not command the same manner of assent. As Cardinal Newman described that authority, "The Roman Pontiff has by divine right the power of passing universal laws pertaining to the *discipline* of the Church; for instance, to divine worship, sacred rites, the ordination and manner of life of the clergy, the order of the ecclesiastical regimen, and the right administration of the temporal possessions of the church" (Emphasis in original).[29] Where the teaching authority is concerned with truth and it appeals to our belief, the disciplinary authority is concerned with commands in the practical order, such as attendance at Mass on Sundays and holy days. It requires obedience and does not concern itself directly with definitions and truth or falsity. Dietrich von Hildebrand described in these terms the obligation which attaches to disciplinary edicts of the Church:

The situation is different when positive commandments of the Church, practical decisions, are at stake. Here we are not faced with the infallible Church. While we must obey such decisions and submit to them in reverence and deep respect, we

need not consider them felicitous or prudent. Here the maxim
Roma locuta est; causa finita est does not apply. If we are
convinced that any practical change or decision is objectively
unfortunate, noxious, compromising, imprudent, or unjust, we
are permitted to pray that it may be revoked, to write in a
respectful manner about the topic, to direct petitions for a
change of it to the Holy Father, to attempt, in a variety of
ways, to influence a reversal of the decision.

Today, many theologians propose to replace the deposit of
Catholic faith with their own subjective opinions about Christ,
His Virginal birth, resurrection, and so on. This is not only clear
apostasy, but also the most ridiculous presumption—as if, in
matters of faith, their subjective opinions could have any weight.
Theologians like Schillebeeckx or Metz cannot base their theologizing about Heaven and Hell and redemption on any real
knowledge, because these mysteries are not accessible to any
natural knowledge or research. But obviously the same is not
true of disciplinary orders or enactments of a pope. They are not
only not infallible, but we can with our reason grasp the
eventual injustice or inadequacy of them.[30]

The objects of the disciplinary authority are such things as the form
of liturgical rites, regulations on fast and abstinence, general administrative matters, and the like. The commands of this governing
authority exact from us a duty of generous obedience, but they do
not demand the assent and submission of mind and will which we
must give to the teaching authority. On the other hand, the
teaching authority, or magisterial office of the Church, relates not
to discipline but to truth. It extends, in the words of Vatican II,
to "matters of faith and morals."[31]

NATURAL LAW

Any Church must be able to answer quite definitely when
great questions of public morals are put. Can I go in for
cannibalism, or murder babies to reduce the population, or any
similar scientific or progressive reform? Any Church with authority to teach must be able to say whether it can be done.
. . . I have no use for a Church which is not a Church militant,
which cannot order battle and fall in line, and march in the
same direction.[32]

When Chesterton wrote this, he had in mind the capacity of the
Church to define the applications of the natural moral law. This

capacity is implied in her general jurisdiction over matters of faith and morals. The infallibility with which Christ endowed His Church "in defining a doctrine of faith and morals extends as far as extends the deposit of divine revelation, which must be religiously guarded and faithfully expounded."[33] As for the content of revelation, Vatican II's Dogmatic Constitution on Divine Revelation declared:

10. Sacred tradition and sacred Scripture form one sacred deposit of the word of God, which is committed to the Church. . . .

The task of authentically interpreting the word of God, whether written or handed on, has been entrusted exclusively to the living teaching office of the Church, whose authority is exercised in the name of Jesus Christ.

The teaching office of the Church, however, is not limited to dogmas of faith. Rather, as stated by Vatican II, it extends also to morals. That is, the Church has the authority and duty to declare that certain types of conduct are moral or immoral. Specifically, this means that the Church has the authority and duty to make binding applications of the natural moral law. The natural moral law has been variously described. A perceptive analysis was made by Father John Courtney Murray:

From the metaphysical premises of natural law follow its two characteristics. It is a law immanent in the nature of man, but transcendent in its reference. It is rational, not rationalist. It is the work of reason, but not of an absolutely autonomous reason. It is immanent in nature in the sense that it consists in the dictates of human reason that are uttered as reason confronts the fundamental moral problems of human existence. These are the problems of what I, simply because I am a man and apart from all other considerations, ought to do or avoid in the basic situations in which I, again simply because I am a man, find myself. My situation is that of a creature before God; that of a "self" possessed of freedom to realize its "self"; that of a man living among other men, possessing what is mine as the other possesses what is his. In the face of these situations, certain imperatives "emerge" (if you like) from human nature. They are the product of its inclinations, as these are recognized by reason to be conformed to my rational nature. And they are formed by reason into dictates that present themselves as demanding obedience. Appearing, as they do, as dictates, these

judgments of reason are law. Appearing, as they do, in consequence of an inclination that reason recognizes as authentically
human, they are "natural" law.[34]

Some critics today deny that the Church has the authority to
rule on the applications of natural law. On the contrary, this authority of the Church is clear and it has been exercised on numerous
occasions throughout the history of the Church.[35] On a number of
occasions, recent Popes have unambiguously asserted this authority.
Although examples could be multiplied, the importance of the issue
justifies a few short quotations to demonstrate the point:

Whatever a Christian man may do, even in affairs of this
world, he may not ignore the supernatural, nay he must direct
all to the highest good as to his last end, in accordance with the
dictates of Christian wisdom; but all his actions, in so far as they
are morally good or evil, that is, agree with, or are in opposition
to, divine and natural law, are subject to the judgment and
authority of the Church. . . . (Pius X, Encyclical *Singulari
Quadam*, 1912)
Christ Himself made the Church the teacher of truth in these
things also which concern the ruling and regulation of moral
conduct, even though some things are not of themselves im-
pervious to human reason. For just as God in the case of the
natural truths of religion and morals added revelation to the
light of reason so that these things which are right and true,
"in the present state also of the human race may be known
readily with real certainty without any admixture of error," so
for the same purpose He has constituted the Church "the
guardian and the teacher of the whole of the truth concerning
religion and moral conduct." (Pius XI, Encyclical *Casti Connubii*, 1930)
It is for this reason that divine revelation must be considered
morally necessary so that those religious and moral truths which
are not of their nature beyond the reach of reason in the
present condition of the human race may be known with a
firm certainty and with freedom from all error. (Pius XII,
Encyclical *Humani Generis*, 1950)
The power of the Church is not bound by the limits of
"matters strictly religious," as they say, but the whole matter
of the natural law, its foundation, its interpretation, its application, so far as their moral aspect extends, are within the
Church's power. For the keeping of the natural law, by God's
appointment, has reference to the road by which man has to

approach his supernatural end. But on this road the Church is man's guide and guardian in what concerns his supreme end. (Pius XII, Allocution *Magnificate Dominum*, 1954)

Therefore as far as Catholics are concerned, this decision (whether the moment has arrived for co-operation with movements based on "false philosophical teachings regarding the nature, origin and destiny of the universe and of man") rests primarily with those who live and work in the specific sectors of human society in which those problems arise, always, however, in accordance with the principles of the natural law, with the social doctrine of the Church, and with the directives of ecclesiastical authority. For it must not be forgotten, that the Church has the right and the duty to intervene authoritatively with her children in the temporal sphere when there is a question of judging the application of those principles to concrete cases. (John XXIII, Encyclical *Pacem in Terris*, 1963)

The Second Vatican Council asserted that "the Church is, by the will of Christ, the teacher of the truth. It is her duty to give utterance to, and authoritatively to teach, that Truth which is Christ Himself, and also to declare and confirm by her authority those principles of the moral order which have their origin in human nature itself."[36] The same point was made by Pope Paul VI in *Humanae Vitae*.

This function of the Church to define the natural law ought not to be regarded as extraneous to its mission. On the contrary, it is difficult to see how the Church could perform its mission at all if it were to renounce the right to define with binding force the applications of natural law. This is not the place for a detailed discussion of the Church's role in defining natural law, but it would seem clear that she could not be deprived of that role without fatally compromising the performance of her function.

The Popes seem to consider that when they pronounce on the applications of the natural law, they are not merely discoursing on questions of philosophy or of human wisdom, but that they are teaching something which is part of the total Christian revelation. Pope Pius XII emphasized this point, that the natural moral law and supernatural revelation have both been entrusted to the Church by Christ:

Both these—the natural law written in the heart and the truths and precepts of supernatural revelation—Jesus, our Redeemer, gave to His Church as the moral treasure of humanity in order that she might preach them to all creatures, explain them, and hand them on intact and safeguarded from all contamination and error from one generation to another.[37]

In principle, the natural moral law, even in its specific applications, can be demonstrated and certainly known from reason alone. Therefore, discussion and argument among theologians and the laity are desirable, since the Holy Spirit works through human agencies in guiding the Church. But reason is not an infallible guide here. As Pope Pius XI put it in *Casti Connubii:*

> But everyone can see to how many fallacies an avenue would be opened up and how many errors would become mixed with the truth, if it were left solely to the light of reason of each to find out or if it were to be discovered by the private interpretation of the truth which is revealed. And if this is applicable to many other truths of the moral order, we must pay attention all the more to those things which appertain to marriage, where the inordinate desire for pleasure can attack frail human nature and easily deceive it and lead it astray. . . .
> On this account, in order that no falsification or corruption of the divine law but a true genuine knowledge of it may enlighten the minds of men and guide their conduct, it is necessary that a filial and humble obedience towards the Church should be combined with a devotedness to God and the desire of submitting to Him. . . . For just as God in the case of the natural truths of religion and morality added revelation to the light of reason so that these things which are right and true, "in the present state also of the human race may be known readily with real certainty without any admixture of error," so for the same purpose He has constituted the Church the guardian and the teacher of the whole of the truth concerning religion and moral conduct.

The guidance of the Church, then, is essential if men are to achieve a consistently correct observance of the law written in their nature. In giving this direction, the Church is not merely seeking to persuade. Rather, although she desires that men should be convinced of the reasonableness of her position, she is primarily expounding the law. It is for this reason that, when the authentic teaching voice of the Church, whether the Pope or the bishops in communion with him, pronounces authoritatively on a matter of natural moral law, the pronouncement's binding force is not limited by the persuasiveness of the arguments advanced:

Therefore, when it is a question of instructions and propositions which the properly established Shepherds (that is, the Roman Pontiff for the whole Church and the bishops for the faithful entrusted to them) publish on matters within the natural law, the faithful must not invoke that saying (which is wont to be employed with respect to opinions of individuals): "the strength of the authority is no more than the strength of the arguments." Hence, even though to someone certain declarations of the Church may not seem to be proved by the arguments put forward, his obligation to obey still remains.[38]

If the Papal teaching need not be accepted by a Catholic unless he is personally convinced of the soundness of the Pope's reasoning, then "the Holy Father is being regarded as nothing more than a wise and morally sensitive man, who deserves to be listened to only because of his human qualifications."[39] The incongruity of this position in light of the intrinsic nature of the Papacy and of the Church is evident.

It is clear, therefore, that the general teaching authority and the guarantee of infallibility extend to the whole of divine Revelation and that this includes the principles and applications of the natural moral law.[40] It is also clear, from the unique character of her commission, that the teaching authority of the Church not only can teach the applications of the natural law, on an infallible or less than infallible basis, as the case may be, but it can also determine whether a particular question is in fact a question of the natural law and therefore within the Church's teaching authority.

In some quarters the argument is made that although the Pope receives a special inspiration or charism from the Holy Spirit, it may occur that in special circumstances the Pope will receive this charism inadequately or misunderstand it and that therefore others might have a clearer view of the truth. This sounds plausible in theory, but we are entitled to ask on what basis the critic is certain that he is receiving and perceiving the Holy Spirit in a manner superior to that of the Pope. How can the critic be so sure of the superiority of his own vision that he feels himself entitled to propagandize against the teaching which the Pope proclaims as the authentic teaching of the Church? To presume that one's own inspiration is superior to that of the Pope would hardly be to give his authentic teachings the "religious submission of will and of mind" required by Vatican II.[41]

If we concentrate only on the structure and content of the Church's authority, we can hardly avoid a distortion of reality. For authority does not exist in a vacuum. It exists in relation to people and its analysis must take account not only of their duty to obey but also of their duty to act according to their own consciences. Conscience was described by St. Thomas Aquinas as "knowledge applied to an individual case."[42] Today, the conscience problem is the most troublesome and complex part of the authority question. However, there are governing principles which are serviceable and distinctively Catholic as well.

Who Must Obey?

"I shall drink—to the Pope, if you please,—still, to Conscience first, and to the Pope afterwards." This was John Henry Cardinal Newman's response to a toast at a banquet tendered to him after his elevation to the cardinalate. Newman, on his entire career, can hardly be dismissed as unduly authoritarian. It is significant, therefore, that his views on Papal authority are of scant comfort to those who today would challenge that authority in the name of conscience. On the one hand, he emphasized "that conscience is ever to be obeyed whether it tells truly or erroneously, and that, whether the error is the fault of the person thus erring or not. . . . Of course, if he is culpable in being in error, which he might have escaped, had he been more in earnest, for that error he is answerable to God, but still he must act according to that error, while he is in it, because he in full sincerity thinks the error to be truth."[43] But Newman denounced the "counterfeit" idea of conscience which many regard as "the right of self-will." For the dictate of conscience "to prevail against the voice of the Pope," he said, it "must follow upon serious thought, prayer, and all available means of arriving at a right judgment on the matter in question. And further, obedience to the Pope is what is called 'in possession'; that is, the *onus probandi* of establishing a case against him lies, as in all cases of exception, on the side of conscience. Unless a man is able to say to himself, as in the Presence of God, that he must not, and dare not, act upon the Papal injunction, he is bound to obey it, and would commit a great sin in disobeying it. *Prima facie* it is his bounden duty, even from a sentiment of loyalty, to believe the Pope right and to act accordingly. He must vanquish that mean, ungenerous, selfish, vulgar spirit of his nature, which, at the very first rumour of a command, places itself in opposition to the Superior who gives it, asks itself whether he is not exceeding his right, and rejoices, in a moral and practical matter, to commence with scepticism. . . . If this necessary rule were observed, collisions between the Pope's authority and the authority of conscience would be very rare."[44]

While conceding its importance, the first thing to recognize is that freedom of conscience is not absolute. In warning against false concepts of freedom, Pope Paul observed that "we are given freedom in order to carry out our duty by our own efforts."[45] The Pope, a week later, rejected the idea that "the whole morality of man should consist in following his own conscience; and this affirmation is made to emancipate him from the exigencies of an extrinsic standard as well as from obedience to an authority that tries to lay down the law to the free and spontaneous activity of man, who must be a law unto himself, without the restraint of other interventions in his actions."[46] The Pope agreed that "to have one's conscience as guide is not only a good thing, but is one's duty. Anyone who acts contrary to his conscience is no longer on the straight path (cf. Rom. 14:23)." But then he qualified his remarks: Conscience, which he described as "the subjective and immediate intimation of a law, which we must call a natural law, in order to be a valid norm for human behavior, must be right, that is, it must be sure of itself and true, not uncertain, not culpably wrong. The latter, unfortunately, may easily occur, owing to the weakness of human reason, when it is left to itself, when it is not educated.

"Conscience needs to be educated," Pope Paul said, echoing the point made by Pius XI and Pius XII that men need the direction of the Church to avoid error in applying the natural law. "Teaching is necessary for conscience," he continued, "as it is necessary for the whole of man. . . . Conscience is not the only voice that can guide human activity; its voice becomes clearer and stronger when the voice of law, and therefore of the lawful authority, unites with it. That is, the voice of conscience is not always infallible, nor is it objectively supreme. And this is particularly true in the field of supernatural action, where reason cannot by itself interpret the way to goodness, and has to have recourse to faith to dictate to man the norm of justice willed by God by means of revelation: 'The righteous shall live by faith' (Gal. 3:11). To walk straight in the darkness, that is in the mystery of Christian life, one's eyes are not enough, one needs a lamp, a light. And this 'lumen Christi' does not distort, does not mortify, does not contradict the light of our conscience, but brightens it and enables it to follow Christ, on the straight path of our pilgrimage towards the eternal vision."[47]

In essence, the teaching of the Church tells me what is morally evil. My conscience tells me whether and to what extent I have violated that teaching so as to be personally guilty of sin. Conscience is not a teacher of doctrine but a practical guide or norm of action in particular cases. "Conscience, in practice," said Pope Paul, "is judgment about the righteousness, that is, the morality, of our actions, both considered in their general aspect and in their individual acts."[48] Catholics have a duty to form their consciences in accord with the teaching of the Church. The Austrian bishops, in their commentary on *Humanae Vitae*, put it well: "That there is a freedom of conscience, but not freedom in the formation of conscience. That is: The formation of a responsible conscience is dependent on the law of God, which cannot be overlooked in making of concrete judgments. And because the law of God has to be applied to thousands of circumstances and ways of life the determining word of the teaching authority of the Church serves to realize our true humanity."[49]

There are two stages, therefore: One must form his conscience and one then must follow it. Conscience must be followed even if it is erroneously formed and is therefore objectively in error. But one still may be culpable for failing to form that conscience correctly in the first place. These limitations on freedom of conscience are not of recent origin. Rather, they have long been recognized. St. Thomas Aquinas, for example, explained that those who act with an erroneous reason or conscience may be culpable:

> If then reason or conscience err with an error that is voluntary, either directly, or through negligence, so that one errs about what one ought to know; then such an error of reason or conscience does not excuse the will, that abides by that erring reason or conscience, from being evil. But if the error arise from ignorance of some circumstance, and without any negligence, so that it cause the act to be involuntary, then that error of reason or conscience excuses the will, that abides by that erring reason, from being evil.[50]

These principles are fully applicable to the contraception issue. The Second Vatican Council emphasized the duty of spouses to "be governed according to a conscience dutifully conformed to the divine law itself . . . and . . . the Church's teaching office."[51] If we concede that the teaching of *Humanae Vitae* is not infallible, we must then admit that it is reformable, in the sense that it would not violate infallible Catholic doctrine for it to be changed at some time in the future. This possibility of change, however, is barely that, a theoretical possibility. It is so unlikely that we can disregard it as a practical consideration. In any event, the crucial fact is that the teaching of *Humanae Vitae* is now, and always has been, the authentic, even if not technically infallible, teaching of the Church. It is in accord with this teaching that we are obliged to form our conscience. "Because the solidly firm teaching of the Church protects us against many erroneous judgments by which we would otherwise have directed our lives," said Patrick Cardinal O'Boyle, "we Catholics are blessed compared with those who do not accept the authority of this divinely established moral teacher."[52]

In its Declaration on Religious Freedom, the Second Vatican Council stressed "the right to religious freedom."[53] But this right refers to the immunity from coercion by the state and does not affect the duty of a Catholic to obey the teaching authority of the Church. As the Declaration phrased it, "Religious freedom, in turn, which men demand as necessary to fulfill their duty to worship God, has to do with immunity from coercion in civil society. Therefore, it leaves untouched traditional Catholic doctrine on the moral duty of men and societies toward the true religion and toward the one Church of Christ."[54] As Cardinal O'Boyle put it, "This decree did not authorize Catholics to judge each precept of the Church's moral teaching for themselves (cf. *Decree on Religious Liberty*, No. 1, and No. 14). The decree does teach that no government may force someone to be a Catholic or not to be one. But a faithful Catholic's own conscience demands that his action not violate the Church's authentic moral teaching."[55]

In summary, we might well quote Pope Paul VI when he spoke to a group of pilgrims three months before he issued *Humanae Vitae*:

> But there are two matters beyond argument; the truth of the Faith, authoritatively sanctioned by tradition and by the ecclesiastical magisterium, and the constitutional law of the Church. . . . Therefore: renewal, yes. Arbitrary change, no. . . . Religious liberty for all in civilized society, and liberty of personal adherence to religion according to the well-considered choice of the individual conscience, yes. Liberty of conscience

as the criterion of religious truth, without reference to the authenticity of serious and authorized teaching, no."[56]

In the aftermath of *Humanae Vitae*, the duty to form one's conscience in accord with the teaching Church has been neglected by some in their effort to avoid the stringency of the Papal edict. As Pope Paul noted, "on the one hand they try to minimize the conception of sin, palliating even grave infractions of the moral norm . . . on the other hand, they suppose themselves to be guided by the Holy Spirit, conferring on their own thoughts and their own conduct a gratuitous and often fallacious charism of certainty and infallibility."[57] The Church has always had schismatics, who reject Papal authority; heretics, who deny points of doctrine; and apostates, who utterly renounce the Faith. But today there is a notable lack of candor in the widespread refusal of obedience. Instead of an open break we have what might fairly be called a "sit-in schism." It was Cardinal Newman who said, "It is a miserable time when a man's Catholic profession is no voucher for his orthodoxy, and when a teacher of religion may be within the Church's pale, yet external to her faith."[58] We are living in such a time. In the words of Pope Paul, "a practically schismatic ferment is dividing" the Church.[59] Dr. Francis E. McMahon, former president of the American Catholic Philosophical Association and of the Catholic Association for International Peace, has charged that "immanent apostasy" is "rife" within the Church. These new apostates, he claims, want "to bring into existence a completely new church though all the while professing allegiance to the old."[60] Members of a "very articulate and influential minority," the immanent apostates, according to Dr. McMahon, "occupy chairs of theology or philosophy in Catholic seminaries of universities. They are editors of so-called Catholic periodicals. They preach from the pulpits of Catholic churches and lecture from Catholic platforms. A number of lay people, some posing as authoritative theologians, exhort Catholics to develop a new religious vision at variance with the traditions of Catholicity." Pope Paul made a similar point in his general audience of January 28, 1970, when he criticized those who "dream of shaping a new kind of Church corresponding to their own ideas, which are sometimes noble and lofty. But it would not be the authentic Church, as Christ willed it, and as it developed and matured in the course of history." It would be presumptuous to call for a purge of those who profess their allegiance to the Church yet withhold their assent to her teachings. Whether excommunication and other spiritual sanctions are appropriate at this time is for the Pope to decide. It is for us to accept his decision. But it is also for us to do our part to counter the prevailing error. There are two things that can be done. One, in the words of Cardinal Daniélou, is to "make our protest." "Rome will not be shaken," the Jesuit Cardinal said, "but it is necessary that in the face of this contestation, an immense wave of the Christian people proclaim their fidelity and declare their confidence to the Sovereign Pontiff, to defend him against those who would drag the Church into decadence."[61] The second thing we can do is to measure our leaders, clerical, religious, and lay, by their adherence to *Humanae Vitae* and the *Credo* of Pope Paul. As Dr. McMahon put it, "Anyone who cannot accept integrally the contents of the creed of Paul VI—accept them in the sense intended by the Pope—should not call himself a Roman Catholic." This is not to suggest a purge. Nor is it to urge anyone to withdraw from the Church. It is only to say that, in troubled times, we should take spiritual direction only from those who are unequivocally receptive to the teaching Church. And it is to urge those Catholics who reject the authority of the Church to recognize the inconsistency of their position. The Catholic bishops of Scotland, in their joint pastoral letter, noted that the willingness to form one's conscience to the teaching of *Humanae Vitae* is a fair test of one's Catholic profession:

> In the encyclical the Holy Father has given us the principles according to which Catholics are to form their consciences in this matter. The obligation of a Catholic to accept the teaching of the Church on any grave moral problem can never justifiably be regarded as an offense against the freedom of his conscience. Rather, the free acceptance of that particular obligation is implicit in the free decision, already made and still continuing, to accept the claim of the Catholic Church to speak with the authority of Christ.[62]

This is not simply an academic problem. It comes to life with the nun in the first grade, the lay confraternity teacher, the priest in the pulpit and the bishop as well. All these have a duty to teach the faith. And we are entitled to insist that they accept the *Credo* and *Humanae Vitae*, without evasion of the plain meaning intended by the Pope, or forfeit their claim upon our acceptance.

The crisis of authority in the Church affects the world as well. For it is not surprising that a Church afflicted by internal disarray is

feeble against the disintegration of civil society. The rebellion in the
Church, by breaking her ranks, has deprived the world of the one
stable force to which it is entitled to look for protection against the
onset of a depraved and ultimately totalitarian society. Basically, of
course, the problem in the Church is one of faith. Given the evident erosion of faith today, it is not surprising that some Catholics
are disdainful of authority, that they are more concerned with
structures than with attitudes and that theology in some quarters
illuminates the fancied loophole more than the truth. In a sense,
the current rejection of authority is a fruit of the Modernist heresy
and is related to the secularism and ethical relativism rampant today.
We will therefore next examine some aspects of these erroneous
ideas. An acquaintance with them will place in better context the
revolt against authority in the Church and also may explain the
otherwise surprising impotence of the Church in countering the
sensual degeneration of civil society.

V.

DISCORDANT IDEAS

The growth of the anti-life society, the rejection of *Humanae Vitae*, and the rebellion against Church authority—these did not occur by accident. They are all related to intellectual currents evident throughout this century within and without the Church. We will examine here some of these ideas that have influenced Catholics and contributed to the rise of discord within the Church. Without some understanding of them, our perception of the authority crisis will be wholly superficial. Without that understanding we can hardly appreciate that the resolution of that crisis requires not only an exhortation to obedience but also a rejection of these contributing errors. For convenience, we can discuss in this chapter the errors of the new morality, secularism, Modernism, and the analogous ideas condemned by Pope Pius XII in his 1950 encyclical, *Humani Generis*.

When a Barnard coed openly shared an off-campus apartment with a Columbia University student in 1968, the Jewish and Protestant chaplains at Columbia came to her defense. The "crucial question," the chaplains said, is "whether or not the relationship is meaningful or worthwhile." The chaplains in turn were criticized by Rabbi Norman Lamm, an Orthodox Rabbinic scholar and professor at Yeshiva University. "The chaplains," Rabbi Lamm declared, "revealed the bankruptcy of the moral relativism showing underneath their ecclesiastical cloaks."[1] Their attitude, he said, "confuses humanistic existentialism expressed in religious vocabulary with an authentic religious stand," and opens the door to the destruction of the family as the "fundamental collective unit." The new morality's "negative rule of not hurting anyone else," said Rabbi Lamm, "is bound to become the sole normative criterion for all legal codes in the Western world. Thus adultery and homosexuality will be legally permitted where both parties consent—and are of the age of consent—and no third party is injured thereby. And what becomes legally permissible tends to become the moral norm as well for society at large."

The people involved in this exchange are not Catholics. But
Rabbi Lamm's conclusion is relevant to the point we are trying to
make in this book. "One can only hope," the Rabbi said, "that the
Christian churches, heretofore the guardians of the moral heritage
common to the great monotheistic religions of the West, will reconsider what appears to be their imminent capitulation to a tri-
umphant moral nihilism which may yet bring down all of civilization."

The moral nihilism to which Rabbi Lamm refers would substitute
a new morality in place of objective standards of right and wrong.
Methodist Bishop Gerald Kennedy, for example, condemns premarital
sex "in general," but adds, "I wouldn't stand in judgment. There
would be exceptions." Professor Ira Reiss, an official of the Sex Information and Education Council of the United States, urges the
adoption of a moral standard of "permissiveness with affection." Dr.
Lester Kirkendall, another SIECUS leader, declares that "a college
should not make a rule that chastity should be the rule." Proponents
of the new ethics emphasize their rejection of "legalism." "We are
not exhorted in the Gospel to love any principle," says Joseph
Fletcher, professor of theology at the Episcopal Theological School
in Cambridge, Massachusetts.[2] In his book *Situation Ethics: The
New Morality*[3] Fletcher rejects "the notion that the good is 'given'
in the nature of things objectively." Rather, "the situationist follows
a moral law or violates it according to love's need." Following this
reasoning, Fletcher would condone, in some cases, abortion, adultery,
compulsory sterilization, suicide, and similar actions. The situationist treats the ethical maxims of his community and its heritage "with
respect as illuminators of his problems," Fletcher believes. "Just the
same he is prepared in any situation to compromise them or set them
aside in the situation if love seems better served by doing so."

In the new morality, the Ten Commandments are regarded as
advisory maxims, not binding precepts. As Anglican Bishop John
A. T. Robinson put it, "I recognize to the full that all of us, especially young people, have to have working rules. My point is that
when these are questioned as they are being questioned, the Christian
is driven back to base them not on law (fornication is always wrong)
but on love, on what deep concern for persons as whole persons, in
their entire society context, really requires."[4] "One cannot, for
instance," Robinson said, "start from the position that sex relations
before marriage are wrong or sinful in themselves. The only intrinsic evil is lack of love."[5] From the condonation of promiscuity,

of course, it is an easy step to urge it as a duty, as Presbyterian minister Richard N. Waugh expresses it, "When maturing people are given their heads and are capable of weighing their responsibilities in the light of pre-marital or extra-marital sexual experience, then, given their situation their decision may be the moral . . . yes, even the Christian thing to do."[6] A more lucid rationale for misbehavior, however, was offered by "Laura," a San Francisco coed commenting in *Life* magazine on her "arrangement" with a male student: "Living together is nice on Sunday mornings when you have nothing to do."[7]

To a disturbing extent, young people have been trained, in Catholic as well as non-Catholic schools, in the notion that the Ten Commandments are not binding but rather that love is the standard of right and wrong. The rightness of an act of fornication, for example, is therefore not to be judged by the intrinsic nature of the act (for there is, they claim, no such thing as an intrinsic, un-changing nature) but rather by the circumstances. Is the relation between fornicator and fornicatee "meaningful"? If so, and if both parties are willing, why, then, no one is getting hurt and therefore the green light flashes on. The new moralist would appear to be less concerned about discouraging promiscuity than he is about pro-moting contraception and abortion so that the parties and society at large will not be bothered by untoward consequences, such as babies.

But ideas have consequences and the new morality can be judged by its results. Consider here the statistics presented in Chapter II, detailing the rise of venereal disease, promiscuity, and marital in-fidelity. While a cause and effect relation cannot be precisely shown, a general inference is valid that the rise of the new morality has contributed to the rise of promiscuity. The impact of the new morality, moreover, is not limited to the sexual realm. Shoplifting, for example, has risen sharply in recent years. In 1969, shoplifters in this country stole three billion dollars' worth of merchandise.[8] A recent survey showed that one out of every ten department store customers is a shoplifter.[9] The United States Office of Education estimates damage by vandals to public schools throughout the nation at $100 million yearly. Arson, vandalism, and pilferage are taking a heavy toll of private as well as public property.[10] In these and other areas that could be cited, many factors are at work to erode the respect for moral law and the rights of others. But it is safe to say that unless something is done to restore respect for the

Ten Commandments and the moral law, it will be impossible to reverse the lawless trend without stringently repressive measures.

The moral rules of the natural law and of revelation should not be regarded as negative restrictions. When we buy a new car, we do not rebel at the instructions that come with it. Rather, they help us to run the car. They make it possible for us to use the car for the purpose for which it was designed. Similarly, the moral rules which are written in human nature or in revelation enable us to accomplish the purpose for which we were created, that is, if the old catechism answer is not passé, to know, love, and serve God in this world and to be happy with Him forever in the next.

The new morality is analogous to the doctrines of Jean Jacques Rousseau. It is premised on an inherent goodness of men. It ignores the defect in human nature resulting from original sin. This is the great practical weakness of the "guidelines" which the new morality would substitute for the definite rules it rejects. Because of original sin and concupiscence, men are simply incapable of taking the detached, wholly objective view required by the new morality. It is illusory to suppose, for instance, that the couple in the back seat of the car will make a detached judgment as to the "meaningful" character of their proposed action. On the contrary, the predictable result is moral anarchy and a rationalized surrender to the concupiscence the new moralists would pretend is not really there. Also, when a vagrant pursuit of "love" is substituted for the objective standards of the natural moral law, the tendency is to interpret that love in terms of self-fulfillment with little regard for the welfare and rights of others. The operative philosophy here is ultimately hedonistic and self-centered. It is the *Playboy* philosophy, as enunciated by Hugh Hefner: "What we believe in, first and foremost, is the individual— and his right to be an individual. If a man has the right to find God in his own way, he has a right to go to the Devil in his own way, also. . . ."[11]

Despite its weakness and its incompatibility with religion itself, the new ethic continues to make headway within the churches. Rabbi Arthur Hertzberg, for example, has criticized clergy of various religions who seem to have accepted situation ethics as a bridge to maintain their relevance to the modern world. Speaking of situation ethics as "a new fad," Rabbi Hertzberg concluded, "No matter how this slogan is dressed up, it means, bluntly put, moral relativism."[12] These clerics can "feel relevant, alive and very contemporary" when they find a basis for agreement with the intellectuals who left the churches because they disagreed with religious moral codes. But, "all that they are," says Rabbi Hertzberg, "is self-deluded. There is no conceivable way of dealing with the Bible that makes of it a paradigm for moral relativism. For that matter, for what do moral relativists need a rabbi, priest, or minister? In situational ethics everyone's situation is unique and must be dealt with in its own terms and in its own context. From what perspective of knowledge and authority does the clergyman have anything to contribute beyond his permissiveness, which is tantamount to the admission of his irrelevance?" Similarly, Pope Paul, in addressing the judges of the Roman Rota on February 12, 1968, condemned "juridical relativism" and affirmed the unchanging character of Divine law and of the "perennial norms engraved in the heart of man." Later, in a speech to the international Congress of Canonists, the Pontiff emphasized the positive and liberating function of law. "For law is naught else but the secure defense that lawfully and authoritatively orders and promotes the common good, while at the same time guaranteeing and protecting against all interference the inviolable autonomy of the individual."

Against the law, the new moralist would oppose a guiding norm of "love." Joseph Fletcher asserts that the end of "love" would justify the use of such means as a mother's smothering her infant child to prevent their trail party from being discovered and slain by Indians. Or, it would be moral for a girl to commit adultery with an official of another nation if thereby her own country's security would be strengthened. Fletcher and other situationists make the intention the decisive factor in determining the morality of any act. And they contend that the use of any means can be justified if it accomplishes a good end, specifically if it contributes to the happiness and well-being of men. It can be said, of course, that these arguments would justify the Nazi extermination of millions of Jews out of "love" for the Jews themselves who were considered unfit to live and therefore better off dead. Curiously, the Nazi compulsory enthanasia program was conceived originally as a benefit to the victims. During its early stages Jews were excluded because they were not considered to deserve the benefit of euthanasia.[13] Later, of course, the Jews were exterminated in large numbers simply because they were regarded as unfit to live. But the point is that, under the new ethic, even the killing of innocents can be justified as a benefit to others or to the victims themselves.

However, there are superficial attractions in the new morality which require more rebuttal than simply reducing it to a logical absurdity. Rather, a few basic principles must be examined.[14] Pope Pius XII analyzed the new morality with great foresight in a message on "The Christian Conscience," broadcast March 23, 1952. The "Christian moral law," he said, is to be found in two places, in "the law written on the heart, that is to say, the Natural law" and in "the truths and precepts of supernatural Revelation" which were "taught by the Divine Master." Christ entrusted both sources of the moral law to the Church, so that she might "preach them to all creatures, make them clearly known and hand them on intact, safeguard against all contamination and error, from one generation to another."[15] Against this doctrine, unquestioned for centuries, said the Pontiff, the "new morality" is now raising a challenge. "We shall not dwell," he continued, "on the evident inexperience and immaturity of judgment of those defending" the relativist standards. "It will be useful, however, to call attention to the central weakness of this 'new morality.' By leaving all ethical criteria to the conscience of the individual, jealously closed up within itself and made absolute master of its own decisions, this new morality, far from making things any easier for conscience, would only lead it away from the main road, which is Christ." In the application of the new morality, the Pope concluded, "the theoretic autonomy in regard to morality becomes in practice a rebellion against morality."

Less than a month later, Pius XII expanded on his analysis in an address on April 18, 1952, to the World Federation of Catholic Young Women:

We have already spoken of the "new morality". . . . What we say today is not merely a continuation of what we said then. We wish today to uncover the hidden sources of this conception. We might term it "ethical existentialism," "ethical actualism," "ethical individualism"—all understood in the restrictive sense that we shall later explain and as expressed in what has otherwise been called "situation ethics" or "morality according to situations."

The distinctive mark of this morality is that it is not based in effect upon universal moral laws, such as, for example, the Ten Commandments, but on the real and concrete conditions or circumstances in which men must act, and according to which the conscience of the individual must judge and choose. Such a state of things is unique, and is applicable only once for every human action. That is why the decision of conscience, as the advocates of this ethic assert, cannot be commanded by ideas, principles and universal laws. . . .[16]

According to the new morality, "If a seriously trained conscience decided that abandoning the Catholic faith and joining another religion brings it closer to God, then such a step would be 'justified,' even though it is generally classified as 'giving up the faith.'" Or "a seriously trained conscience would decide that, because of a sincere mutual inclination," sexual intimacies between the unmarried are allowable as expressions of that inclination. "Such judgments of conscience, howsoever contrary they may seem at first sight to Divine precepts, would be valid before God because—they say—in the eyes of God, a seriously formed conscience takes precedence over 'precept' and 'law' . . .

"The new ethic," said the Pope, "is so foreign to the faith and to Catholic principles that even a child, if he knows his catechism, will be aware of it and will feel it." Parenthetically, it might be observed here that one reason why the new morality is gaining ground today is because too many children, educated in Catholic schools, simply do not know their catechism.

The new morality raises the basic issue of how the moral law, which is universal, "can be sufficient and even have binding force in an individual case which, in the concrete, is always unique and 'happens only once.'" Pius XII answered this objection:

> It can be sufficient and binding, and it actually is, because precisely by reason of its universality, the moral law includes necessarily and "intentionally" all those particular cases in which its meaning is verified. In many cases it does so with such convincing logic that even the conscience of the simple faithful sees immediately, and with full certitude, the decision to be taken.
>
> This is especially true of the negative obligations of the moral law, namely, those which oblige us not to do something or to set something aside. Yet it is true not only of these obligations. The fundamental obligations of the moral law are based upon the essence and the nature of man and on his essential relationship, and thus they have force wherever we find man.

While the precepts of the natural moral law are based on the essence of man, "The fundamental obligations of the Christian law, in the degree in which they are superior to those of the natural law, are based on the essence of the supernatural order established by the Divine Redeemer." According to these essences, said Pius XII, some things are always wrong under all circumstances:

> From the essential relationship between man and God, between man and man, between husband and wife, between parents and children; from the essential community relationships found in the family, in the Church and in the State, it follows, among other things, that hatred of God, blasphemy, idolatry, abandoning the true faith, denial of the faith, perjury, murder, bearing false witness, calumny, adultery and fornication, the abuse of marriage, the solitary sin, stealing and robbery, taking away the necessities of life, depriving workers of their just wages, monopolizing vital foodstuffs and unjustifiably increasing prices, fraudulent bankruptcy, unjust maneuvering in speculation—all this is gravely forbidden by the Divine Lawmaker. No examination is necessary. No matter what the situation of the individual may be, there is no other course open to him but to obey.

Against the situationist arguments of the new morality, Pius XII set forth three "maxims":

> *First:* We grant that God wants, first and always, a right intention. But this is not enough. He also wants the good work. A *second* principle is that it is not permitted to do evil in order that good may result. Now this new ethic, perhaps without being aware of it, acts according to the principle that the end justifies the means. A *third* maxim is that there may be situations in which a man, and especially a Christian, cannot be unaware of the fact that he must sacrifice everything, even his life, in order to save his soul. . . . (Emphasis added)

It must be borne in mind here that to affirm the objective evil of an act, say contraception, is not to affirm necessarily the culpability of all who perform that act. Here it is useful to remember the distinction between material and formal sin. An act is materially sinful if it is a sin as it is in itself; contraception, or lying, for example, is always objectively wrong and therefore it is always materially a sin. We can say that it is objectively evil. But one who performs an objectively evil act is culpable only if it is a formal sin, that is, only to the extent that he did it with sufficient knowledge of its evil and with consent of his will. "Formal sin is a voluntary transgression of the dictate of conscience; material sin is not a violation of the dictate of conscience, but is an act in disaccord with unsuspected moral obligation."[17] Here, too, the principle of probabilism enters, that a doubtful law has no binding power. "The principle of Probabilism is that in cases of doubt as to the lawfulness of any concrete action, if there exists a really probable opinion in favor of liberty, i.e., of disregard of the law, although the opinion in favor of the law is more probable, I may use the former opinion and disregard the latter, and in doing so I am acting with complete moral rectitude."[18] Of course, no law of God is doubtful in objective fact. But the actor's vision might be so clouded that he did not perceive that the act was prohibited. His guilt would be eliminated or reduced, subject of course to his responsibility if he were ignorant of the prohibition through his own culpable neglect. But, as Bishop Edward Ellis, of Nottingham, England, said, "It is one thing for a friend, a spiritual director or a confessor to be compassionate and merciful like Christ. . . . It is quite another thing to say that God's laws concerning purity and chastity, marriage and the family do not bind in certain cases. Conscience must never be considered a law to itself . . . it is so easily blinded by the fierce desires of our lower nature and inner weaknesses."[19]

Unfortunately, however, the clear teaching of the Church on the new morality is not shared by all the clergy, including some in influential positions. Father Joseph Champlin, for instance, has written approvingly of "the approach increasingly common among religious authors. Petting is neither condemned nor condoned. It depends on the persons involved. Premarital sexual intercourse is neither approved nor discouraged. Its value and moral appropriateness can be judged only in terms of the couple. Does it help their total relationship? Do they grow as individuals, as a couple through their intimacy? Is theirs a deep love relationship already present that seeks and finds best expression in deep petting or sexual relations? Or would this foster in the particular couple selfishness and diminish their love?"[20] Father Champlin proved his acceptance of these concepts when he set out to "offer the young some fairly precise norms to govern their courtship":

I do not like to stress that it is a sin if you do this or do that. I would rather say, "You don't do this unless you really care for the girl or the boy. And if you go beyond these boundaries, you can normally be sure that it is not real love, but selfishness on your part. You were using her (or him)." . . .

Later on, in the older couple, the engaged one, the issue is not so categorical. Petting, sexual intercourse may not be selfish on either part. I would say it is better to wait, better for their love relationship and for their inner peace. But I would not say they automatically are selfish if they do not wait.[21]

Father Champlin, incidentally, holds an important position in the American Church as assistant executive secretary, the second in command, of the Committee on the Liturgy of the National Conference of Catholic Bishops.

The new morality concerns us here because its popularity is a contributing cause of the authority crisis in the Church. The rejection of *Humanae Vitae* arises in part from a widespread refusal to accept moral absolutes in sexual matters. This refusal, of course, is an incident of an acceptance of the new morality. But, as Paulist Father Robert E. Burns has pointed out, the spread of the new morality has been facilitated by the parallel growth of secularism and Modernism.[22] These two basic errors have prepared the way, not only for the new morality but also for the overall crisis of authority in the Church. The materialistic philosophy of secularism, as the term is used here, would separate God and spiritual considerations from government, from society, and, ultimately, from religion itself. Secularism has been defined as "that characteristic of our world according to which life is organized apart from God, as though God did not exist."[23] Or, it is "the ordering and conducting of life as if God did not exist."[24] Secularization is the process of turning away from a religious world view toward one "limiting itself to life on the human plane."[25] Under the influence of secularism, it is easy to conclude that adultery, for example, is not wrong unless it can be shown to us to be such under standards of human temporal welfare and convenience. Prohibitions based on a divine command, transcending the standards of this world, are unthinkable in a secularistic morality. Also, when spiritual realities are discounted or ignored, a teaching Church which has no authority or sanction other than the spiritual will soon find its authority spurned. Essentially, a secularistic attitude flourishes to the extent that faith is weak. It follows that the remedy for secularism is a regeneration of spiritual faith, which depends upon prayer.

Modernism, too, is related to secularism in its denial of the fact that the faith is built upon known and objective spiritual realities.

It is related to the new morality in its denial of objective standards and in its exaltation of subjective judgment and experience. Modernism was a strong movement in Europe and, to a lesser extent, in America at the turn of the twentieth century. Modernism discounts the inspired character of Sacred Scripture and instead evaluates the Bible according to a rationalistic standard. It was condemned by Pope St. Pius X in 1907 as "the synthesis of all heresies" in his encyclical *Pascendi* and his decree *Lamentabili,* listing sixty-five Modernist errors. After the condemnation by Pius X, Modernism was generally thought to have come to an end, but analogous errors have since germinated underground in the Church.

Father Philip Hughes, in his *A Popular History of the Catholic Church,* described the Modernist heresy in these words: "The heresy that goes by the name of Modernism was an attempt to make Catholicism palatable to the thought of the day by repudiating its objective supernatural character, and reducing it to a matter of individual religious psychology. The Modernists were never, indeed, very numerous and Pius X's acts against them—the decree *Lamentabili* in July and the encyclical *Pascendi,* September 1907—were to most Catholics the first news of their existence. But the group occupied important posts in various seminaries and universities, and the danger anticipated was that it would gradually corrupt the faith of the clergy and of the educated laity, perverting theology and philosophy and the whole theory of the spiritual life."[26]

Father George D. Smith, in his book *The Teaching of the Catholic Church* says of the Modernists:

> More recently certain restless spirits within the Church, anxious to reconcile Catholic doctrine with the so-called exigencies of "Modern Thought," formed the school known as Modernism. Rejecting with Kant all rational demonstration of religious tenets, and borrowing from his disciple Schleiermacher "the religious sense" as a criterion of truth, the Modernists found the source and explanation of all religion in a subconscious "need of the divine." Thus the revelation which the Traditionalists (rightly) sought from God the Modernists (wrongly) thought to find within the nature of man himself. From this the way lies open to pantheism, to the rejection of all dogmas, and indeed of all objective religious truth.[27]

The Modernists were particularly strong in their aversion to scholastic philosophy. One characteristic of the Modernists, as described by Anne Freemantle, was "their rejection of traditional scholastic metaphysics, substituting for it hegelian immanentism and nineteenth century historicism."[28] It follows from this that one way of nullifying the influence of modernism is a solid grounding in scholastic philosophy. Nor is it surprising that the current ascendancy in Catholic colleges of doctrines analogous to Modernism has coincided with the exclusion from those schools of the rigorous grounding in scholastic metaphysics which formerly anchored their curricula.

In his first encyclical, *Ecclesiam Suam*, Pope Paul VI renewed the Church's strictures against Modernism:

> Was not the phenomenon of modernism, for example, which still crops up in the various attempts at expressing what is foreign to the authentic nature of the Catholic religion, an episode of abuse exercised against the faithful and genuine expression of the doctrine and criterion of the Church of Christ by pyschological and cultural forces of the profane world?

Since 1910, priests have been required, before ordination to the subdiaconate and at other later times, to take an oath of assent to the Church's condemnation of Modernism. The oath also contains five affirmative propositions, as summarized in the New Catholic Encyclopedia: "(1) God can be known and proved to exist by natural reason; (2) the external signs of revelation, especially miracles and prophecies, are signs giving certainty and are adapted to all men and times, including the present; (3) the Church was founded by Christ on earth; (4) there is a deposit of faith and the assertion that dogmas change from one sense to another one different from that held by the Church is heretical; (5) faith is not a blind sense welling up from the depths of the subconscious under the impulse of the heart and of a will trained to morality, but a real assent of the intellect to truth by hearing from an external source."[29] A renewed awareness of these propositions and their truth would go a long way toward curing the ills that afflict many of the clergy today.

We should also examine here the encyclical *Humani Generis*, issued by Pope Pius XII in 1950. *Humani Generis* has been neglected, particularly in recent years. But it is worth discussing because it analyzes a broad range of intellectual errors which have assumed great importance within the Church over the past twenty years.

Pius XII said he wrote *Humani Generis* to expose these errors while they were still of small magnitude because "we prefer to withstand the very beginning rather than to administer medicine after the disease has grown inveterate." The encyclical first attacked three erroneous views, evolution, existentialism, and historicism, which prevail outside the Church. "Some imprudently and indiscreetly hold," said the Pope, "that evolution—which has not been fully proved even in the domain of natural sciences—explains the origin of all things, and audaciously support the monistic and pantheistic opinion that the world is in continual evolution. Communists gladly subscribe to this opinion so that, when the souls of men have been deprived of every idea of God, they may the more efficaciously defend and propagate their dialectical materialism."

The repudiation of absolute values has paved the way, said the Pope, for a philosophy of "existentialism," which "concerns itself only with the existence of individual things and neglects all consideration of their immutable essences." Thirdly, "there is also a certain historicism, which, giving value only to the events of man's life, overthrows the foundation of all truth and absolute law in regard to philosophical speculations and especially to Christian dogmas."

The encyclical next rebuked some "Catholic theologians and philosophers" who, "desirous of novelty, and fearing to be considered ignorant of recent scientific findings, tend to withdraw from the sacred teaching authority" and propagate instead these erroneous doctrines. Further, the encyclical criticized those who promote "an imprudent 'irenism.'" Seeking to promote Christian unity, they tend to minimize the teachings and dogmas of the Church. Then, the Pope exposed the manner in which these false opinions are insinuated into every level and corner of the Church:

> Theories that today are put forward rather covertly by some, not without cautions and distinctions, tomorrow are openly and without moderation proclaimed by others more audacious, causing scandal to many, especially among the young clergy and to the detriment of ecclesiastical authority.
>
> Though they are more cautious in their published works, they are more open in their writings intended for private circulation and in conferences and lectures. Moreover, these opinions are published not only among members of either clergy and in seminaries and Religious institutions, but also among

the laity, and especially among those who are engaged in teaching youth.

Not only do the adherents of these views minimize doctrine, but some even "hold that the mysteries of faith are never expressed by truly adequate concepts but only by approximate and ever changeable notions, in which the truth is to some extent expressed, but is necessarily distorted.

"Wherefore, they do not consider it absurd, but altogether necessary that theology should substitute new concepts in place of the old ones in keeping with the various philosophies which in the course of time it uses as its instruments, so that it should give human expression to Divine truths in various ways which are even somewhat opposed, but still equivalent, as they say."

In his commentary on *Humani Generis*, Jesuit Father A. C. Cotter observed that "this conception of the history of dogma . . . favored by the new theology . . . resembles rather closely the conception of the Modernists of 50 years ago, which was exposed and condemned by Pius X as involving dogmatic relativism."[30] Pius XII was not condemning here the linguistic refinement of doctrinal statements to develop the nuances of the teaching. The progressively more precise development of the teaching on birth control, especially by Pius XI, Pius XII, and Paul VI, as we discussed in Chapter III, illustrates such a refinement of an authentic teaching. What Pius XII was rejecting here was the substitution of concepts, so that the new formulations would convey a meaning different from the old. An example of this is the recent tendency in some quarters to replace the Eucharistic doctrine of transubstantiation with a new concept of transignification which does not affirm the Real Presence. This concept was rejected by Pope Paul in his encyclical *Mysterium Fidei*. In *Humani Generis*, Pius XII explained at length this unchanging nature of doctrinal truth:

However, even in these fundamental questions, We may clothe our philosophy in more convenient and richer dress, make it more vigorous with more effective terminology, divest it of certain scholastic aids found less useful, prudently enrich it with the fruits of the progress of the human mind; but never may We overthrow it or contaminate it with false principles or regard it as a great but obsolete relic. For truth and its philosophic expression cannot change from day to day, least of all where there is a question of the self-evident principles of the human mind or of those propositions which are supported by the wisdom of the ages and by the Divine revelation.

Whatever new truth the sincere human mind is able to find certainly cannot be opposed to truth already acquired, since God, the highest truth, has created and guides human intellect, not that it may daily oppose new truths to rightly established ones, but rather that, having eliminated errors which may have crept in, it may build truth upon truth in the same order and structure that exist in reality, the source of truth.

Let no Christian, therefore, whether philosopher or theologian, embrace eagerly and lightly whatever novelty happens to be thought up from day to day, but rather let him weigh it with painstaking care and a balanced judgment, lest he lose or corrupt the truth he already has, with grave danger and damage to his faith.

It is characteristic that the advocates of the new ideas reject scholastic philosophy and theology, which teach that truth can be known and expressed with finality and certainty. "Unfortunately," continued the Pope, "these advocates of novelty easily pass from despising scholastic theology to the neglect of and even contempt for the teaching authority of the Church itself, which gives such authoritative approval to scholastic theology." Rejecting the teaching authority of the Church, the new theologians "judge the doctrine of the Fathers and of the teaching Church by the norm of Holy Scripture, interpreted by the purely human reasoning of exegesis, instead of explaining Holy Scripture according to the mind of the Church which Christ Our Lord has appointed guardian and interpreter of the whole deposit of Divinely revealed truth." Further, "It is now doubted that human reason, without Divine revelation and the help of Divine grace, can, by arguments drawn from the created universe, prove the existence of a personal God; it is denied that the world has a beginning; it is argued that the creation of the world is necessary, since it proceeds from the necessary liberality of Divine love; it is denied that God has eternal and infallible foreknowledge of the free actions of men—all this in contradiction to the decrees of the Vatican Council.

"Some also question whether angels are personal beings, and whether matter and spirit differ essentially." The Pope continued with a catalogue of the errors resulting from these false teachings:

Disregarding the Council of Trent, some reject the very concept of original sin, along with the concept of sin in general as an offense against God, as well as the idea of satisfaction performed for us by Christ. Some even say that the doctrine of Transubstantiation, based on an "antiquated" philosophic notion of substance, should be so modified that the Real Presence of Christ in the Holy Eucharist be reduced to a kind of symbolism, whereby the consecrated species would be merely efficacious signs of the spiritual Presence of Christ and His intimate union with the faithful members of His Mystical Body.

Some say that they are not bound by the doctrine, explained in Our encyclical letter of a few years ago and based on the sources of revelation, which teaches that the Mystical Body of Christ and the Catholic Church are one and the same thing. Some reduce to a meaningless formula the necessity of belonging to the true Church in order to gain salvation. Others finally belittle the reasonable character of the credibility of Christian faith.

The Pope next emphasized the importance of scholastic philosophy according to "the method of Aquinas," especially in the training of priests. He criticized those who reject scholastic philosophy because, "while scorning our philosophy, they extol other philosophies of all kinds, ancient and modern, Oriental and Occidental, by which they seem to imply that any kind of philosophy or theory, with a few additions and corrections if need be, can be reconciled with Catholic dogma. No Catholic can doubt how false this is." The encyclical went on to attack those who misapply the theories of evolution so as to cast doubt on the Church's teaching that "souls are immediately created by God." Similarly, the Pope rejected the notion of polygenism and maintained, on the contrary, that "the faithful cannot embrace that opinion which maintains either that after Adam there existed on this earth true men who did not take their origin through natural generation from him as from the first parent of all, or that Adam represents a certain number of first parents." The theory of polygenism, according to the Pope, particularly undermines the doctrine of original sin. On the "historical sciences," the Pontiff then took issue with certain scriptural interpretations which place some stories from the Bible "on a par with myths."

Finally, expressing a hope that was not to be realized, the Pope said, "We charge Bishops and Superiors General of Religious orders binding them most seriously in conscience to take most diligent care that such opinions be not advanced in schools, in conferences or in writings of any kind, and that they be not taught in any manner whatsoever to the clergy or faithful."

Humani Generis is critically important to our examination of the present disobedience and division in the Church. But there is a danger of overemphasizing its condemnation of errors and ignoring its affirmative summons to sound methods of research and interpretation. As Father Cotter summarized this point:

> But though a superficial reading may leave the impression that the Encyclical is mainly negative, condemning modern errors and erroneous tendencies, a more attentive study should correct that impression. All through its pages the Pope appears far more concerned with putting before the reader the positive norms which should guide Catholic scholars in their work. I should say that the modern trends were only the occasion for him to inculcate the positive doctrine of the Church, in particular on the *teaching authority of the living Magisterium* which some Catholics had flouted in their writings and lectures. It is for this positive doctrine that *Humani Generis* will be remembered long after the glittering theories condemned in it are buried and forgotten. (Emphasis in original)[31]

In *Humani Generis*, Pius XII exposed the errors of evolutionism, existentialism, and historicism. These errors have more than a superficial kinship to the new morality, secularism and Modernism. In fact, the errors described by Pius XII might fairly be called a New Modernism, which inherently entails a repudiation of the teaching authority of the Church. In any event, it is clear that the errors discussed in this chapter are separately and collectively responsible as contributors to the erosion of respect for authority and to the division in the Church.

Thus far in the book we have noted some characteristics of modern society which involve a lessening of respect for innocent life, for the process by which life is begun and for the family in which it is meant to mature. We have examined the Pope's response, in *Humanae Vitae*, to these anti-life tendencies. But we have also seen how obedience to the Vicar of Christ is refused, in defiance of the clear teaching of the Church on the nature and effect of Papal authority. This rejection of authority, however, cannot be considered in a vacuum. It is related to the new morality in its subjectiveness and permissiveness. For if one admits no unchanging moral precepts, it should not be surprising that he does not submit to a church that proclaims those precepts as binding. But, like the new morality itself, the origins of the spirit of disobedience can be traced to the more basic errors of secularism and the New Modernism. For this reason we have discussed these related trends.

It remains, however, to consider the impact of the authority crisis on the Church and her mission and also to consider ways in which matters might be improved. Many areas could be selected for analysis. But we can make the essential points with just a few: the clergy, ecumenism, the liturgy, elementary and high schools, colleges and universities, and Church-State relations. We shall therefore proceed next to consider, not only the impact of erroneous ideas in these areas, but also the corrective measures that can be taken without going to extremes.

VI.

THE CLERGY
AND RELIGIOUS

Throughout the world some priests are questioning their vocations while some chase from study group to seminar seeking for—what Lord, for You? Our mission priests here in the midst of the battle are like the three children in the fiery furnace; they pray, they sing, as though the fire were not burning—as though it were the dew.

For them no problems. Having a clear faith, abandoning themselves to God they have a free spirit and clear heart. They are working in humanly impossible conditions but they know from experience that "God is the Master of the impossible." Hundreds of refugees, injured and sick are asking for our help and protection daily. They are never refused whatever we can give.

This was written in 1969 by Bishop Paul L. Seitz of Kontum in South Vietnam. The clerical attitude he describes is, of course, not universal today. In the United States, it is fair to say, there are few, if any, bishops who could make such an optimistic assessment of the attitudes of their priests. The American Church, said Harvard sociologist Father Joseph Fichter, is "disunited, polarized and pluralized to the point of open disagreement on important issues." In this address to the convention of the National Federation of Priests' Councils, which purports to represent thirty-five thousand of the nation's sixty thousand priests, Father Fichter said, "The so-called 'clergy crisis' has brought the moment of truth at last to the hierarchy." The bishops, he claimed, "are pushing the panic button. They are losing their constituents, their employees, their subjects. All of a sudden they realize that the sacred priesthood is no longer attractive enough as a life-long profession to draw new recruits or to hold men who have already been ordained."[1]

We should neither exaggerate nor overdramatize the clergy crisis described by Father Fichter. But at the same time we should not be blind to its seriousness and its basic elements. There is an

obvious connection, too, between the problems of the clergy and
the general authority crisis with which this book is concerned.

When the Third Study Congress of National Directors for Vocations met at Lucerne in March 1969, Gabriel Cardinal Garrone,
the prefect of the Sacred Congregation for Catholic Education,
commented on the growing shortage of vocations to the priesthood:

> Of course, . . . no specific measure in favour of vocations
> must be omitted. But three things leap into the foreground:
> the absolute necessity to keep firmly to the essential values of
> the faith in this great upheaval; *the consequent necessity not to
> lose sight of the Church, her Tradition, her Magisterium, in
> order to be sure of not going astray, with everyone understand-
> ing values in his own way;* finally, the necessity of keeping practi-
> cal and strict solidarity with all others engaged in studying and
> cultivating vocations, whatever kind these may be: diocesan,
> missionary, religious. (Emphasis added)[2]

What Cardinal Garrone infers is that adherence to the teaching
authority of the Church is not only correct in itself, but that it
has a further practical utility through imbuing the young with the
sense of commitment and discipline necessary to sustain a priestly
vocation today. In short, if we would arrest the decline in vocations,
we ought to begin impressing upon our children and on Catholics
generally that the Church is indeed endowed with the authority
of Christ and that she is therefore to be loved and obeyed.

"The fact is," said Cardinal Garrone, "that the problem of
vocations is tending to get more serious year by year, except in
a few countries, which have been kept at exceptional spiritual levels
and close to the source of exceptional graces by terrible trials of
yesterday or today. Examples are Poland, Yugoslavia and also
Mexico. . . ."

In 1965 there were 48,992 seminarians in the United States
at the high school, college, and theological school levels. At the
end of the calendar year 1969 there were only 28,819. If the
figures are restricted to theological students, or seminarians in the
last four years prior to ordination, the decline is clear but less
pronounced than for seminarians of all ages considered together.[3]

There are several reasons for this decline in vocations. Essentially, however, the explanation is one of faith. According to the
study issued by the vocation directors at Lucerne:

The present crisis is not solely in the sociological and psychological order; it also results from difficulties inherent in the faith. . . . The young are now faced with the atheism and indifference of their surroundings, and consequently have to ask themselves about numerous problems, amongst which are, the relations between faith and culture; faith and technology; faith and contestation, etc. Today it is the very capacity to believe that is being called into question.[4]

So it is not only the prevailing disdain for the Church's authority that discourages vocations. It is also an atmosphere hostile to belief itself. Here we can see the impact, too, of the relativist, secularist, and New Modernist errors we discussed in the preceding chapter.

As Cardinal Garrone put it, "The young come from a world in which every sort of definite commitment is viewed with incomprehension and repugnance."[5] The students are the products of a relativist world. But this is all the more reason for presenting to them without equivocation the certitudes of the Faith, the Church and her authority. For the Church cannot rightly be reconciled with a world that refuses to recognize the reality of a higher commitment. The imprudent efforts of some to force that reconciliation have contributed to the drop in vocations. For a secular Church has little capacity to inspire. Pope Paul commented in 1969 on this point: "We wonder, is Christianity suited to temperaments weak in human strength—in moral conscience? To faint-hearted, lukewarm, conformist men, heedless of the austere requirements of the Kingdom of God? We sometimes wonder if the superficial presentation of a sweetened Christianity, a Christianity without heroism and without sacrifice, without the Cross, and therefore deprived of the moral greatness of complete love, is not among the causes of the drop in vocations in following Christ generously, without reserve, without looking back."[6] It is time, it would seem, to present to the young the Church and her authority as they really are.

This chapter intends briefly to show a connection between the problems that beset the clergy and the general authority crisis in the Church. However, even in a short discussion, some cautions are required. The first, in Pope Paul's words, is "that the majority of the clergy are outstanding for their religious and moral virtues, for their dedication to their own ministry, for their convinced fidelity to the Church . . . and for their spirit of service."[7] Nonetheless, there is reason for concern. The Pope has emphasized two

elements of the clergy problem, one involving attitudes and the
other actions. The first, which is "fairly widespread," is "the uncertainty of the priest about his status; an uncertainty that concerns
faith in the very nature of the priesthood, the priest's human
and ecclesiastical formation, his religious and apostolic function,
his hierarchical and sociological position, his inner and outer manner
and his mission in the modern world." The second "phenomenon
is the falling away of a small, but ever too noticeable number of
Priests and Religious from their sacred duties, to which before Christ,
the Church and their consciences they were solemnly, freely and
lovingly dedicated. This is Our crown of thorns."[8]

One difficulty, said the Pontiff, is that "today's facile publicity
and the curiosity of public opinion" bring these unfavorable trends
"more into evidence than other more generous and comforting
phenomena." The notoriety adds fuel to the fire but even were
there no publicity there would still be serious cause for concern.

Considering here first the second trend described by the Pope
—the defections from the priesthood—let us remember that though
the defectors are "ever too noticeable," their number is nonetheless
"small." Between 1963 and 1968, 7137 priests petitioned formally
to be released from their vows. But these are fewer than 2 percent
of the world-wide total of priests.[9] These figures compare favorably
with Our Lord's own batting average—He lost one out of twelve
or 8⅓ percent.

Of course, we are concerned, not only with those who formally
petition to be dispensed from their vows, but also with those who
simply drop out and those who stay in the ranks but discredit
the Church through their disregard of her teaching authority. In
all these categories, though reliable figures are not attainable, the
problem is big enough to cause real concern. Nevertheless, it is
not so big that inferences can be drawn about priests in general.
Of those who leave the priesthood, many are authorized to do so
by the appropriate dispensation from vows. Of the total number
who leave, only a small proportion create open scandal in so doing.
And those who stay but foster discord in their priestly roles cannot
as yet be more than a comparative few. So, in considering the
priesthood, it is important not to lose a sense of proportion and
allow the failings of a few to incline us toward anticlericalism.
Also, to criticize those who dishonor the priesthood is not to disparage those who offer a helping hand to priests, nuns, and
religious who are seeking to adjust to lay life. So long as such

efforts do not involve an encouragement of defections, they are charitable and praiseworthy.

The priestly defections about which the Pope is concerned are caused in turn by the first element of the clergy problem which he mentioned—"the uncertainty of the priest about his status." The priesthood, said the Pope to a recent audience of priests and brothers, is suffering from a crisis "in the very minds of those who have chosen it as a form of life."[10] This crisis, he said, is "one of the things which today considerably disturbs the life of the church and which gives us—we confide in you as brothers— the greatest concern and sorrow." Some priests, he noted, "abandon the holy ranks of the priesthood because of moral collapse, spiritual tiredness, and fear of being mistaken in their choice of the sacred ministry."

There are many reasons why men leave the priesthood. Priestly defections are widely attributed to the Church's requirement of celibacy. But it is doubtful that this is generally the case. "There are four reasons why priests leave," said Dennis Barry, a Catholic layman connected with *Look* magazine. "Either they are priest- worker types who want to get more involved in social action than their superiors allow, or they have lost their faith, their mind, or their virginity."[11] One survey conducted at the Jesuit-run University of San Francisco indicated that the main motive for quitting was what the former priests called the stifling of progressive ideas.[12] For some, the reason is an identity crisis, as John Cardinal Heenan of England commented: "Apart from the priest, and perhaps the politician, no normal man is obsessed with his own image. It is sad that priests who otherwise would be busy about God's work should be so constantly told to look at their image."[13] Some priests are unduly concerned about the impression they make on others and about their own self-fulfillment. There is a tendency, too, to regard the priestly calling not as a vocation that consumes a man's potential but as a profession or as merely a role that must be supplemented by the playing of other, secular roles if personal completion is to be attained. When Jesuit Father John McLaughlin, associate editor of *America* magazine, was nominated by the Repub- lican Party to run for the United States Senate in Rhode Island, he said, "Too many people think priesthood exhausts a man's identity. I have many functions—writer, educator, social critic, priest. Now I am taking on a new one."[14]

Sometimes the priest in search of his identity will discard the externals of his calling in an effort to remove fancied barriers to communication which, if they exist at all, probably arise from his own attitude more than from his Roman collar. Father Gregory Baum maintains that "today we are witnessing a reaction against the 'reverend father' business—on the part of both people and priests. That is why so many priests have put aside their Roman collars and asked to be called by their given names; they are seeking to escape a fatherhood that has denied them their role as true leaders—a role they hope to assume by becoming brothers among brothers."[15] Pope Paul, however, has warned against:

> the attempt, rather widespread today, to make the priest a man like any other, in dress, in secular profession, in going to places of entertainment, in worldly experience, in social and political commitment, in the formation of family of his own with renunciation of holy celibacy. People say this is an attempt to integrate the priest into society. Is this the way to understand the masterly words of Jesus, who wants us in the world, but not of the world? Did He not call and choose His disciples, those who were to extend and continue the announcement of the kingdom of God, distinguishing them, in fact separating them from the ordinary way of life, and asking them to leave everything to follow Him alone? The entire Gospel speaks of this qualification, this "specialization" of the disciples who were afterwards to act as apostles.[16]

The leading symbol of the clerical identity crisis is the controversy over celibacy. Although the issue has not reached the breaking point in the United States, agitation for a relaxation of the celibacy edict is strong in this country as well as in Europe. Less than a month after thirty-one Brooklyn priests announced that they no longer consider themselves bound by the celibacy law, a like stand was taken by thirty-eight priests of the Archdiocese of Detroit.[17] Other priests, too, have rejected celibacy, either in theory or in fact, sometimes with publicity far out of proportion to their numbers or significance. Frequently, scandal results.

Celibacy is not essential to the priesthood. Rather, it is a rule of Church discipline. It is theoretically possible to have a married Catholic priesthood. But there never has been a time in the history of the Church when the rule has been otherwise. It is true that the Orthodox Church has a married clergy, but the Orthodox Church does not allow its priests to marry. A married man may become an Orthodox priest. But once he is ordained he cannot thereafter marry. Every priest ordained today knew of the celibacy rule when he accepted ordination and he freely chose the celibate priesthood. There are no shotgun ordinations. Yet the agitation continues for a relaxation of the celibacy rule. "The new Jesuit," wrote Father John L'Heureux, S.J., "fears that not to marry may in some important way stunt his personal development, that he will be less the man he ought to be."[18]

The Second Vatican Council strongly reaffirmed the rule of celibacy in the *Decree on the Ministry and Life of Priests.* Pope John XXIII expressed the same view. So has Pope Paul, in his 1967 encyclical on priestly celibacy and on numerous occasions since. The American bishops have supported him strongly in this stand.[19] Recently, the Pope emphatically rebuffed the opposition to celibacy of the Dutch clergy, Belgian Cardinal Suenens, and others.[20] In reply to the Dutch assertions, Pope Paul stressed the rule of celibacy more firmly than ever. The Pope spoke because "the link between the priesthood and celibacy established for centuries by the Latin Church constitutes for this Church an extremely precious and irreplaceable good."[21]

There is no evidence that the abandonment of celibacy would halt the decline of priestly vocations. Instead, said the Pope, "the young will feel themselves even less attracted to the ideals" of the priesthood. "Where preparation for the priesthood," he continued, "takes place in an atmosphere of prayer, charity and self-humiliation, the problem of celibacy does not even arise."[22]

At root, the clamor over celibacy is a sign of immaturity in the minority of priests who are excited about it. John Cardinal Wright, head of the Vatican Congregation for the Clergy, recently told of a woman who dragged her husband—a priest who had married her outside the Church and then requested laicization—into Cardinal Wright's office. "In God's name," the cardinal said the woman demanded, "why did you ordain that?" She went on: "Two weeks after we were married, I discovered I had not married a man; I had adopted a small boy. I think I love him, but I pity him more. I think I'll take about two years to make a man out of him, then kick him out." She asked that their marriage not be regularized in the Church because then it would be a valid marriage and she would be "stuck" with him.[23]

In some cases the celibacy issue appears to underlie other complaints. When a priest climaxes a period of public dissent on doctrinal issues by suddenly running off and getting married, the inference is fair that he was really less troubled by the literal reality of the Resurrection than he was by the desire to marry. The cover of *The Critic*, published by the Thomas More Association in Chicago, showed a priest responding to a news reporter's questions:

> I am leaving the priesthood because I believe that the parochial school system is obsolete. . . .
> Because I am disturbed by the church's failure to meet the social needs of the poor. . . .
> Because the American Bishops are not implementing the decrees of the Vatican Council. . . .
> Because of the irrelevance of the church's message for the modern mind. . . .
> Because I have doubts about the literal sense of the scriptures. . . .
> And my fiancée is leaving the church for the same reasons.[24]

This example is fictional and irreverent. But it reflects an unpleasant reality. The agitations of a minority of priests over celibacy are exposing all priests and the priesthood itself to the danger of ridicule and futility. Having chosen that state in life with full awareness of what it entails, they now paint a picture of frustration, sexual anxiety, irrelevance, and uselessness which cannot help but repel some who otherwise would choose to serve God in the clergy. The positive values of the priesthood are muted. So, too, is the privilege involved in being another Christ to men.

This is a short chapter because it has a limited purpose. Much could be said about the failings of priests. But much could be said, too, about the failings of laymen. In neither case do the real troublemakers constitute even a substantial minority. We are concerned in this book with a rejection of authority that crosses vocational lines. Both priests and lay people are affected. The aim of this chapter is only to note the effect of that rejection on priests and the importance of a renewed respect for authority as a means for improving the quantity and quality of present and future vocations. Indeed, there are hopeful signs that this reaffirmation of authority is taking place, including, especially, recent actions of the Vatican and the bishops to improve the course of instruction in seminaries. The Catholic bishops of the United States approved a program in this direction in November 1969. More recently, the Vatican's Sacred Congregation for Catholic Education issued the first comprehensive guidelines for seminaries since 1556. Entitled *Ratio Fundamentalis Institutionis Sacerdotalis*, they are intended to provide general guidance for documents on seminary reform which are to be drawn up by each bishops' conference. The Congregation urged various seminary reforms, including the continued teaching of Latin and the traditional stress on philosophy, theology, and the teachings of St. Thomas Aquinas. Also, it urged improved preparation of priests in modern languages, sociology, psychology, and other secular subjects. Gabriel Cardinal Garrone, who heads the Congregation, commented that the new guidelines are based on the Second Vatican Council's *Decree on Priestly Formation* and the deliberations of the 1967 bishops' synod. The major concern in drafting the document, he said, was to form a priest in contact with the world. The *Ratio* therefore emphasizes pastoral training, studies of atheism, ecumenism, and sexual matters and some relaxation of rules which tended to isolate seminarians unrealistically from the world.

One significant recommendation in the Vatican guidelines is the suggestion that bishops choose as instructors of priests those theologians who are adept in "solving problems laid before them" rather than those characterized by "reputation, research in novel ideas or in the exposition or enunciation of arguments."[25] The faculty will determine the character of any seminary as of any institution of learning. Clearly, those who teach future priests ought themselves to be characterized by an unreserved loyalty to the teaching Church. Today, on the contrary, some professional theologians, including some seminary teachers, seem to regard themselves as virtually equal partners with the Pope and bishops in the teaching function of the Church. From this, it is not surprising that some young priests seem more impressed with intellectual novelties than with the teaching of the Church and the spiritual life she approves.

"There is nothing wrong with the priesthood," Frank Sheed recently commented, "that spirituality cannot cure. If priests would call a moratorium on Chardin and spend the time in study of the Gospels of Christ, much of the confusion would evaporate."[26] This is a simple suggestion but it is not unreasonable.

Thus far in this chapter we have talked about the priesthood. But similar problems are found among brothers and nuns. The uncertainty among nuns is particularly important because of their central though diminishing importance in Catholic education. The number of nuns in this country fell in 1969 from 167,167 to 160,931. At the beginning of 1968, there were 176,341.[27]

The unrest among the sisters is related in some respects to the general movement for the "liberation" of women. One incident of this is the tendency to blur the canonical distinction between men and women and priests and nuns. As Mrs. Philip A. Hart, wife of the Democratic senator from Michigan, said, "There is no reason why a woman isn't a full human being and why she shouldn't be a priest."[28] A joke currently making the rounds is that bishops attending the next Vatican Council will be accompanied not only by their theological advisors but by their wives. At the council after that, it runs, some bishops may bring along their husbands.[29] However, L'Osservatore Romano, the Vatican newspaper, responded in a different tone when the Dutch National Pastoral Council proposed women priests in January of 1970. After noting that Christ "has chosen men," the paper concluded, "Not even the Church could alter or ignore this will. It is precisely this will that founds the Church and is the law of its nature and of its existence."[30]

As with the priests, the Vatican has also specified guidelines for the training and community life of women religious.[31] Father Edward L. Heston, C.S.C., secretary of the Vatican's Sacred Congregation for Religious, recently outlined principles which he described as "the minimum required by competent authority in the Church as a basis for approval of a religious institute in the Church."[32] The minimum requirements, according to Father Heston, include: corporate witness; sharing of community life; community prayer; religious dress; primacy of the spiritual in their purpose; and collaboration with local ordinaries. In his speech to the annual meeting of the Conference of Major Superiors of Women's Religious Institutes, in St. Louis, Father Heston stressed the importance of collaboration with the local ordinary. This is a further indication of the indispensability of respect for authority in the renewal of the religious life.

The crisis of faith and the authority problem that comes in its wake have had a serious impact on all in religious life, whether male or female. And it places on them a greater responsibility than ever before to follow the teaching Church. Addressing the International Union of Superiors General of Women, Pope Paul strongly made this clear:

Like the priest and the male religious—but with a different perspective from theirs—the woman religious is faced with a terrible dilemma—either to be a saint, totally and without compromise, and attain the greatest measure of sanctity possible; or to be reduced to a joke, a caricature, an unsuccessful and, let us say, abortive being. The dangers of secularization are evident in every aspect, especially as regards poverty, when an attempt is made to obtain an economic autonomy that contrasts with the spirit of renunciation proper to the Gospel and to religious life.

Then there is the temptation to individualism, for which modern man is as solicitous as for his own inviolable property. It can injure your communities, as when little "fraternities" are formed, sometimes even composed of members belonging to differing congregations. This entails the danger of a leveling and impoverishment of religious life. Obedience can also be seriously threatened if proper collaboration with the episcopate and an organic overview in plans for the aspostolate are lacking.[33]

Increasingly, the choice is presented to priests, brothers, and nuns: follow the teaching Church or be reduced to futility and become a detriment to the Church. While the problem is serious, it would be well for us to pay more attention to the faithful among the clergy and religious and less to the disruptive few. Whatever the abuses committed by a minority, there is no warrant for Catholics to lessen their respect for the priesthood and for priests in general. The same applies, of course, to brothers and nuns.

It is true, however, that the recalcitrance of some requires us to confront the painful duty of separating in our minds those priests and religious whom we would follow from those we would not. We are not likely to meet a disembodied Modernist heresy walking down the street. Our problem, instead, is to gauge the reliability of those with whom we deal. This is not with a view to personal condemnation, but rather simply as a means to discern the true leader from the false. A fair test here would be the attitude of the individual priest, brother, or nun toward *Humanae Vitae* and the *Credo* of Pope Paul. Acceptance or rejection of the encyclical and the *Credo* will fairly measure the reliability or orthodoxy of any Catholic, clerical, religious, or lay. But it is particularly relevant with respect to priests and religious. If a priest, brother, or nun disdains *Humanae Vitae* or will not subscribe to the *Credo* of

Pope Paul without evasion, we ought to pray for him or her.
We should avoid all unkindness. But let us also follow the suggestion of St. Paul to the Romans:

> Not I exhort you, brethren, that you watch those who cause
> dissensions and scandals contrary to the doctrine that you have
> learned, and avoid them. For such do not serve Christ our Lord
> but their own belly, and by smooth words and flattery deceive
> the hearts of the simple.[34]

Finally, we can do something to alleviate the disorder among
some clergy and religious by prayer and by promoting respect
for the Pope and the Church's authority. Particularly, in dealing
with the young, we should know the case for authority and do
our best to present it sensibly. Thereby we serve the cause of
truth. But we may incidentally also help in this way to increase
the flow of sound vocations. And we ought to regard this as a
duty of the first rank. As Archbishop Timothy Manning of Los
Angeles recently said, "We have an obligation to sustain the priesthood. It is of crucial value for the permanency of the Church. . . .
Without it there is nothing left."

VII.

ECUMENISM

There will always be in every movement the false prophets who want to clean up the problem by sweeping it out of sight; who seek the slick solution, the quick anodyne, the ready aspirin. Remove the pain and forget the cause. Solve the mixed marriage problem, admit the validity of Anglican Orders, allow joint churches, pulpits, divorce and the pill, and all will be well. All won't be well. We have removed the very troubles which drive men to seek unity.

Non-Catholic ecumenists are often more aware of this than we give them credit for. Archbishop Ramsey, praying in the Sistine Chapel, asks God, "to enable us to feel the pain of our diversion." His predecessor, Archbishop Fisher, once warned the World Council of Churches, that "united action can become a narcotic rather than a stimulant." And the secretary of the same World Council, Dr. Visser t'Hooft, warned everyone against "ecumenical varnish covering up real differences." *It could be said of false ecumenism that it is more concerned with avoiding the embarrassing than promoting the truthful.*[1] (Emphasis in original)

These observations by Archbishop John Murphy of Cardiff, Wales, could be readily supported by examples. There are those who construe Vatican II as a license to diffuse religious distinctions in a fog of sentimentality. Other Catholics, however, look with a jaundiced eye on the very idea of ecumenism despite the opening declaration of the Second Vatican Council's *Decree on Ecumenism* that "promoting the restoration of unity among all Christians is one of the chief concerns of the Second Ecumenical Synod of the Vatican."[2] At both extremes, the balanced approach of the Council and the Pope is neglected. The ecumenical movement has shared the fate of other Church endeavors in being thrown off course by the prevailing disregard for the teaching authority of the Church.

The point of this chapter is, first, to note that the authority crisis in the Church has had the incidental effect of undermining the ecumenical movement and, second, to suggest ways in which adherence to the Church's authority can promote an authentic and effective ecumenism. "All divisions, quarrels, separatisms, all egoism within our Catholic Communion," said the Pope, "harm the cause of ecumenism."[3] On the one hand, it is a scandal and a discouragement for non-Catholics to see Catholics refuse to the authentic teachings of the Pope that "religious submission of will and of mind"[4] enjoined upon them by Vatican II. On the other hand, their own rejection of authority in general inclines some Catholics to reject as well the teachings of that authority on ecumenism.

The first thing we ought to do, however, is to fix in our minds what the ecumenical movement actually is. For this we can turn to the Second Vatican Council. "Number four of the conciliar *Decree on Ecumenism*," said Pope Paul, "deserves to be read and meditated upon by everyone."[5] In Article No. 4 of the *Decree on Ecumenism*, the Second Vatican Council said:

> The "ecumenical movement" means those activities and enterprises which, according to various needs of the Church and opportune occasions, are started and organized for the fostering of unity among Christians. These are: first, every effort to eliminate words, judgments and actions which do not respond to the condition of separated brethren with truth and fairness and so make mutual relations between them more difficult; then, "dialogue" between competent experts, from different Churches and Communities. In their meetings, which are organized in a religious spirit, each explains the teaching of his Communion in greater depth and brings out clearly its distinctive features. Through such dialogues, everyone gains a truer knowledge and more just appreciation of the teaching and religious life of both Communions. In addition, these Communions cooperate more closely in whatever projects a Christian conscience demands for the common good. They also come together for common prayer, where this is permitted. Finally, all are led to examine their own faithfulness to Christ's will for the Church and, wherever necessary, undertake with vigor the task of renewal and reform.[6]

The ecumenical movement, properly so called, involves our relations with non-Catholic Christians. The Council stated that "men

who believe in Christ and have been properly baptized are brought
into a certain, though imperfect, communion with the Catholic
Church." Also, that "all those justified by faith through baptism
are incorporated into Christ. They, therefore, have a right to be
honored by the title of Christian, and are properly regarded as
brothers in the Lord by the sons of the Catholic Church."[7] The
object of the movement is unity, but a unity within the Catholic
Church. "The result" of a properly conducted ecumenical movement, said the Council, "will be that, little by little, as the obstacles
to perfect ecclesiastical communion are overcome, all Christians
will be gathered, in a common celebration of the Eucharist, into
that unity of the one and only Church which Christ bestowed on
His Church from the beginning. This unity, we believe, dwells
in the Catholic Church as something she can never lose, and we
hope that it will continue to increase until the end of time."[8]
While it is true that it is possible for a non-Catholic, acting in
good faith, to be saved, nonetheless "it is through Christ's Catholic
Church alone, which is the all embracing means of salvation, that
the fullness of the means of salvation can be obtained."[9]

The Second Vatican Council is a summons to Christian perfection for all followers of Christ.[10] Since the Catholic Church is
the pre-eminent means toward perfection, it is fitting that the
ecumenical movement seeks unity only within her fold. A failure
to insist on that condition would amount to a failure of charity
toward separated Christians since it would imply that we are satisfied with a condition in which they are deprived, not of the means
to bare salvation, but of the means to the perfection desired of
us all by God. It is in this context that the Church's insistence
on her unique position becomes an essential condition of authentic
ecumenism rather than an obstacle to it. This unique position
of the Church is a positive factor but it is sometimes regarded
in a negative light by those who get carried away by their desire
for unity at any cost.

There are basically two dangerous attitudes prevalent "in this
sudden enthusiasm for reconciliation between Catholics and Christians separated from us."[11] "These threaten," said Pope Paul, to
frustrate the ecumenical movement through "misunderstanding, indifference," and "false irenicism." *First,* those "who see everything
perfect in the camp of the separated Brothers, and everything heavy
and blameworthy in the Catholic camp, are no longer able to pro-

mote the cause of union effectively and usefully. As one of the best contemporary ecumenists, a Protestant, pointed out with sad irony: 'the greatest danger of ecumenism is that the Catholics should become enthusiastic about everything that we have recognized as being harmful, abandoning everything the importance of which we have rediscovered' (cf. Bouyer)."

Beyond this "servile attitude," continued the Pope, there is a *second* attitude, "even more widespread today which claims to reestablish unity at the expense of doctrinal truth. The creed, which makes and defines us Christians and Catholics, seems in this way to become the insuperable obstacle to the restoration of unity; it does raise very severe and grave requirements—but the solution of the difficulties to which it gives rise cannot consist . . . in sacrificing faith, in the illusory confidence that charity suffices to recompose unity, that is, that empirical practice, stripped of dogmatic scruples and disciplinary norms . . . suffices. . . . Let us remember the Council, which 'urges the faithful to abstain from any superficiality or imprudent zeal, for these can cause harm to true progress towards unity.' "

A "servile attitude" and a willingness to compromise doctrinal truth—these are the primary misdirections that exist in ecumenical matters. The latter abuse, however, is the one that bears more closely upon the general issue of Church authority.

Three Points on Doctrine

In considering ecumenism, doctrine, and authority, three points should be made:

1. *Adherence, without exception, to the defined doctrines of the Church is essential to an authentic ecumenism.*

The necessity of preserving doctrine unchanged was underscored by Agostino Cardinal Bea, who, until his death, was the foremost exponent of ecumenism in the Church:

First and foremost the fundamental teaching of the Catholic Church will not be changed. Compromise on points of faith that have already been defined is impossible. It would be quite unfair to our non-Catholic brethren to stir up false hopes of this nature. Nor is there a possibility that the Church—even in its zeal for eventual union—will ever be content with a recognition only of "essential dogmas," or that she will reverse or withdraw the dogmatic decrees drawn up at the Council of Trent. Again it would be simply dishonest to suggest that there is any likelihood that the dogmas of the primacy or the infallibility of the Pope will be revised. The Church has solemnly proclaimed all these doctrines to be of faith, that is to say, truths revealed by God Himself and necessary for salvation. Precisely because of these solemn declarations made under the guidance of the Holy Spirit, the action of the Church in this field is severely limited. She must guard these truths, explain them, preach them, but she cannot compromise them. For the Church founded by Christ cannot tamper with the Word of God which He preached and entrusted to her care. She must humbly subject herself to Him with whom she is inalterably united.

I am sure that my non-Catholic brethren will understand this. For they maintain, just as strongly as we, that unity cannot be achieved at the expense of truth. As Dr. Ben Mohr Herbster, the President of the United Churches of Christ, put it: "A unity based on the least common denominator would be a curse and not a blessing."[12]

There are influential voices in the Church, however, who do not accept the orthodox view of dogma enunciated by Cardinal Bea. Father Avery Dulles, S.J., believes not only that "the Catholic dogmas as presently formulated and understood may be significantly changed," but also that "positive acceptance of all the dogmas may not be absolutely necessary for communion with the Roman Church."[13] To the extent that Father Dulles' view would countenance changes in the meaning of doctrine, as opposed to the mode of expressing the unchanging meaning, and to the extent that it would tolerate substantial differences in doctrine within the Catholic Church, its inconsistency with the view of the teaching Church is clear.[14]

2. *The preservation of doctrine does not preclude the development of new ways of stating the same truths.*

The preservation of doctrine does not rule out all changes in phrasing. We discussed this point in Chapter V, noting that the development of new formulations is permissible so long as they do not change the meaning of defined doctrine. Pope Paul recently expanded on this point in ecumenical terms:

> This does not mean that discussion about the dogmas of the faith is barred between Catholics and Christians separated from us. On the contrary, it is from a common theological examination, objective and serene, of revealed truth and truth that has been faithfully lived by the genuine tradition of ecclesiastical teaching, that we may see what is the essential Christian doctrinal heritage, what in it can be enunciated authentically, and at the same time, in different terms, substantially the same or complementary, and how it is possible for everyone to discover that identity of faith, in the freedom and variety of its expressions, from which union can be happily celebrated with one heart and one soul (cf. Acts 4:32).[15]

In its *Decree on Ecumenism,* the Second Vatican Council urged that Catholics "preserve a proper freedom . . . in the theological elaborations of revealed truth" and said that "the formation of doctrine . . . must be carefully distinguished from the deposit itself of faith."[16] At the opening of the Council, Pope John XXIII emphasized the necessity of preserving doctrine unchanged. But he carefully noted that "the Deposit of faith is one thing; the way that it is presented is another. For the truths preserved in our sacred doctrine can retain the same substance and meaning under different forms of expression."[17]

> 3. *While every Catholic has a role to play in the ecumenical movement, the important discussions on doctrine are primarily the province of experts delegated by the proper Church authority. This is no place for self-directed amateurs and officious theologians unresponsive to the teaching Church.*

Some people love conferences, round tables, and dialogues. The ecumenical fad, as distinguished from the authentic movement, is made to order for these types, whether they be clerical or lay, abundantly or indifferently qualified. "Interfaith-conference-hopping," said Rabbi Howard Singer, "is a great deal more glamorous than visiting old ladies in the hospital. And by now a kind of permanent interfaith civil service has developed with a strong vested interest in calling still more meetings. It helps to remember that dialogue is a wondrous puffer-upper of clerical reputations [and] a new way to gain social status."[18] This tendency would be a matter of small concern, but for a built-in escalation that occurs. The success of a meeting and its potential for publicity are frequently gauged by whether "progress" has been made. Progress, in this context, is often understood as a new agreement or a new concession. As the meetings go on and the game continues, the ante is predictably raised. The result can be a public assertion of agreement by participants who appear to represent the Church but who are themselves misguided and wholly unauthorized to commit the Church to anything. The remedy for this sort of thing is to leave the doctrinal negotiations to authorized experts operating under the control of the magisterium. Pope Paul made this plain in his audience of January 22, 1969:

> But this examination involves the responsibility of qualified theologians and scholars in the first place, of the ecclesiastical magisterium in the second place, and it cannot easily ensue from the discussion of opinions at every level. You will be glad to know that this examination is already going on, on different fronts of ecumenism; and it is not surprising if it calls for caution, time, gradualness: It is ecumenism in progress, to which the great, pious and elect figure of the late Cardinal Agostino Bea has directed the steps of Our Secretariat for the union of all Christians. Let us pay tribute to his memory by remaining faithful to his method, at once courageous and prudent.[19]

This does not imply that discussions cannot profitably take place at lower levels. But it does mean that participants, when discussing doctrinal formulations, should be scrupulous not to go beyond the expressed conclusions of the Pope, the bishops teaching in communion with him, and their authorized representatives.

Intercommunion

Apart from doctrinal formulations, ecumenical abuses occur in other respects when the guidance of the teaching Church is ignored. Intercommunion is an example. There is an emotional satisfaction to be gained by sharing the Holy Eucharist with non-Catholic believers in Christ, and by receiving their communion from them. And it is occasionally done. At the 1969 convention of the Lutheran

Church-Missouri Synod, the Reverend Thomas Rauch, a Catholic priest, celebrated an interdenominational communion service, unauthorized by both Catholic and Lutheran rules, with a Lutheran minister and the Reverend Malcolm Boyd, the Episcopal priest who alternates between theological innovation and opposition to the war in Vietnam.[20] In the Netherlands, Protestant and Catholic clergymen regularly and openly conduct joint Eucharistic services.[21] The Pope, however, as noted above, has described the "episodes of so-called 'intercommunion'" as "a practice which we must frankly condemn."[22]

Whether one agrees with him or not, all Catholics are bound to obey the Pope on this disciplinary matter of intercommunion. However, upon reflection his position can be readily seen to be sound on its own merits. Nothing will be solved by papering over this difference on the most fundamental question of the Real Presence of Christ in the Holy Eucharist. Intercommunion creates a façade of unity where real unity is absent and it removes a powerful spur toward the genuine resolution of differences.

Non-Christians

The subject of ecumenism strictly covers our relations with non-Catholic Christians. But it should be remembered that a comparable attitude was urged by the Council toward members of non-Christian religions, since "all peoples comprise a single community, and have a single origin, since God made the whole race of men dwell over the entire face of the earth (cf. Acts 17:26). One also is their final Goal: God."[23] The Council recognized the potential for dialogue here, too: "The Catholic Church rejects nothing which is true and holy in these religions. She looks with sincere respect upon those ways of conduct and of life . . . which . . . nevertheless often reflect a ray of that Truth which enlightens all men. The Church therefore has this exhortation for her sons: prudently and lovingly, through dialogue and collaboration . . . acknowledge, preserve and promote the spiritual and moral good found among these men, as well as the values in their society and culture."[24] The Council also urged that the questions raised by atheism be "examined seriously and more profoundly" and that atheists not be subjected to unjust civil discrimination.[25]

As to all three groups, non-Catholic Christians, non-Christian believers in God and atheists, the attitude of the Catholic should be open and receptive to discussion, while avoiding compromise with error. The problems are different with all three groups, but the principles are comparable. In no case should enthusiasm for harmony lead us to renounce the Church's claim to the truths of doctrine and the moral law. In all cases, the surest means to success will be adherence to the teaching authority of the Church.

Discrimination in Dialogue

One weakness in the ecumenical movement in this country, however, is that it tends to concentrate on dialogue with liberal spokesmen for other creeds while paying insufficient notice to others who seem to be closer to the Church on basic doctrine. Dr. Harold O. J. Brown, director of the International Fellowship of Evangelical Students, has urged cooperation between Catholic and Protestant "conservatives" to halt what he termed "the headlong rush" of liberals in both religions.[26] Dr. Brown acknowledges that there are serious differences between Catholicism and traditional Protestantism. But, he maintains, there are many points of agreement, such as the reality, personal nature, and power of God, the existence and authority of God's revelation in the Bible, the reality of the fall of man which actually occurred in time and space, the Divinity of Christ, the Virgin Birth, the Atonement, Resurrection, Ascension, and Final Judgment. By contrast, according to Dr. Brown, there is far less pre-existing ground for agreement between orthodox Catholicism and liberal Protestantism:

while the ecclesiastically inclined theologians of Protestantism are stretching out their hands (to each other, to the Orthodox and most recently to the Catholics) a larger group of Protestants is continuing to undermine, in the name of reason and science, all the great convictions of evangelical faith—beginning with the lesser miracles of the Bible, going on to important doctrines such as that of the Virgin Birth, and finally seeking to discredit even the Atonement and the Resurrection. And this attack on central evangelical doctrines is not confined to the churches which call themselves "evangelical," i.e., Protestant. It has deeply infected Catholicism as well. Its spread from Protestant to Catholic seminaries seems to have been facilitated by the ecumenical movement, although Catholicism too has produced its own "Modernism" independent of Protestant contagion.[27]

There is merit in Dr. Brown's point. If the objective is unity, it would seem reasonable to give due attention to those whose beliefs, at the outset, appear, in many respects, to be closer to those of the Church. Also, a broadening of the ecumenical effort could lessen the danger of Catholics absorbing, through an unbalanced overexposure, the secularistic and Modernist ideas which are current in some Protestant circles.

Similar considerations apply to non-Christian religions and to Marxists and other atheists. There is a strong Orthodox Jewish movement in the United States which, incidentally, is committed to preventing the total secularization of American society. These elements, however, have been underemphasized in a concentration on dialogue with more liberal Jewish groups which actively promote secularism in this country. As Rabbi Israel Mowshowitz said, "We should not be guilty of indulging in the old-type inter-faith meetings which were described by someone as occasions when a Jew who does not believe in Judaism meets a Christian who does not believe in Christianity and they find they have much in common."[28]

A broadening of the dialogue would be desirable, too, with respect to Marxists. Too often, Catholic spokesmen, in dealing with Marxists and other atheists, have been afflicted with a diffidence and failure of the will to instruct. There is a tendency in some Catholic circles, including especially the academic, to moderate the Church's opposition to Communism and to regard the Catholic Faith and Communism as broadly reconcilable. In fact there is an irreducible contradiction between the two creeds, one acknowledging God the Creator and the reality of the spiritual, and the other denying God and affirming the reality only of matter. Nor is it true that the Church has softened her stand against the Marxist creed. On the one hand, Pope John and Pope Paul have promoted prudent discussions and have offered the love of Christ to individual followers of Communism. On the other hand, they have reiterated the Church's condemnation of the Marxist creed both in theory and as it is practiced in reality. For example, in 1966, on the seventy-fifth anniversary of Pope Leo XIII's social encyclical, *Rerum Novarum*, Paul VI told a group of Christian workers' representatives that the

Church cannot adhere to "social, ideological and political movements which take their origin and strength from Marxism and have preserved its principles and negative methods, because of the incomplete and hence false concept of man, history, and the world, which goes with radical Marxism. The atheism which it professes and promotes is not in favor of the scientific concept of the universe and of civilization, but is a blindness that man and society in the end will have to pay for with the gravest consequences. The materialism which derives from it exposes man to experiences and temptations which are extremely harmful. It extinguishes his genuine spirituality and his transcendent hope."[29]

In dealing with Marxism, we should avoid the implication that discussion confers approval. But also, we ought to pay more attention to those who have suffered under Communism. For instance, we could profit from the experience of the Reverend Richard Wurmbrand, an Evangelical minister from Romania. A former representative of the World Council of Churches in that country, Pastor Wurmbrand was imprisoned in Romania for "illegal preaching" in 1948, released after eight years, but imprisoned again from 1959 through 1964, when he was released in a general amnesty. In April 1966 he was ransomed from Romania by Church organizations and came to the United States. When Pastor Wurmbrand testified before the Senate Internal Security Subcommittee, he bared himself to the waist to show the senators the eighteen scars he bore from his interrogations by the Communists.[30]

Before he left Romania, the secret police told him, "You may preach Christ as much as you like. We know that you are a preacher but don't touch us. Don't speak against Communists." They threatened him with death, or kidnapping, and a return to prison, or with moral destruction through circulation of false rumors "and people will be stupid enough to believe it." "And under these conditions I was allowed to come out. And very sorrowfully in the West I found people in the West, even religious leaders, who told me the same thing: 'Preach Christ as much as you like but don't touch Communists.'"

The Evangelical cleric criticized Western religious leaders for courting favor with the oppressors but not with the oppressed:

So I asked Christian leaders—I will not tell names—"Why have you sat at banquets with our inquisitors? I am a little pastor, I cannot interrogate you, but I speak for the others who cannot speak for themselves. Why have you sat at banquets with our inquisitors?"

I was answered, "We are Christians and must have friendship and fellowship with everybody, with the Communists, too. Don't you agree?"

I said, "I can't polemicize with you. I have not read the Bible for fourteen years. You must know Christianity better than I. Faintly I remember in the Bible it is written that friendship with the world is hatred toward God. But supposing you must have friendship and fellowship with everybody. How is it that you have had friendship and fellowship only with our inquisitors, and with us never?"

An unbalanced approach in this delicate area can easily frustrate the aims of the teaching Church. Whether we are dealing with atheists, Jews, or Protestants, the objective should be to lead others to the truth and not to confirm them in error. If we discourage those who are close to us in basic beliefs, we cast doubt on our pretension that we desire the unity of all men. If we focus unduly on those who are basically hostile to our creed, we confer on their beliefs an unwarranted legitimacy, we raise false hopes of reconciliation, and we demoralize those Catholics who wrongly infer, from the excesses of a few, that the Church herself is yielding on doctrine.

Converts

One frequent misconception is that the ecumenical movement has lessened the importance of obtaining converts. In fact, ecumenism and convert-making are two entirely distinct operations and "the work of preparing and reconciling those individuals who wish for full Catholic communion is of its nature distinct from ecumenical action. But there is no opposition between the two, since both proceed from the wondrous providence of God."[31] But the Council also emphasized the mission of the Church to obtain conversions: "Therefore, the Church announces the good tidings of salvation to those who do not believe, so that all men may know the true God and Jesus Christ whom He has sent, and may mend their ways (cf. Jn. 17:3; Lk. 24:27; Acts 2:38)."[32]

"The great danger which faces our country (the same applies to the United States) is that if it is not converted to the true religion

of Jesus Christ it will be converted to humanism and paganism."
Father Francis J. Ripley, director of the Catholic Information Center in Liverpool, England, said this in an article urging the reacti-
vation of the Catholic inquiry classes which began to grow a decade
ago and then lapsed in the wake of Vatican II. "The tragedy at the
present day," observed Father Ripley, "is that some of us seem to be
questioning the very nature of the Church and asking whether or
not the days of making converts and engaging in missionary activity
are not over."[33] Father Ripley also criticized those who imply that
"we should make no effort to convert people because their good
faith will save them in any case." This attitude, according to Father
Ripley, particularly as it is applied to humanists and Marxists, "is
a denial of the universal law of love which commands us to share
our treasures with all who do not possess them," and a rejection of
the mind of Christ whose "last injunction to his apostles" that they
preach the gospel to every creature included no exception that good
faith was not to be disturbed.

The conversion of individuals and the ecumenical unity of
Christian religions are both works of the highest importance. But
there are indications that misdirections of the ecumenical spirit
have not only impeded the ecumenical movement but discouraged
prospective individual converts as well. The declining rate of converts in the United States, as mentioned in Chapter I, indicates
this to be the case. The impression is conveyed by some that to
seek converts is somehow a denial of the respect that is owed to
non-Catholics and to their beliefs. In truth, however, we owe a
duty to the non-Catholic to seek his conversion by prudent means.
The reason for this was stated by Pope Pius XII in his 1943
encyclical on the Mystical Body of Christ. Non-Catholics, he said
"are in a condition in which they cannot be sure of their salvation,
since they still remain deprived of those many heavenly gifts and
helps which can only be enjoyed in the Catholic Church." His
predecessor, Pius XI, also emphasized that charity requires that we
"strive by every means to increase the flock and unite to Christ
those estranged from Him and those outside the Church."[34]

Interior Conversion

Ecumenism is crucial, both in the broad sense and in the more
proper sense of relations with other Christians. There have been

abuses. But our aim here is not to catalogue abuses. It would be possible to extend this chapter to great length with a parade of horrors, illustrating excesses committed by those who disregard, in one direction or another, the guidance of the teaching Church in this area. But the purpose of this chapter is merely to relate ecumenism to the overall authority crisis in the Church. For this reason it is brief and limited in its scope. Essentially, it is a call for obedience to the teaching authority of the Church as the first condition for fruitful relations with non-Catholics of all creeds and of none. The Popes and Vatican II have pointed the way to achieve the desired union of all in Christ. For us it remains to comply. It is our duty to know and understand other beliefs more than we have in the past and to remain open to discussion and an honest, but neither overbearing nor sentimentalized, exchange of views. It is also our task to present the Church and the Faith to others to the best of our ability. But this cannot be done if the essential authority of that Church is treated as a transient accident of history.

Most importantly, however, it is our responsibility to pray so that all might freely come to choose the Faith. As Pope Paul observed in his 1969 address to the World Council of Churches Assembly in Geneva, "There can be no ecumenism worthy of the name without interior conversion."[35] This interior conversion would seem to be as important for us as it is for those non-Catholics who are the objects of our attention. As Vatican II declared, the "primary duty" of Catholics in ecumenical terms "is to make an honest and careful appraisal of whatever needs to be renewed and achieved in the Catholic household itself, in order that its life may bear witness more loyally and luminously to the teachings and ordinances which have been handed down from Christ through the apostles."[36] It is important, therefore, for us to know the case for the Church's authority and to present it well. But it is more important to conform ourselves to the mind of the Church in our interior life as well. This latter effort can do more for the ecumenical movement than any amount of argument. Hopefully, this brief chapter will contribute to an awareness that interior conversion, no less than dialogue, is essential for its own sake and for the sake of the ecumenical movement.

The discussion of ecumenism and of the need there for obedience to Church authority leads naturally into the subject of the liturgy. For changes have been made there speedily and radically with the partial motivation among many of making the Church more understandable to non-Catholics and thereby promoting the ecumenical cause. Also, the liturgy is another area where strict obedience to authority is essential if abuse is to be avoided.

VIII.

THE LITURGY

Yet the majority of people in York must have submitted to the changes under Edward, must have sat through the hearing of the *Book of Homilies* which contradicted most of their beliefs and poured scorn upon their practices. They must have seen some of their beloved statues removed from the parish churches in perfunctory obedience to royal Injunctions. In 1548 they were amazed to be offered Communion in both species, bread and wine, in the course of a new Communion Service in English, and to be told in advance that the Sacrament of Penance need not be received in preparation, even if they were in a state of sin. In 1549 the Latin Mass ceased to be the normal daily service, the Missal being replaced by an entirely new *Book of Common Prayer* in English. In November 1550 the very altars were ordered to be destroyed and replaced by wooden tables; in the diocese of York, however, many parish priests avoided this destruction.[1]

These were among the steps taken during the reign of King Edward VI, son of Henry VIII, "to complete the destruction of the Catholic Church in England, not merely materially, but spiritually, by the abolition of the Mass, which was the object of the Reformers' peculiar hatred, and of almost the whole sacramental system."[2] The description has a familiar ring today. Liturgical changes have been made which some regard as a capitulation to Protestant ideas, as if the Church in the twentieth century were doing of its own accord what Henry VIII and his successors sought vainly to do in the sixteenth by force. But the changes today, however much they may resemble the Protestant edicts, have been authorized by Vatican II and the Pope for legitimate reasons.

What can be said of both the sixteenth century and our own day is that in each era the liturgy provides a natural avenue of approach for those who seek to undermine the authority and the doctrine of the Church. This is especially true of the Mass and the Holy Eucharist. Today, as four centuries ago, there are too many who are prominent in the Church because of their liturgical excess.

"Catholic bishops have no monopoly on Christ and the body of Christ may appear just as validly if not more so in the Eucharist celebrated by a Negro woman around a kitchen table as in the one celebrated by the Pope in St. Peter's."[3]

Dr. Rosemary Ruether, a prominent figure in the liturgical underground, made this statement quite seriously. Of course, it does not conform to the teaching of the Church. But it also reflects the readiness of some to throw off all liturgical restraints while maintaining that they are still in the Church.

On the first anniversary of *Humanae Vitae*, an "innovative" Mass was celebrated in Washington under the sponsorship of the Center for Christian Renewal. The Center is the headquarters for the forty recalcitrant priests who were penalized by Cardinal O'Boyle for their public opposition to the encyclical. Attended by two hundred persons, the Mass was notable in several respects. It was held, to begin with, in a Lutheran church. Father John Corrigan, leader of the dissident priests, was the celebrant. Sal Caruso's orchestra provided the accompaniment. Mass opened with the congregation singing "Georgy Girl." Another number played was "The Impossible Dream." Holy Communion was distributed by James Colaianni, executive director of the Liturgical Conference, Mrs. Philip Hart, wife of the Michigan senator, and several of the dissident priests. Colaianni preached the homily. *Humanae Vitae*, he said, has caused some Catholics to "slip back into servitude," thereby denying the liberty of spirit which Christ can effect in the believer. Colaianni denied a report that a woman who opposed the Mass was kept from speaking when she tried to address the group near the end of the service. It was purely coincidental, he said, that the orchestra struck up the recessional, "When the Saints Go Marching In," when the woman tried to speak.[4]

Perhaps this zany affair confirms the observation of Father Mark Hegener, O.F.M., that there is evident in the underground Church, "a Waldensian smugness in a little church of its own—underground, where all hold hands and feel fellowship in a kind of ecclesiastical felony that brings the excitement of conspirators in crime." Not all abuses, however, are on the side of innovation. Some who describe themselves as traditionalists, such as the followers of Hugo Maria Kellner, have questioned the validity of liturgical changes introduced by Pope Paul, even to the point of accusing the Pope himself of heresy.

We deal with the liturgy here for two limited reasons. First, it is one area where the rejection of Church authority is highly discernible and measurable. Partly for that reason, but mostly because the liturgy pervades and sets the tone for the entire life of the Church, it is an area where the defiance of authority can have profoundly damaging effects. The second reason for our attention to the liturgy here is because it offers a clear example of the distinction between the obedience owed to a doctrinal or moral teaching, such as *Humanae Vitae,* and that owed to a disciplinary regulation such as the New Order of the Mass.

In approaching the liturgy, the first essential is to maintain balance. This requires adherence to the norms authoritatively decreed by the Church. And it requires that we avoid both extremes, those on the one hand who spurn any restrictions on their right to cultivate new forms of worship as the spirit moves them, and those on the other hand who hold so firmly to the old way that they refuse to recognize the validity of authorized changes.

The New Rite of the Mass

The liturgy is "the oustanding means by which the faithful can express in their lives, and manifest to others, the mystery of Christ and the real nature of the true Church."[5] In his 1947 encyclical, *Mediator Dei,* the charter of the modern liturgical movement, Pope Pius XII defined the "sacred liturgy" as "the public worship which our Redeemer, the Head of the Church, offers to the heavenly Father and which the community of Christ's faithful pays to its Founder, and through Him to the Eternal Father; briefly, it is the whole public worship paid by the Mystical Body of Jesus Christ, Head and members."

The effort to increase lay participation in the liturgy was stressed by Vatican II[6] and has assumed even greater importance since then. It will be appropriate to gauge the success of that endeavor by its impact on the central act of worship, the Mass. The Mass, the "Eucharistic Sacrifice," was described by the Council as "the center and culmination of the whole life of the Christian community."[7] This does not imply that the Mass is the sum total of the liturgy.

But the changes in the Mass have been the most dramatic and controversial. And they present in sharp relief the issues of authority with which we are concerned.

On April 28, 1969, the Pope announced the publication of the new Order of the Mass, the *Novus Ordo Missae*, which he described as "the reform that the Council Fathers desired. Its aim is to give even greater assistance to living, conscious participation by the faithful in the Divine Sacrifice."[8] This was the first overall revision of the Mass since the Roman Missal was promulgated by Pope St. Pius V, by decree of the Council of Trent. Its promulgation by Pope Paul terminated a period of official study and experimentation that began in March 1964. Writing in *L'Osservatore Romano*, the Very Reverend Annibale Bugnini, secretary of the Sacred Congregation for Divine Worship, explained that with the new Ordo "the experiments, however, have come to an end, the provisional indults, the temporary concession and personal initiatives have finished."[9] The New Ordo went into effect in Italian dioceses on November 30, 1969, and was to be applied throughout the Latin Church over the next two years. During the transition period, national bishops' conferences were authorized to permit the use of the old rite "side by side" as an alternative to the new rite.[10]

The New Order of the Mass, however, did not meet with unanimous approval. On September 25, 1969, Alfredo Cardinal Ottaviani, perfecte-emeritus of the Sacred Congregation for the Faith, sent the Holy Father a letter with a Study of the new rite and of the official General Instructions, the *Institutio Generalis*, issued to accompany it. The Study was written by a group of Roman theologians and it demonstrated, in Cardinal Ottaviani's words, "that if we consider the innovations implied or taken for granted, which may of course be evaluated in different ways, the *Novus Ordo* represents, both as a whole and in its details, a striking departure from the Catholic theology of the Mass as it was formulated in Session XXII of the Council of Trent. The 'canons' of the rite definitively fixed at that time provided an insurmountable barrier to any heresy directed against the integrity of the Mystery" of the Mass. The Study claimed that the *Novus Ordo Missae* was virtually the same as the "normative Mass" that had been submitted to the Episcopal Synod of October 1967. Out of 187 bishops voting, a majority either opposed the new Mass or had substantial reservations about it. The absence of any evidence that the people desired a new Mass was also alleged by the Study. Beyond that, the Study charged that the new Mass contained dangerous equivocations on such topics as the nature of the Mass as a sacrifice as well as a meal; the real change of the bread and wine into the body and blood of Christ; the Real Presence of Christ in the Eucharist; and the character of the priest as a "consecrated minister celebrating *in persona Christi* instead of 'a mere president or brother.'" "He now appears as nothing more than a Protestant minister," was the way the Study described the role of the priest in the new Mass.

In concluding his letter, Cardinal Ottaviani implored the Pope "not to deprive us of the possibility of continuing to have recourse to the fruitful integrity of that Missale Romanum of St. Pius V, so highly praised by Your Holiness and so deeply loved and venerated by the whole Catholic World."[11]

Before the new rite went into effect in Italy on November 30, 1969, some public opposition developed to it in that country. To allay these misgivings, the Pope devoted his General Audiences of November 19, 1969, and November 26, 1969, to the subject. These addresses were definitive in their treatment and they should be understood before any judgment is formed on the new Mass rite or on liturgical changes in general.

In the audience of November 19, Pope Paul addressed himself to three questions raised by the new rite. The first question is, "How could such a change take place?"

The answer is that it is due to the express wishes of the recent Ecumenical Council. The Council says: "The rite of the Mass is to be revised in such a way that the intrinsic nature and purpose of its several parts, as well as the connection between them, may be more clearly manifested, and that devout and active participation by the faithful may be more easily achieved. For this purpose the rites are to be simplified, due care being taken to preserve their substance; elements which, with the passage of time, came to be duplicated, or were added with but little advantage, are now to be discarded; other elements which have suffered injury through accidents of history are now to be restored according to the pristine norm of the holy Fathers, to the extent that they may seem useful or necessary."[12]

"The reform," he continued, "corresponds to an authoritative mandate of the Church. It is an act of obedience. . . . It is not a whim. . . . It is not some dilettante's improvisation. It is a law thought out by authoritative scholars of the sacred liturgy, who studied it long and carefully." The reform "puts an end to uncertainty, debate and abusive whims. It recalls us to the oneness of rites and sentiments that is proper to the Catholic Church. . . ."

The "second question," the Pope went on, is: "What does this change consist of?" He hastened to answer, first of all, that "none of the substance of our traditional Mass has been changed." There are two reasons for saying this: "first of all, because the rite and its related rubric are not in themselves a dogmatic definition." And "secondly, because the Mass of the new rite is and remains the Mass it always was—in some of its aspects even more clearly so than before."

Then the Pope explained why the new rite remains the same as the Mass it always was:

> The unity between the Lord's Supper, the sacrifice of the cross, and the re-presentation of both in the Mass, is inviolably affirmed and celebrated in the new rite, as it was in the old. The Mass is and remains the memorial of the Lord's Last Supper, at which He instituted the sacrifice of the New Testament by changing bread and wine into His Body and Blood and willed, by virtue of the priesthood that He conferred on His Apostles, that it be repeated identically but in a different manner—that is, in an unbloody and sacramental manner—in perpetual memory of Him until His last coming.
>
> In the new rite you will find clearer light shed on the relationship between the Liturgy of the Word and the properly Eucharistic Liturgy—the latter being the response which realizes and effects the former.

The third question is: "What consequences will this have for those who assist at holy Mass? The consequences expected, or rather desired, are more intelligent, more satisfying, more real and more sanctifying participation by the faithful in the liturgical mystery—participation, that is, in the hearing of the word of God which lives and resounds through the centuries and the annals of our own souls, and in the mystic reality of Christ's sacramental and propitiatory sacrifice."[13]

In his audience of November 26, the Pope went into more detail. He warned his hearers that they might be disturbed at the changes which will distract "them from their usual personal devotion or their habitual torpidity." He reiterated the reasons behind the change: "The first reason is obedience to the Council, which then becomes obedience to the bishops who interpret and carry out its prescriptions." The second reason, a product of "the prophetic impulse that is running through the Mystical Body of Christ, which is the Church . . . rousing the Church from slumber and obliging her to revitalize her mysterious art of prayer," is: "to associate the assembly of the faithful more closely and effectively with the official rite—that is, with the Liturgy of the Word of God and the Eucharistic sacrifice, of which the Mass is composed."

Next, the Holy Father addressed himself to the fact that "no longer Latin, but the vernacular, will be the principal language of the Mass." He acknowledged that "we do have reason for sadness, and perhaps even for bewilderment at sacrificing an inestimable treasure." The Pope then asked what reason could justify the sacrifice of Latin and he answered in these words:

> The answer may seem banal and prosaic, but it is valid because it is both human and apostolic. Our understanding of prayer is worth more than the regal antique garments in which it has been clothed. More important is the participation of the people, of modern men who are saturated with clear, intelligible and translatable speech in their worldly conversation.

On the Latin question, the Second Vatican Council had this to say:

> 1. Particular law remaining in force, the use of the Latin language is to be preserved in the Latin rites.
> 2. But since the use of the mother tongue, whether in the Mass, the administration of the sacraments, or other parts of the liturgy, may frequently be of great advantage to the people, the limits of its employment may be extended.[14]

However, the introduction of the vernacular in the Mass does not mean that the Church is abandoning Latin. The Pope made this clear in his audience of November 26:

> Moreover, the new Mass rite lays down the proviso that the faithful "should be at least able to chant in unison, in Latin, the Ordinary of the Mass—in particular, the Creed and the Lord's Prayer, the Our Father."

We also do well to remember something else, which should

give us comfort and second thoughts. Latin will certainly not disappear in our Church. It will remain the lofty language of the Apostolic See's official pronouncements. It will remain the pedagogical instrument for ecclesiastical studies, and the key that unlocks to us the heritage of our religious, historical and humanistic culture. Perhaps it may flourish with new splendor in this respect.

The first sentence of the above quotation may surprise some American Catholics who might never suspect, from the implementation of the new liturgy in the United States, that they should be able to chant in Latin the Ordinary of the Mass.

The Pope then emphasized again "that the fundamental design of the Mass remains what it always was, in terms of its theological and spiritual import." But he went further and asserted that if the new rite is properly carried out, its greater richness will show itself in several ways:

It will be made evident by the greater simplicity of the ceremonies, by the abundant and varied scriptural texts, by the combined actions of the various ministers, and by the silences that mark the deeper moments of the rite. Above all, it will be made evident by two indispensable requirements: the intimate participation of each individual present, and the outpouring of hearts in communal charity. These requirements should make the Mass, more than ever before, a school of deep spirituality and a serene but compelling training ground in Christian social living."

The Pope concluded by establishing the technical norms and schedules for introducing the New Mass, noting incidentally that there is no problem with the vernacular "for those who celebrate Mass in private, because they are to celebrate Mass in Latin."[15]

This Papal explanation is crucial to our understanding of the Mass. It served, too, to allay the basic fears of Cardinal Ottaviani. On February 17, 1970, Cardinal Ottaviani expressed his "regret that my name was misused—in a manner that I did not want— by the unauthorized publication of a private letter which I had sent to the Holy Father." He expressed his pleasure at the Pope's clarification of the New Order and said:

I have been greatly cheered in reading the Discourses of the Holy Father on the questions raised by the new *Ordo*

Missae. . . . After these, I believe that no one can sincerely find fault henceforth. It remains, however, that a prudent and intelligent work of catechesis must be given in order to remove some legitimate perplexities that the text can raise.[16]

Without going into detail here, it can be said that the "legitimate perplexities" to which Cardinal Ottaviani refers are magnified in the English translations used in the United States. But, as John Cardinal Carberry noted in his pastoral letter to the people of his Archdiocese of St. Louis, "the Congregation of Rites has only given what is known as an interim or temporary approval to the English text of the translation. The Congregation has not given final or official approval. This is important, for it means that questions of translation can still be raised and they will be studied."[17] This study will doubtless take a long time before it is finally completed. As of this writing, at least, the translations in the United States are primitive in some respects.

With some appreciation of what the Pope had in mind in instituting the new *Ordo*, we ought to consider the Mass in the context of the authority crisis in the Church.

The Second Vatican Council decreed that "in the restoration and promotion of the sacred liturgy, this full and active participation by all the people is the aim to be considered above all else; for it is the primary and indispensable source from which the faithful are to derive the true Christian spirit."[18] To increase this participation was the expressed aim of the Pope in promulgating the new rite. While the Council did not decree an entirely new rite of the Mass, it made it clear that decisions of this sort are the prerogative of the Holy Father: "Regulation of the sacred liturgy depends solely on the authority of the Church, that is, on the Apostolic See and, as laws may determine, on the bishop."[19] After noting that Church laws may confer power to regulate the liturgy on "competent territorial bodies of bishops legitimately established," the same article concluded:

3. Therefore, absolutely no other person, not even a priest, may add, remove, or change anything in the liturgy on his own authority.

The Duty to Participate

The new rite has been promulgated. We have the Pope's assurance that the Mass and its rubrics are free from doctrinal error. We can rely on that assurance. Our duty, therefore, is to obey and to do our best to take part in it according to the mind of the Holy Father. Indeed, this attitude is required of us with respect to the rest of the liturgy as well as the Mass. Just as we ought to reject those who prefer clandestine liturgies to the authorized rites, so we should reject those who, out of an excess of zeal for orthodoxy, accuse the Pope himself and the bishops teaching in communion with him, of heresy in this regard. However, while we owe the duty of full and unreserved obedience, the liturgy is not irreformable and Catholics are entitled, if they so desire, to regard the changes as impractical or unwise and to petition the Pope and, where appropriate, the bishops, for such modifications as seem necessary. There are more than a few doctrinally orthodox Catholics who regard the new rites as undesirable. According to Dietrich von Hildebrand, for instance, "it would be disastrous to identify the God-willed response of faith to the infallible theoretical authority of the Church with the completely different response of obedience to the practical authority of the Church." Therefore, Von Hildebrand concludes, "though we must obey such a practical decision, we must not approve it; nay, we must even pray for its revocation, and in full respect, strive with all legitimate measures to persuade the Holy Father of its danger. . . ."[20]

Von Hildebrand's distinction between the teaching and the disciplinary authority—or what he calls the theoretical and the practical authority—is well founded. But his objections were primarily to the *Institutio Generalis* issued with the new rite of the Mass in 1969. However, since it was issued, the Pope has affirmed in detail the doctrinal regularity of the Mass—particularly in his general audiences of November 19 and 26, 1969—and the *Institutio* itself has been clarified. On April 9, 1970, Monsignor Annibale Bugnini, secretary of the Sacred Congregation for Divine Worship, announced the revision of the *Institutio*. While denying that the original version contained doctrinal error, Monsignor Bugnini announced that the *Institutio Generalis* "will be preceded in the new Missal by a foreword . . . in which there shall be explained at greater length the continuity of the tradition, as well as its legitimate progress and enrichment, from Trent to Vatican II on the priesthood, the Eucharist, Sacrifice and the Real Presence."[21]

These points—the special ministry and consecrating function of the priest; the intrinsic value of the Eucharist; the sacrificial character of the Mass; and the Real Presence of Christ in the Eucharist —were the major points on which Cardinal Ottaviani's study charged the original version was weak.

The Mass in English

It is clear that the New Order of the Mass cannot be attacked, itself or in its explanatory *Institutio*, as a contradiction of doctrine. But the implementation of the new rite in English leaves much to be desired. For some years the Church in the United States has had its liturgy controlled from above by a tight band of liturgists in the Bishops' Committee on the Liturgy, the International Committee on English in the Liturgy, and allied committees.[22] Archbishop Robert J. Dwyer, of Portland, Oregon, recently attacked the International Committee on English in the Liturgy for having "performed its task so poorly as to raise serious questions as to its competence. Never was there the slightest consultation with the bishops of the English-speaking world; here is a signal instance of bureaucracy inflicting its will by methods which can only be described as high-handed."[23] "Translators and consultants both," said Archbishop Dwyer, "have demonstrated their incompetence, their insensitivity, and their indifference to the demands of absolute fidelity when dogmatic considerations make this obligatory."[24] One interesting note is that the secretary of the International Committee on English in the Liturgy until early 1970 was Father Gerald Sigler, who was suspended from certain of his priestly functions by Cardinal O'Boyle on October 1, 1968, for rejecting the cardinal's directive that the priests of the Washington Archdiocese should teach nothing contrary to *Humanae Vitae*.[25]

In view of the potential of the liturgy for reinforcing or undermining doctrinal beliefs, it is clear that only those who adhere without reservation to the teachings of the Church and the authority of the Pope should have any responsible part to play in the translation of the liturgy.

One weakness of the liturgy in English is evident below the

level of doctrine. This is the failure of the new liturgy, including other rites as well as the Mass, to respond to the felt modern need for the sacred and the mysterious in worship. Instead, the English liturgy tends to be commonplace, pedestrian, and boring. Sociologist Father Andrew M. Greeley recently asserted that "the Pentecostal hysteria, rock mass, folk music, guitars, to say nothing of astrology, divination and oriental mysticism, are all a judgment on the Western churches," he said, "for their failure to respond to man's yearning for the sacred and the ecstatic."[26] Justus George Lawler, editor-in-chief of the publishing house of Herder and Herder, made a similar point:

It seems rather apparent that everywhere outside of the churches people are seeking an experiential, self-directing reality—what in earlier days was called an "interior life": they are trying to develop the contemplative side of their person, a side they rightly feel has been atrophied by the dominant culture of this society . . . The irony is, of course, that this is precisely the tradition now abandoned by the churches. Zen kicks, assorted hybrid yogisms, communal life, grass—all are crude expressions of a universal urge for what an older and better heritage called "the hart panting after the waters." And this urge is being frustrated by the churches which are still offering the poverty-struck language of a chamber-of-commerce press release. The children of the flower children have more in common with the mystical fervor and freedom of the desert fathers than with all the guitar-strumming rotarians who presently constitute the most visible segment of our parish ministry.[27]

The obliteration of Latin, particularly in the hymns, the labored activism and the banal translations all contribute to an inadequacy in the English liturgy that can be felt rather than proven. Perhaps one difficulty is that the emphasis in the Mass, as implemented in the United States, seems to be on role-playing and the performance of a task. As Father Joseph M. Champlin, assistant executive secretary of the Bishops' Committee on the Liturgy, commented, the "new epoch in the liturgy" will have the characteristic of being "technically excellent," with a "concentration on having each person fulfill his appointed function *well*." (Emphasis in original)[28]

For some, the new rite in English is undoubtedly helpful. But for others, it is an impediment to devotion and real participation.

For those who find the English renditions inadequate, it would be appropriate to inform the bishops and the Pope of their reaction and of their desire for a new translation. An effort in this direction is being made by the Laymen's Commission on the English Liturgy. This group, organized at the *Wanderer* Forum in 1970, has urged that the bishops of the United States provide "a more faithful and majestic translation of the 'New Ordo' of the Mass . . . as befitting the sacred dignity of the Eucharistic Sacrifice."[29] The work of this lay commission must be sharply distinguished from the refusal of some others to accept the new *Ordo* itself. All Catholics are bound to accept the new rite and do their best to join in it according to the desires of the Pope and the directives of the bishops. To seek an improved translation is clearly consistent with this duty, provided that a new translation is sought in a prudent manner without casting discredit on the new rite itself. In principle it is legitimate, too, for Catholics to request that the Pope authorize an alternative rite, whether it be the Tridentine Mass of Pius V or some other variation. This is essentially the position of the editors of *Triumph* magazine and some others, who emphasize their full acceptance of the new rite as an exercise of Papal authority and whose petition for an alternative involves no challenge to that authority or to the legitimacy of the new rite.

The practical judgment on which the new rite is based is that it will best achieve the greater understanding and participation desired by Vatican II. But the achievement of this goal can be measured only by experience. It is in helping to gauge that experience that it could be beneficial for Catholics to inform the Holy Father and the bishops of their reactions and opinions. This would be a process of information and in no way a demonstration or pressure campaign. The reaction of the people would seem to be one of the data from which the Pope would be able to judge the practical efficacy of the English Mass in achieving the goals he has set for it.

Four cautions, however, are necessary here:

1. A hasty judgment must be avoided. The new rite of the Mass is a change from the practice of four centuries. Under the best of conditions it should be expected to cause some inconvenience and irritation. However, we are obliged to give it a fair chance. This requires participation and a receptive mind.

2. The inadequacies we see in the new rite in the United States are evidently due to the manner in which the new rite has been translated and implemented rather than to the rite itself. If the American bishops strictly follow and enforce the Pope's instructions, if they provide an adequate translation and if lay Catholics do their best to participate, it is likely the new rite in English will fulfill the highest expectations of the Pope.

3. For those who are dissatisfied with the new rite in English, the first recourse should be to petition the bishops of the United States for an improved translation and such other modifications as may be appropriate and within their jurisdiction. A petition to the Pope for an alternative rite should be regarded as a last resort.

4. In no event should the liturgy be embroiled in the sort of contention that has surrounded the issue of priestly celibacy. The requirement of celibacy and the promulgation of the liturgy are both within the disciplinary authority of the Pope. In both cases, we are obliged to accept that authority generously and to avoid any public controversy that could impede the attainment of the purposes sought by the Pope.

Other Innovations

Other liturgical issues would be interesting to cover in detail, but space forbids. Neither Vatican II nor the Pope intended the new liturgy to disparage the importance of personal prayer, devotion to the Real Presence in the Blessed Sacrament, devotion to the Mother of God, and other incidents of Catholic life. There is a danger that the new liturgy can create what Dan Herr called a "piety void."[30] Nor is it necessary that personal devotions be eliminated. Rather they are indispensable to the proper functioning of the liturgy and their importance has been underscored by the Council and Pope Paul.

Another issue we can only mention in passing involves the special Masses for youth. There is no clear evidence that these Masses have increased the attendance or devotion of young people at Mass. One reason is that if the youth do not really believe in God and the Mass, all the fancy footwork and psychedelic lighting in the world is not going to hold them. It may be coincidental, but the heaviest leakage of young people from the Church has occurred during the new liturgical era. Perhaps we tend to underestimate the young. Perhaps they perceive that the youth Mass, in at least some circumstances, is a kind of patronizing put-down. The implication is that young people are incapable of responding to an adult appeal, to the reality of the Mass, and that they have to be conned, or amused, into assisting at Mass. As Pope Paul pointed out, the youth Mass, properly done, can be helpful and should be encouraged:

> We also refer to the Masses for youth, excellent initiatives to be cordially encouraged, where they are free from polemical inspiration with regard to other Masses, and free from novelties which debase the celebration, weakening it in the rite, in the texts, in the music and chants, in its duration and in the homily under the pretext of adapting it to the modern mentality.[31]

But there is a tendency in some quarters to force the youth-oriented liturgy on the young due to a misconception of what they really want. Father Andrew M. Greeley recently warned that while young people have been seeking new forms of spiritual experience in mystical creeds and practices, church leaders have been "busy trying to eradicate as much of the sacred as possible from their own behavior and worship."[32] An interesting footnote here was written in Vietnam where the Catholic chaplains at the Army posts at Pleiku and Long Binh said the traditional Latin High Mass with Gregorian chant, for Christmas 1970. The special Masses were requested by their congregations, most of whom were in the nineteen-to-twenty-one age bracket.[33] If the men were stateside in their parishes, they could never have had that Mass.

Maybe there should be a poll. When the bishops of the United States asked the opinion of the people in the parishes, they discovered that the people, by a vote of two to one, wanted no change in the number of Holy Days of Obligation.[34] This was a striking demonstration that sometimes changes are promoted on behalf of the people that the people do not want. Sometimes the innovating clerics in the middle bureaucracy of the liturgical apparatus appear to be out of touch with the people. It would be interesting to see the results of a poll in the United States on several liturgical questions, including the English translations, optional use of Latin and Gregorian chant, standing to receive Communion, the reception of Communion in the hand, and others.

Professional liturgists are resourceful, to say the least, in devising new practices to impose on the people without any prior indication of a popular demand. The judgment of scholars and liturgists as to what the people want and need bears no necessary relation to reality. We might recall here Christopher Derrick's comment, "A liturgist is an affliction sent by God, so that at a time when there is no overt persecution, a Catholic need not be denied the privilege of suffering for the faith."[35]

A minor point, that tells us something of the prevailing attitude toward authority in liturgical matters, involves the custom that women should cover their heads in Church. Canon 1262 of the Code of Canon Law reads in part, "Women will assist at divine services in modest dress and with heads covered, especially when they approach Holy Communion." Confusion arose when a Vatican spokesman, in answer to a reporter's question, said the new Mass regulations contained nothing about women's headdress. He failed to add that the Mass regulations never did. Monsignor Annibale Bugnini, secretary of the Sacred Congregation for Divine Worship, removed the confusion:

> The custom goes back to St. Paul. Of course, there is nothing in the new regulations about women covering their heads at Mass, but there never was. And there is certainly nothing in the new regulations to repeal the custom.[36]

The head-covering rule might be changed in the future. But at this time it remains in force. Yet the bareheaded practice continues, without significant clerical remonstrance. This is a curious but perhaps significant indicator of attitude among priests and the people.

To Follow the Pope

In all these matters, but pre-eminently in the Mass, the liturgy offers a striking proof that the only way to achieve both participation and devotion—and the only way to avoid excess—is to adhere to the Holy Father's expressed desires on the subject. Regrettably, that compliance with the Pontiff's will has been notable for its absence in some quarters. In concluding this chapter, it would be appropriate to quote from an address of Pope Paul in which he described three categories of people who are failing in their duty to respond to the liturgy:

The *first category* is perhaps the largest one. It is composed of those souls who are spiritually asleep. . . .

. . . One indication of this spiritual sluggishness is the heavy weight that prayer exerts on pious practices when no inner devotion is present. The exercises always seem to be too long, their format is accused of being incomprehensible and alien. Prayer lacks wings. . . .

[The] *second category*, which has become more numerous and anxiety-ridden since the Council's liturgical reform, is composed of suspicious critics and malcontents. With their habitual pious practices disturbed, these souls are reluctant to accept new ways. They do not try to understand the reasons behind the new forms of worship, nor are they happy with them. They take refuge in complaining, which takes away all the old flavor from their ancient formulas and prevents them from enjoying what the Church, in this liturgical springtime, now offers to souls who are open to the language and message of the new rites.

[The] *third category* is composed of those who are satisfied with charity toward their neighbor, so much so that they neglect or reject love of God as superfluous. Everyone knows the negative turn that this spiritual attitude has taken, claiming that it is action, not prayer, that keeps Christian life alert and authentic. The social sense replaces the religious sense. This devouring reaction spreads from radical and even open-minded literature to the area of public opinion and popular thinking, moving on into so-called "underground groups." Restless souls, seeking a more intense personal life of the Church, which they describe as authoritarian and artificial, end by losing authentic religious life. For it is replaced with a notion of human sympathy which, beautiful and noble in itself, has been stripped of theological truth and religious charity.

How much substance and transcendent value can there be in a religious form where doctrines of the faith, of man's relationship with the Absolute, with the one and triune God, the drama of Redemption and the mystery of grace and the Church, are usually passed over in silence, or replaced by comments about the social, political or historical situation? . . . (Emphasis added)[37]

We ought not to find ourselves in any of these categories. Rather, as Pope Paul said, "We would want to be classified with those alert souls whom Jesus would have carry lighted lamps. . . . The fact is that it is prayer which lends light to life, maintains our vigilance, and prods our conscience."[38] But beyond prayer, docility and obedience to the Holy Father are required. It may be that if we were Pope we would have done otherwise. But the decision is his to make. And it is ours to follow his will as completely as we can.

IX.

ELEMENTARY
AND HIGH SCHOOLS

Harmful Monopoly
the Public School System Should Be
Broken Up

With this startling headline, *Barron's*, the respected business weekly, introduced an article in 1967 calling for the elimination of the public school system.[1] After detailing the academic and disciplinary failures of the public schools, *Barron's* urged the substitution of a free choice plan:

> Innovation, in short, is running wild except where it counts, i.e. in the basic structure of the school system. On this score one of the more daring—and promising—proposals has come from a downtrodden minority for whom nobody seems to take up the cudgels, the tiny group of scholars who oppose collectivism in any form and champion the individual. They urge a switch from public to private schools, or what Milton Friedman, in "Capitalism and Freedom," has aptly called the "denationalization of the education industry." Under such a scheme the state would continue to enforce standards and school attendance through some kind of voucher system, it also would finance universal schooling. However—here is the major breakthrough —parents would be free to patronize privately owned and operated schools of their own choice. There is ample precedent: in both Britain and France, the government pays the fees of some students who attend private schools, while this country, in the original G.I. Bill of Rights, in effect furnished veterans with educational vouchers.

This could be a time of great opportunity for private education. Parents and taxpayers in many places have had enough of public schools that fail to do their primary job of basic education. If private schools could solve their financial problems they could provide an effective alternative for those parents. This is especially true of the Catholic schools, which alone offer, in Pope Paul's phrase, "the wealth and firmness of religious and pedagogical principles derived from Christ's Divine Magisterium."[2]

At the end of 1969 there were 558 fewer Catholic elementary and high schools in this country than there were at the end of 1968. During 1969, enrollment in those schools dropped by 313,052. And no reversal of the downward trend is in sight. According to Monsignor James C. Donohue, director of the Division of Elementary and Secondary Education of the United States Catholic Conference, "In the next five and a half years, Catholic elementary schools will lose almost 2,000,000 pupils, half their enrollment, unless Catholics vastly increase support of their school system."[3]

Between September 1963 and September 1969, 1023 Catholic schools closed in the nation and enrollment dropped 771,000 or fourteen percent. At the start of the 1969–70 school year, parents of the 740,000 children in Catholic elementary and secondary schools in New York State were warned in a joint statement, issued by the eight dioceses of the state, that, "for the schools to continue to operate and educate New York State's children, increased revenue is essential. Within one or two years parents and other supporters will not be able to keep the schools operating at their present size and effectiveness without government aid."[4] Private, nonparochial school enrollment, however, continues to rise in many places, reflecting the widespread dissatisfaction with the public schools. In New York City, for instance, private school enrollment rose fifty percent between 1952 and 1967, while Catholic parochial school enrollment was rising by twenty-six percent and public school enrollment rose by twenty-two percent.[5]

Parochial schools are particularly vulnerable to inflation and rising costs. Declining vocations to religious orders have necessitated the hiring of more lay teachers at full salaries. In September 1969, lay teachers outnumbered priests and nuns for the first time in the Catholic elementary and secondary schools in New York City.[6] The increased concentration of the public schools on programs requiring expensive equipment, in science and other areas, has made it difficult for parochial schools to keep pace without overstraining their budgets.

Catechism

These and other financial pressures are real. But the reasons for the declining enrollments and the closings of parochial schools cannot be found in the ledger books alone. Although it cannot be demonstrated conclusively, there is reason to believe that parochial schools, both elementary and secondary, are in trouble because they are not performing their function. Consider, primarily, the catechism crisis. In recent years, parochial school children have been exposed to catechisms which are dubious in their theology and, not incidentally, repulsive in their art. It is not within the scope of this work to analyze in detail the various catechisms used in Catholic schools. Analyses of this sort have been competently done elsewhere and are readily available.[7]

It would be possible to fill many pages with quotations from the unsound catechisms to show their doctrinal irregularity. But their essential content can be seen from the Declaration of the Commission of Cardinals appointed by the Holy See to evaluate the "New Catechism," the so-called Dutch Catechism, first published in Holland in 1966 by the Dutch bishops. The Commission issued its report on October 15, 1968. While it did not condemn the catechism, the Commission called for the catechism to clarify certain points where it failed to present the true teaching of the Church. The cardinals required that the catechism be improved so as to present the following truths:

1. *Points concerning God the Creator.* "It is necessary that the Catechism teach that God, besides this sensible world in which we live, has created also a realm of pure spirits whom we call Angels. . . . Furthermore, it should state explicitly that individual human souls since they are spiritual . . . are created immediately by God."

2. *The Fall of Man in Adam.* Original sin is a reality, through which man lost for himself and his offspring "that sanctity and justice in which he had been constituted, and handed on a true state of sin to all through propagation of human nature."

3. *With regard to the conception of Jesus by the Virgin Mary.* The perpetual virginity of Mary and the virginal conception and birth of Jesus must be taught "clearly" as "factual truth" and not merely in a "symbolic signification."

4. *The "Satisfaction" made by Christ Our Lord.* Jesus, the Son of God, "freely and with filial love," died for our sins and His death "more than abundantly compensated for the sins of the world."

5. *The Sacrifice of the Cross and the Sacrifice of the Mass.* "The sacrifice of the Cross is perpetuated in the Church of God as eucharistic sacrifice. . . . That celebration is both sacrifice and banquet."

6. *The Eucharistic Presence and the Eucharistic Change.* It must be "brought out beyond doubt that after the consecration of the bread and wine the very body and blood of Christ is present on the altar and is received sacramentally in Holy Communion."

7. *The Infallibility of the Church and the Knowledge of Revealed Mysteries.* The "infallibility of the Church" gives her "the truth in maintaining doctrine of faith and in explaining it always in the same sense."

8. *The Ministerial and Hierarchical Priesthood and the Power of Teaching and Ruling in the Church.* The "ministerial priesthood . . . in its participation of the priesthood of Christ, differs from the common priesthood of the faithful, not only in degree, but in essence. . . . Furthermore . . . the teaching authority and the power of ruling in the Church is given directly to the Holy Father and to the Bishops joined with him in hierarchical communion, and that it is not given first of all to the people of God to be communicated to others." Also, "the Holy Father and the Bishops in their teaching office do not only assemble and approve what the whole community of the faithful believes. . . . Finally, that authority by which the Holy Father directs the Church is to be clearly presented as the full power of ruling, a supreme and universal power which the Pastor of the whole church can always freely exercise."

9. *Various points concerning Dogmatic Theology.* As to the three Persons in God, the Trinity, "Christians do well to contemplate them with faith and love them with filial devotion not only in the economy of salvation where they manifest themselves but also in the eternal life of the Divinity, whose vision we hope for. The efficacy of the Sacraments should be presented somewhat more exactly." The Catechism should not imply "that miracles can only be brought about by divine power insofar as they do not depart from that which the forces of the created world are able to produce." It should be emphasized that the souls of the just, "having been thoroughly purified, already rejoice in the immediate vision of God."

10. *Certain points of Moral Theology.* "The text of the Catechism is not to make obscure the existence of moral laws which we are able to know and express in such wise that they bind our conscience always and in all circumstances. Solutions of cases of conscience should be avoided which do not sufficiently attend to the indissolubility of marriage. . . . The presentation of a conjugal morality should be more faithful in presenting the full teaching of Vatican II and of the Holy See.[8] (Emphasis in original)

The Dutch Catechism is not directly used in classroom instruction of elementary and secondary school children. But its influence is considerable because its approach has sifted down to the teachers of religion through the perennial workshops to which they are exposed and through the promotion of its ideas in the Catholic press. One sixteen-year-old student in a midwestern Catholic high school recently said, "Now that I am in high school I find that what I learned in religion class in grade school was all wrong. Adam and Eve did not exist. You sit there and discuss whether or not the Resurrection was or was not an historical fact. Sophomore year we threw almost everything out. Now that I am a Junior we are still discarding. And now I just don't know what to believe. I find I am mixed up about many things, now—not only with things having to do with religion."[9] A seventeen-year-old girl student put it this way:

It's like finding out there's no Santa Claus. Here you are in high school and now you know. You know that all that hokus pokus you learned in grade school about God was all wrong— irrelevant, you might say. We are the "now" generation and we are concerned with our neighbors.

None of this "pie in the sky" kind of religion for us. We do help our neighbors. I boycott the supermarket that sells grapes every chance I get. Religion classes are all discussion-oriented. And boy, do you learn this way—at first. After a while, though, you sort of know what everybody's going to say.

My religion teacher last week said that if she ever had a child she didn't think she'd bother to have it Baptized. She just didn't believe in that water bit. A few of the girls argued with her about this. Some really seem to care that this is important enough to argue about.

Me—not anymore. Once in a while I do stop and think and wonder when I stopped caring. Because, actually, what diference does it make whether she believes in Baptism or not? She sees Christ in each and every one of us. She tells us this all the time. And I believe her. She is really sincere.[10]

It is not difficult to see the influence of the new morality, secularism, and the new Modernism in all of this. Nor is it difficult to see that it is a fraud to present teaching of this sort in Catholic schools. "I trusted that cross on the school," said one father. "I thought they were being taught the Catholic faith. I had no reason to suspect that my children were being fed secular humanism. Now I know." "What bothers me," said a New York mother, "is that we *paid* for this unbelief." [Emphasis in original][11]

It should not be surprising that catechism instruction is in a deplorable state. One reason is that some leading figures in the dominant catechetical movement in this country appear to be adherents of the errors we described in Chapter V. When Pope Paul VI issued his encyclical *Humanae Vitae*, one of the most significant dissents was issued by the Catechetical Forum, described by the *National Catholic Reporter* as "a 73-member organization of key people who shape the teaching of religion in grassroots Catholicism."[12] Among the signers of the statement was Brother Gabriel Moran of Manhattan College in New York, "the chief theoretician of the catechetical movement" in the United States. It is interesting, therefore, to note Brother Moran's response to *Humanae Vitae* and especially to the *Credo* of Pope Paul: "Well, these are nice statements," said Brother Moran. "We'll put them in the folder and consider them as part of a long tradition which has survived worse things than this. We really won't change anything." On the Pope's *Credo*, he said: "To me it was irrelevant. I don't know if what I'm teaching is at variance or not. He just doesn't use any of the language that I use. I can't figure out if what I teach is absolutely contradictory because his statements don't say anything to me. It's not that they're false. They just don't say anything."

Brother Moran's concept of authority is indicated by the fact that he considers it "intellectually irresponsible" for any teacher to make changes simply because someone says so and "that's true all the way down the line—right to the teacher in the first grade." He simply does not believe doctrine should be taught to children, and he thinks that "the questions posed by the *Credo* should not arise on this level." These views of Brother Moran are extreme. But they could be complemented by statements from other catechists who are similarly alienated from the authentic formulations and the mind of the teaching Church.

Brother Moran was one of the five theologians hired in 1968 by Monsignor Russell Neighbor, head of the United States bishops' national catechetics office, to help in the preparation of national catechetical curricula. Of the five theologians hired, four are public dissenters from *Humanae Vitae*. Monsignor Neighbor claimed he had not been asked to fire any of the theologians and that if he were asked he would refuse: "They stay on. They have a right to express their opinion. Just because a man might not seem 100% orthodox in the eyes of some in Rome on one point doesn't mean he can't be purely orthodox on other points."[13] Monsignor Neighbor himself would seem to be having some difficulty adhering to the authentic doctrine of the Church on certain basic questions. For instance, among the problems raised by Pope Paul's *Credo*, according to Monsignor Neighbor, is the question of original sin: "This is under study. Nobody denies that something happened, but just what it is, and how it affects man, is a big question." Monsignor Neighbor's attitude should be a warning to Catholic parents because of his position. However, even if his attitude were more in harmony with the teaching authority of the Church, it is doubtful that orthodoxy could be easily enforced against the entrenched catechetical establishment in the Catholic schools. Brother Moran, for example, claims there is no practical way for the bishops to get at dissenters in the universities. He believes it is a healthy development for the church to have a tension between the "scholarly, university-based theologizing and the pastoral, clerical and organizational side of the Church." Father John Reedy, C.S.C., editor and publisher of the now-defunct *Ave Maria* magazine, made a similar observation to the effect that the policing of classrooms by chanceries is impossible because "the whole spirit of the last ten years will not be turned off. What is going to happen is that there will be some administrative policies put out which won't be observed."[14]

We cannot take comfort in the assumption that the catechism crisis is accidental and unrelated to the deeper storms agitating the Church. For the errors and ambiguities in the questionable textbooks are fairly close derivations from the errors we discussed in Chapter V. When John Cardinal Carberry, Archbishop of St. Louis, announced in October 1969 that he was launching an inquiry into the teaching of catechism in his archdiocese, he noted "the dominant impact of three trends in the secular academic world which have had their influence even on Catholic thinking today." He emphasized these trends because their effect is clearly discernible in some of the catechisms now in use:

> The first trend is that which proposes a Christianity, or a form of religion, whose central feature is a *denial of the Divinity of Jesus Christ*. . . . In our own more recent times, this denial reached a kind of peak in the person of Adolph von Harnack, whose influence, from his prestigious position as the head of the School of Theology in the University of Berlin and from his many writings, seemed to permeate much of the Christian world. Indeed, though he himself died in 1930, four of his students have become world famous in our time, all of them accepting, under one guise or another, the denial of the Divinity of Christ as a starting point of their religious systems.

They are:

> 1. *Paul Tillich*, whose three volume work *Systematic Theology* was to call the worship of Christ as God a form of idolatry;
> 2. *Rudolph Bultmann*, whose famous principle of demytholization denies anything miraculous or supernatural to the life and teachings of Christ;
> 3. *Albert Schweitzer*, who despite the inspiring humanitarianism of his later life among the poor in Africa, had, in his book entitled *The Quest for the Historical Jesus*, presented to the world what he thought were the final convincing arguments against the Divinity of Christ;
> 4. The unfortunate *Dietrich Bonhoeffer*, who in the prisons of Adolf Hitler's Gestapo, in one of which he was to be hanged in April of 1945, found himself struggling with his faith in Christ and jotting down notes about a "world without God," a "religionless Christianity," and "Christ as merely the man for others." . . .
> The second trend is that of the philosophy of *existentialism*, which at times becomes a theology, because it attempts to answer the ultimate questions that can be raised by the mind of man. We know that existentialism is a reaction against its opposite extreme: A rigid essentialism, which had been inclined to neglect or even deny the individual differences among human beings.
> In its extreme form, however, as we find it in the writings of Martin Heidegger, of Karl Jaspers, of Jean Paul Sartre, and many others, existentialism makes the individual supreme,

accountable to no law of truth or of God or of origin or of destiny. It is this that has led to the exaggerated notions of freedom and personalism and even lawlessness today. Again its pervasive influence is bound to engulf some of the Catholic thinkers and writers and educators of our time.

The third trend that may be detected in almost all fields of education today is that which endeavors to make a religion out of *agnostic secular humanism*. We find this presented, for example, in the books of the Anglican Bishop John A. T. Robin-son—*Honest to God* and *But I Can't Believe That*, and the books of Harvey Cox—*The Secular City* and *On Not Leaving It to the Snake*, and of Joseph Fletcher—*Situation Ethics* and *The New Morality*. It is the belief that man's sole and entire purpose in life is to make a better world out of this visible world in which he briefly lives. . . .

Many of the contemporary so-called theologies of hope are nothing other than veiled forms of secular humanism. They are based on the unrealistic foundation that if only we have good will, if only we love one another, if only we work together for what is good for us all, we can make a paradise out of this world. And the words of the Psalmist have never been more true: "Unless God builds the house, they labor in vain who build it; unless God guards the gates, they watch in vain who stand guard." (Psalm 126) (Emphasis added)

As in other areas, the response that should be made to the catechism problem should be firm but balanced. There is no basis for opposing as a matter of principle the introduction of new educational techniques into the teaching of religion. These techniques should be judged by the standards proper to educational concerns. To the extent that they are worth while, new techniques should be welcomed. However, there can be no compromise on doctrine. This is essentially the position adopted by Vatican II: "The bishops should present Christian doctrine in a manner adapted to the needs of the times, that is to say, in a manner corresponding to the difficulties and problems by which people are most vexatiously burdened and troubled."[15] In these terms the Council called for the use of modern techniques in religious instruction. But this did not imply that doctrine could be distorted or omitted. On the contrary, the very next sentence reminded the bishops that "they should also guard that doctrine, teaching the faithful to defend and spread it." And the bishops were enjoined to "see to it that this instruction is based on sacred Scripture, tradition, the liturgy, the teaching authority, and life of the Church."[16] Unfortunately, some catechisms widely used in this country are seriously defective and dangerous. The catechism series published by Allyn & Bacon, Benziger Brothers, the Paulist Press, W. H. Sadlier, and some other publishers are all deficient in their substantive content. Yet the bishops of this country, with few individual exceptions, have done nothing significant to correct the situation. It is important to note, moreover, that there are plentiful alternatives to the defective catechisms widely used.[17]

As a national body, the bishops continue to tolerate a catechetical structure that has grown bureaucratic and less than diligent about preserving the orthodoxy of the schools under their care. But here and there we can see hopeful signs. Cardinal Carberry's reassessment of the catechisms in his St. Louis Archiocese has already been mentioned. Bishop Leo A. Pursley of Fort Wayne and others have taken comparable stands. In June 1968, Lawrence Cardinal Shehan, Patrick Cardinal O'Boyle, and the other bishops of Baltimore and Washington, D.C., issued guidelines to govern the teaching of religion. The statement noted the new era of theological speculation and said, "There is nothing wrong or even unusual about this—they are simply doing for our day what the Fathers and Scholastics did for theirs." But the bishops emphasized that theological speculation and opinion "ultimately rely on human reason" while the magisterium "ultimately relies on the words Christ first spoke to the twelve and through them to their successors." The bishops said it was important "for every Catholic teacher of religion to bear in mind the difference between the findings of theologians and the teaching of the magisterium." Every Catholic, they stressed, "must not rely merely on his own opinions but must take into account the pre-eminence of the sacred and certain doctrines of the Church."[18] What is needed now is stern enforcement of these pronouncements.

One very hopeful sign was the recent establishment in Middleburg, Virginia, of the Institute for Advanced Studies in Christian Doctrine. Monsignor Eugene Kevane, former dean of the School of Education at the Catholic University of America, is the head of the new center. He explained its purpose to adhere to the magisterium of the Church: "As Pope John XXIII pointed out explicitly, every teacher concerned with the Doctrine of the Catholic Faith functions by mandate of the Sacred Magisterium. The new Institute intends to hold fast to this principle as its most basic position."[19]

The promotion of orthodox centers for advanced study by teachers of religion is a task of the greatest importance. For the attitude of the teacher will determine the character of religious education. "Altogether too many of our Catholic educators are determined to stay with the so-called 'New Theology' and 'New Morality,'" says the Reverend Robert E. Burns, C.S.P., "despite the Holy Father's *Credo* and the condemnation of Situation Ethics by the Holy See. Thus, there is at the root a crisis of authority, with these educators lining up with the liberal theologians and sociologists, instead of supporting the Holy Father, the Vicar of Christ on earth."[20] John Cardinal Wright, Prefect of the Congregation of the Clergy, reminded the 1969 Congress of Catechists, in Italy, that "Christ was never a professional theologian. He chose rather to be a prophet to a specified truth." In warning the catechists not to assume for themselves the role of professional theologians and not to abandon themselves to idle speculation, the cardinal said, "We are in danger of losing the specific truth in this very theological renewal which we encourage, because a new presentation with a substitution of terms can cloud over, change entirely, or turn completely around the very truth itself.[21]

If a parochial school teaches religion from unsound books and with little regard for the teaching authority of the Church, then it should not be surprising if some Catholic parents feel more secure entrusting their children to the public schools where the children at least will be on guard against the potential subversion of their religion. As one parent in South Bend, Indiana, remarked, "When your daughter says 'my religion teacher told me that I don't have to go to Mass on Sundays anymore if I don't feel like going'—and when the yearly retreat features an avowed atheist on its panel— a mature man who is 'available' to talk to your children—in the name of what I wouldn't know—well, then, I would say parents have 'had' it."[22] Despite their secularization, the public schools may have the advantage of not lulling the children and their parents into a false sense of security. Generally speaking, it might well be safer for children to be exposed in school to no truth than a half-truth, where religion is concerned. In the words of retired Bishop William L. Adrian of Nashville, Tennessee, if the catechism "situation cannot be corrected by a vigorous and persistent protest to the proper authorities, the pastor or bishop, the parents are bound in conscience to remove their children from the Catholic school and teach them religion at home or in private classes. The state schools will at least not teach, or should not teach, the students false doctrine."[23] This conclusion would be reinforced in areas where the public schools still maintain adequate academic and disciplinary standards. There are no statistics available on this, but it is a safe deduction that the failure of Catholic schools to teach the Catholic religion has caused the alienation of a significant number of parents who frankly prefer to take their chances with public or private schools.

Sex Education

A similar parental attitude clearly exists with respect to sex education. The Family Life Division of the United States Catholic Conference, under the leadership of Father James T. McHugh, is actively promoting classroom sex education in Catholic schools. To keep this subject in perspective, however, it is important to remember just what is involved. The sex education controversy does not involve the usual courses in hygiene and biology which have commonly been taught in schools. Nor should there be a challenge to the right of the Catholic school to provide moral instruction in sexual matters. This instruction has always and properly been given in Catholic schools and it incidentally involves the imparting of information. You cannot teach that adultery is wrong without teaching what adultery is. No one can properly object to this sort of moral formation in Catholic schools.

But what is at issue is the introduction into Catholic schools of "sex education" as such, of instruction in human "sexuality." This sort of instruction is not merely incidentally informational. Its main purpose, rather, is to expose the child to detailed information concerning the clinical, social, and behavioral aspects of such things as intercourse, reproduction, venereal disease, masturbation, homosexuality, and the various methods of birth control including abortion and the different types of contraception.

Sex education programs, in this context, are objectionable morally and psychologically. The moral considerations were outlined by Pope Pius XI in his encyclical *Christian Education of Youth* issued on December 31, 1929:

> Another grave danger is that of naturalism which nowadays invades the field of education in that most delicate matter of

AUTHORITY AND REBELLION

purity of morals. Far too common is the error of those who with dangerous assurance and under an ugly term propagate a so-called sex education, falsely imagining they can forearm youth against the danger of sensuality by means purely natural, such as a foolhardy initiation and precautionary instruction for all indiscriminately, even in public; and, worse still, by exposing them at an early age to the occasions, in order to accustom them, so it is argued, and as it were to harden them against such dangers.

The encyclical proceeds to analyze the modern denial of original sin and the corollary belief that knowledge is virtue. The Pope criticized the erroneous assumption of the perfectibility of man and the consequent lack of dependence on God. These considerations are all involved in the sex education concepts he rejected:

Such persons grievously err in refusing to recognize the in-born weakness of human nature . . . particularly in young people, evil practices are the effect not so much of ignorance of intellect as of weakness of a will exposed to dangerous occasions, and unsupported in the means of grace.

Psychologically, the prevailing sex education programs are primarily objectionable because the subject matter is inappropriate for group instruction. From the age of five until adolescence, there is a phase of personality development known as the latency period in which the child's interest in sex is passive and dormant. Any parent can attest to the reality of this phase. To disturb this period by forcing the child's attention upon sex, in the words of Dr. Rhoda Lorand, author of *Love, Sex and the Teenager*, "very likely will lead to sexual difficulties later in life."[24] As psychiatrist William McGrath wrote, "Premature interest in sex is unnatural and will arrest or distort the development of the personality. Sex education should not be foisted upon children; should not begin in the grade schools."[25]

In short, you cannot turn a ten-year-old into an amateur gynecologist without risking serious trouble. Classroom sex instruction is unacceptable because you cannot take forty children and expose them to this material, en masse, as if they were all equally ready for it, without someone getting hurt. Teaching about sex is not comparable to teaching mathematics or history, because the subject of sex is uniquely personal and sacred. Sex is the channel by which life is transmitted from God and instruction in its mysteries is properly the province of the family just as the ultimate use of the sexual faculty is reserved for the married state. To subject children to classroom instruction in sexuality as part of a school curriculum, would be to intrude upon the privacy of the parent-child relation and it would violate the individual right to privacy of both the parent and the child.

We delude ourselves if we think that sex education can be instituted without the inclusion of imprudently excessive detail. The parochial school program in the Diocese of Rochester is a clear and fairly typical example of such excessive detail. Also, the New York Archdiocesan sex education program includes a bibliography, entitled "Books, Films, and Recordings on Sex Education," which was prepared and is highly recommended by the Family Life Bureau of the United States Catholic Conference. This bibliography has been mailed by the United States Catholic Conference to every grammar school convent in the United States. It is heavily loaded with material oriented toward the amoral and imprudently detailed approach recommended by the Sex Information and Education Council of the United States. An earlier bibliography, "Selected Resources on Sex Education for Parents-Teachers-Children," prepared by the Archdiocese of New York, is similarly defective.[26]

It is also significant that one of the stated objectives of the Rochester diocesan program is to "avoid, as much as possible, a separate *course*, utilizing rather the opportunities presented in the normal program (religion, social studies, science, etc.)" (Emphasis in original)[27] The only way you could excuse your child from such a program would be to withdraw him from the school.

Even if the sex instruction were isolated in a separate course and children allowed to be excused, the program would still be intolerable because of the inherent danger of such a program to all participating children and because the children would be subjected to the sort of "indirect coercive pressure" to conform which the Supreme Court found objectionable in its decisions outlawing prayer in the public schools.[28] This would not be merely a short prayer recited in the classroom. It would be a course in the curriculum and to require the dissenting child to slink out of the classroom would be to treat him unfairly.

It is important to note here that Pius XI stipulated that sex instruction should be given in private and he cautioned that excessive detail should be avoided even in private instruction:

In this extremely delicate matter, if, all things considered, some private instruction is found necessary and opportune from those who hold from God the commission to teach and who have the grace of state, every precaution must be taken. Such precautions are well known in traditional Christian education, and are adequately described by Antoniano cited above, when he says:

Such is our misery and inclination to sin, that often in the very things considered to be remedies against sin, we find occasions for and inducements to sin itself. Hence it is of the highest importance that a good father, while discussing with his son a matter so delicate, should be well on his guard and not descend to details, nor refer to the various ways in which this infernal hydra destroys with its poison so large a portion of the world; otherwise it may happen that instead of extinguishing this fire, he unwittingly stirs or kindles it in the simple and tender heart of the child. Speaking generally, during the period of childhood it suffices to employ those remedies which produce the double effect of opening the door to the virtue of purity and closing the door upon vice.

Pope Pius XII reiterated this teaching in his address to the women of the Catholic Action organization, on October 26, 1941: "Finally . . . you will not fail to watch for and to discern the moment in which certain unspoken questions have occurred to their minds and are troubling their senses. It will then be your duty to your daughters, the father's duty to your sons, carefully and delicately to unveil the truth as far as it appears necessary, to give a prudent, true and Christian answer to those questions, and set their minds at rest. If imparted by the lips of Christian parents, at the proper time, in the proper measure, and with the proper precautions, the revelation of the mysterious and marvelous laws of life will be received by them with reverence and gratitude, and will enlighten their minds with far less danger than if they learned them haphazard, from some disturbing encounter, from secret conversations, through information received from over-sophisticated companions, or from clandestine reading, the more dangerous and pernicious as secrecy inflames the imagination and troubles the senses."[29]

The Second Vatican Council said that, "as they advance in years," children "should be given positive and prudent sexual education."[30] This short statement, as analyzed by Bishop Mark J. Hurley,

in no way contradicts the encyclical whose strictures on natural-
ism, "so-called sex education," early exposure to the occasions
of sin and denial of original sin in the matter still stand valid.
Actually it changes, and indeed develops, only one word of the
encyclical—"if":

"If, in this extremely delicate matter, all things considered,
some private instruction is found necessary and opportune from
those who hold from God the commission to teach and who
have the grace of state, every precaution must be taken."

The Council has deleted the one word and in effect is saying
that, all things considered today, private instruction *is* necessary
and those with the commission to teach and the grace of state
should see to a positive and prudent education in the matters
of sex. The mood of the imperative has replaced the con-
ditional "if." (Emphasis in original)[31]

The bishops of the United States acted on the Vatican Council's
teaching in their collective pastoral of November 1968. They urged
a proper sexual education in words that we should set out at length:

In accord with the "Decree on Christian Education" of
Vatican Council II we affirm the value and necessity of wisely
planned education of children in human sexuality, adapted to
the maturity and background of our young people. We are
under a grave obligation, in part arising from the new circumstances of modern culture and communications, to assist
the family in its efforts to provide such training. This obligation
can be met either by systematic provision of such education
in the diocesan school curriculum or by the inauguration of
acceptable educational programs under other diocesan auspices,
including the Confraternity of Christian Doctrine.

Parents are those primarily responsible for imparting to their
children an awareness of the sacredness of sexuality; this will
ordinarily be best accomplished when both parents discharge
this duty in mutual consultation and shared responsibility.
The necessity for greater communication and cooperation between parents and teachers is highlighted in this problem; the
consequent role of parent-teacher guilds and similar home-
school associations is apparent.

Parents are sometimes fearful that their right to teach the
norms of sexual morality to their children may be usurped or
that programs such as we envision may lead to the sexual misdirection of their children if the teachers involved are in-

162   AUTHORITY AND REBELLION

adequately prepared or emotionally immature. In the light of such legitimate concerns, the careful selection of instructors for these discussions is a serious responsibility to be shared by priests, school authorities and parents, perhaps best under the auspices of parent-teacher associations.

The content of these instructions should provide an appreciation of "the true values of life and of the family" (*Humanae Vitae*, 21), in addition to a healthy inculcation, from the earliest years of moral and intellectual formation, of how conjugal love involves a harmonious response from the emotions, the passions, the body and the mind. At the same time, healthy Christian attitudes toward life will be developed in young people if they are given an understanding, consistent with their years, of why the Council insists that those "actions within marriage by which the couple are united intimately and chastely are noble and worthy ones" (*Gaudium et Spes*, 49).

It is true that the bishops recognized that limited classroom instruction might be appropriate in some circumstances, provided that parental involvement is maintained, and especially that parents have coequal responsibility for the selection of teachers. But the bishops reaffirmed the emphasis of the Popes on private instruction by parents as the best method of sex education. They stressed absolute need for moral "inculcation" as an intrinsic and indispensable part of any sexuality instructions.

The most important aspect of the pastoral on this question, however, is that it does not mandate classroom sex instruction. Nor could it do so without contradicting the clear opinion of Pius XI. Rather, the pastoral allows "the inauguration of acceptable educational programs under other diocesan auspices." It thus leaves room for local flexibility in the application of the Vatican Council's recommendation that as children "advance in years, they should be given prudent and positive sexual education."[32]

The need in this area today is for formation, not information. No proponent of "sex education" has ever presented an adequate justification for the program. Their proposals are based upon unexamined assumptions. Why do we need a sex education program? To discourage premarital intercourse? To prevent venereal disease? You cannot do these things by teaching children, as the Rochester and similar programs teach them, how to have intercourse and how to cure venereal disease. Or perhaps the goal is to prevent premarital pregnancies. After teaching the children how to have intercourse, usually in the sixth grade, the sex education programs teach them in the eighth grade how to prevent births.

In Orange County, California, however, the introduction of sex education in the public schools was followed by a definite increase in teen-age pregnancies and venereal disease.[33] Nor should this be surprising. A committee of Swedish doctors and teachers, including Dr. Ull Nordwall, physician to the King of Sweden, blamed that country's sex education program for the rise in teen-age promiscuity in that country:

It has bombarded school children with sexual instruction for which their immaturity ill fits them and the result has been an unnatural over-sexualization of the rising generation [in which] . . . the young have confused instruction in method with encouragement to practice.[34]

The fact is that systematic classroom sex instruction from the elementary grades is an indispensable prerequisite to the development of the contraceptive mentality and the anti-life society.

It is true that the Catholic schools have a function to assist the parents in discharging their primary duty of giving sex instruction to their children. But this should be done through providing classes for the parents, if desired, and printed or other materials for the parents to use as they see fit. If some parents desire to have their children see a particular film or hear a particular lecture, they can make arrangements for that and the school can assist them, apart from school hours and the school curriculum. And the appropriate school authorities, of course, including the nurse or spiritual advisor, can provide counseling and information to children in special cases where it is needed, on an individual basis and with parental approval. The irreducible point, however, is that there should be no group sex instruction in the school curriculum or during school hours. The constructive alternative of assisting parents should be pursued instead of the harmful course of classroom instruction.

Contrary to the apparent assumption of the proponents of sex education, parents generally are willing and ready to perform their obligations in this matter. The schools should assist the parents to do so. If it be objected that some parents will choose not to give their children the detailed information envisioned by the school, two things can be said. One is that it is the parents' right to make the ultimate decision here, even if that decision does not conform to the concepts of the school authorities. The other is that the harm arising from the neglect of their duty by some parents is far less than the harm that would occur from the introduction of sex instruction into the classroom. One incidental reason why the introduction of such a program would be intolerable is the disarray within the Church itself. In view of this it would be illusory to expect that any sex education program could be implemented with a uniformity of adherence to the teaching authority of the Church. Clearly, no one who does not accept fully, without equivocation or reservation, the teaching authority of the Church, including the encyclical on birth control, should have any part in any parochial school program in this area.

In summary, the Catholic Church and the Catholic schools should introduce a constructive program of helping parents to provide the necessary information and formation for their children. Finally, Catholics should protest the exposure of Catholic children in public schools to sex instruction. Such instruction would be indefensible in Catholic schools even where it is accompanied by instruction in morality. Where it is given in the secular atmosphere of the public school, there would seem to be a clear invasion of the rights of the parents and children to privacy and the free exercise of their religion. For the public schools are barred, by the Supreme Court's school prayer decisions, from affirming as truth that any particular conduct is morally right or wrong. The most that the public school can do is to present the conflicting moral views without indicating to the children that one is right or wrong. This suspension of judgment on the moral and religious issues involved would clearly violate the mandates of Pius XI, Pius XII, and of the United States bishops' pastoral of November 1968.

The introduction into Catholic schools of classroom sex instruction is a powerful inducement for parents to withdraw their children from those schools. On a related front, a number of Catholic schools are adopting sensitivity training programs for their students, under various names and forms. Accurately described by Russell Kirk "as a form of induced hysteria, meant to break down norms, manners, and the traditions of civility,"[35] the sensitivity training regime of mind-probing has been well documented by a number of groups.[36] Without discussing it in detail, we can merely note the problem here as another element in the spreading alienation of responsible Catholic parents from their schools.

What the Bishops Could Do

The responsibility for halting the doctrinal erosion in the Catholic schools rests upon the bishops, individually and as a national body. While some bishops have taken effective action, the bishops as a national body have been largely immobile. This inaction is doubly unfortunate because the restoration of the Catholic schools is not an insuperable task. Rather, there are certain specific things the bishops might well consider.

Of the problems afflicting the parochial schools, the catechism crisis is most important. If we were to search for one means to improve the catechism situation, it would be found in the *Credo* of Pope Paul VI, which he issued during the Mass marking the end of the 1967–68 Year of Faith. Let the bishops require, and enforce, that Catholic schools expressly and faithfully teach every single truth affirmed in that *Credo*, in the language used by the Pope, and teach nothing contrary to it. It will be objected that the *Credo*, as the Pope said, is not "strictly speaking a dogmatic definition." But he described it as a "solemn utterance," a "profession of faith," and "a firm witness to the divine Truth entrusted to the Church to be announced to all nations." In fact the *Credo* is an excellent compendium of the infallible definitions and the authoritative teachings of the Church. Needless to say, a proper emphasis on the *Credo* would entail the removal of catechisms containing dubious theology.

As a corollary to emphasizing the *Credo*, the bishops could require, with appropriate enforcement, several other things. They could forbid the promotion of the erroneous theories of Teilhard de Chardin and the Dutch Catechism. They could require that the importance and relevance of the Ten Commandments be emphasized. They could promote the virtue of purity, including, to that end, the removal of classroom sex instruction from the curriculum, the termination of sensitivity training, and the prohibition of recommending books and films to students which are likely to be the occasion of sin. They could require that the spiritual and corporal works of mercy be given a sorely needed emphasis while not diluting Catholicism to a sociological cult. They could prevent the presentation of the Bible to students as a collection of myths and fables, and they could emphasize instead the principles laid down by Pius XII in *Humani Generis*. They could require that the importance of the

Holy Sacrifice of the Mass be emphasized and that students not be told that attendance at Mass on Sundays and Holy days is less than a grave obligation.[37] Other measures could be suggested, including a proper emphasis on the importance of frequent Confession. But the point is that change for the better is not impossible if the will can only be summoned to do it.

Two Bureaucracies: Clerical and Civil

It is plain that effective action by the bishops is urgently needed to restore the Catholic schools to their accustomed position of reliability. But a more basic reform is needed, too. While the bishops have the responsibility of correcting the abuses in the Catholic schools, a lasting improvement can hardly be expected as long as the official schools, sponsored by the hierarchy, enjoy a practical monopoly of Catholic education. Financial stringencies have led the Catholic schools to seek and obtain government aid. But, as will be explained in Chapter XI, various forms of that aid bring in their train government controls, including the requirement that the subsidized schools purge themselves of sectarian characteristics. In effect, the aided parochial schools are required to conform to the secularizing mandates applied by the Supreme Court's school prayer decisions to the public schools. The sale of their independence to the government accounts in large measure for the unsatisfactory conditions in parochial schools. Under the existing federal and state laws, the schools are in a spiral downward in this respect. The more money they need, the more government aid they seek. The more government money they get, the more entrenched the parochial school bureaucracy, which solicits and receives the aid, becomes and the more secularized and deviant their instruction becomes. The more the parochial schools become secularized and deviant, the more do parents withdraw their children and reduce their contributions. The more the tuition and contributions fall, the more the schools need money. And so on.

Inevitably the parochial schools are conforming to what is expected of them by a subsidizing, secular state. In the process their independence is bartered away and those schools are inflexibly brought under the control, not of pastors or local parishioners, but of governmental and clerical bureaucracies.

"The Catholic Church in America," said Archbishop Robert

Dwyer of Portland, Oregon, recently, "has long been in the process of building up its own bureaucratic structure." It is largely located in the Nation's Capital, at the headquarters of the United States Catholic Conference and the National Conference of Catholic Bishops. "Here are bureaus, ever proliferating, set up to carry out the programs and to implement the decisions of the American Hierarchy," continued Archbishop Dwyer. After noting that most of the men and women in these bureaus are outstanding for their ability, loyalty and unselfishness, Archbishop Dwyer continued:

> If we note, however, that certain sections or elements of this American Catholic bureaucracy exhibit from time to time signs of irresponsibility, or of willfulness, or of what could be interpreted as contempt for ecclesiastical authority, and specifically the authority of the Bishops, this should hardly come as a surprise to anyone inured to the ways of this less than perfect world.
>
> If high-handedness has ruled in several of the bureaus, those for example, concerned with the implementation of the liturgy and with the promotion of catechetical instruction and adult education, the wonder comes not so much from the fact, regrettable as it is, that such tendencies should emerge, as that they should be tolerated, or, what is worse, encouraged.

"It would make us look just a little silly," the Archbishop concluded, "if, after demanding that the Holy See clear up its bureaucracy, the Church in America should saddle herself with one quite as bad. Or maybe worse."[38]

It is not the intent to disparage here the efforts of the many priests and laymen in diocesan educational commissions and elsewhere in the parochial school structure who are manfully trying to do their jobs under adverse conditions. What is at fault here primarily is the system which militates toward increased control of the Catholic school system by those functionaries, especially on the national level, who are most adept at fishing for government grants and at baiting the hook with progressively greater dilutions of the authentic and religious character of those schools.

The system ought to be opened up. Fortunately, there is a way to do it which offers the promise of preserving the religious character of parochial schools, infusing adequate money into authentically religious schools without secularizing government controls and, most importantly, ensuring an ultimate freedom of choice in the parents who, according to Vatican II, "have the just and the un-alienable duty and right to educate their children."[39]

These goals can be achieved through a Federal tuition-tax credit, a straight tuition grant, or an educational voucher system. These plans will be discussed in more detail in Chapter XI. Any of them would relieve the financial stringencies of church-related schools without secularizing government controls. As we will note in Chapter XI, there is a trend toward increased government support of nonpublic schools. The main reason for this trend appears to be economic, to prevent the greater burden on public schools which would result from increased closings of church-related schools. But the main consideration here is not economic. It is one of liberty and authentic religion. Parents, as the Second Vatican Council pointed out, "should enjoy true freedom in their choice of schools."[40]

Parents' Alternatives

At the same time, the Council reminded Catholic parents of "their duty to entrust their children to Catholic schools, when and where this is possible, to support such schools to the extent of their ability, and to work along with them for the welfare of their children."[41] Catholic parents are therefore not at liberty to ignore, for trivial reasons, the parish or diocesan schools. In a sense, those schools have a prior claim on the attendance of Catholic children, apart from the exceptional case where private Catholic schools are available and preferred for a legitimate reason. But while the general duty to support and attend parish or diocesan schools cannot be disregarded, it should be remembered that the parents' duty toward those schools is not absolute. If those schools present a spiritual danger to their pupils, with the existence of that danger to be honestly and prudently determined by the parents, in consultation with competent advisors where appropriate, then the parents should be considered relieved of their duty to send their children to those schools. The burden of proof here should not be on the parents. While their first choice should normally be to send their children to parish or diocesan schools, their prime consideration should be the welfare of their children rather than the maintenance of a school system that is Catholic in name only. If the parents have serious reason to doubt the orthodoxy of the school in question, they should not trifle with the souls of their children.

For the dilemma of parents who cannot trust the parish or diocesan schools, there are two solutions, one long term and one short term. The long-term solution depends on the enactment of federal or state legislation, as described above, to make it economically feasible for parents to form or support other schools to teach the full academic course and religion as well. Some parents are economically able to inaugurate and support such schools, or to pay tuition to existing private Catholic schools, without governmental aid. But for most parents, this solution is economically unattainable in the absence of a tuition tax credit, a tuition grant, or a voucher. For these parents, a short-term solution must be sought to preserve their children from the spiritual misdirection they would receive in some Catholic schools.

The short-term solution involves the establishment of separate schools of religion. These schools would not teach academic subjects. Rather they would teach only the Catholic doctrine appropriate for each of the eight years of grade school and the four years of high school. Classes could be held on one or two afternoons or evenings a week or on Saturday or Sunday mornings. They should not be held in anyone's home, but rather classroom space should be sought, for a rental or donated, in private or public school buildings in the area. Because of their limited scope these schools would be fairly inexpensive to run. A few parental groups in various parts of the country have already established schools of this sort, with considerable success. One suggestion might be in order, however. It is that these schools of religion should not be run on a gratuitous basis. Rather, parents should be expected to pay, if they could afford it, whatever reasonable sum is necessary to maintain the school. Teachers should be adequately compensated, as should administrators who organize and run the program. This monetary point is more important than it might at first appear. For the requirement of a reasonable fee would ensure that only the seriously concerned would apply for admittance and the payment of compensation to the teachers and administrators would help to ward off the dilettantism that has plagued the after-school instruction provided by the Confraternity of Christian Doctrine. There should be no real difficulty in obtaining competent teachers for these schools of religion, particularly among interested and orthodox graduates of Catholic colleges. Nor would there be any shortage of pupils, even considering the requirement of a monetary payment.

The schools of religion would not undertake to be centers of moral formation. Nor would they provide counseling or spiritual exercises. Rather, their function would be simply to provide the children with the authentic information, from valid source materials, which they should be getting from the diocesan schools. Moral formation would be a task for the parents.

It has been suggested by some that the private school of religion should even guarantee the parents that their children would learn the desired information. If the child failed to pass an examination in the subject, the parent would get back the money he paid for the course. Correspondingly, the child who failed would be ineligible to advance to the next course in the series without successfully repeating the course he failed. There is merit in this idea. If it seems radical and unrealistic, it will seem less so when it is remembered that the teaching of Catholic doctrine is today a very serious affair. There should be no room in such schools for those who do not approach it as such.

Finally, the schools of religion should not be connected with the diocesan school system. They should solicit advice from competent and orthodox priests. But they should not be under the supervision of diocesan or governmental authorities. These schools would be the parents' schools and they would be authentically Catholic schools, teaching the doctrine according to the magisterium of the Church rather than the theories of Brother Gabriel Moran. They would have the mission of transmitting authentic doctrine to a generation that would otherwise be subverted. They would also enable their students to meet other young people of the same religious faith, i.e., orthodox Catholicism. The importance of this last advantage is self-evident.

Where the parents prudently decide that separate schools of religion are necessary, it would be up to them to decide whether to enroll their children in the public or the parish or diocesan schools for their regular academic instruction. The parish or diocesan schools may be sufficiently bad so as to dictate the immediate withdrawal of the children and their enrollment in public or other private schools. But if the public schools are unacceptable academically or in disciplinary matters and if other private schools are unavailable or too expensive, the parents may have no alternative to keeping the children in the parish or diocesan schools. The private school of religion, and prayer, would have to be relied upon to offset the bad influence of the parish or diocesan schools. Also, it would be appropriate in such cases for the parents to petition the parish or diocesan school authorities to have children excused from religion classes on the ground that the children profess a different religion from the religion taught in the school. If a Protestant or Jewish student could be so excused, so should a Catholic who desires to adhere to the teaching authority of the Church.

It should be emphasized that the private schools of religion would be only a short-term expedient. The long-term solution must be a real freedom of choice in education for all parents. This can best be attained through the governmental programs described above. The tuition tax credit, the tuition grant, or the voucher would encourage real competition in education. To a lesser extent, the private schools of religion described above can provide it in the interim as far as the teaching of Catholic doctrine is concerned. But in any case, it is important to break the monopoly of Catholic education which is currently enjoyed by the national and diocesan school bureaucracies.

The introduction of real competition would make both the public and the diocesan schools improve or go out of existence. We ought to regard with some pleasurable anticipation the reduction of the public school system by a process of free competition. But we can expect, too, that the parish and diocesan Catholic schools would show a vast improvement in their fidelity to the teaching authority of the Church. Those which did not, would go out of business and we would have no regrets. For they would be supplanted by authentically Catholic schools conceived in parental freedom and loyalty to the teachings of the Church.

X.
THE CATHOLIC UNIVERSITY

BENSALEM the farthest-out college in the U. S. today. No exams, no compulsory classes, or papers. Study what, when and if you like. Sleep all day or night. Mixed apartment sharing for students and faculty. No curfews, no house rules. Credit for time spent traveling or working. Thirty students are admitted each year by interview with two students and one faculty member. Grades? Forget them. You don't even need a high school diploma to get in. Nobody can expel you. And if you survive three years, you get a B.A. from Jesuit-run Fordham University in New York.[1]

In the building housing the college, "Four-room apartments are shared by couples, two girls and a boy, two boys and a girl, or all-the-same-sex roommates." As bearded Dean Kenneth Freeman points out, no one cares who is sleeping with whom. "Promiscuity has lost its shock value." For this, the parents pay $2300 a year tuition plus $50 a month room rent, plus "extras for groceries, movies, cigarettes, maybe books." Bensalem, named after the land in Francis Bacon's *New Atlantis* where weary seafarers were made welcome, is the creature of former Fordham president Father Leo McLaughlin, S.J., and British poet Elizabeth Sewell. Envisioned as a kind of intellectual Walden Pond, Bensalem in practice "isn't quite so placid." "By night, Bensalem rocks. A band practices in the basement, a combo plays in a fifth-floor apartment. Dogs, ubiquitous and unhousebroken, bark. Cats yowl. . . . An ex-Jesuit novice, affectionately dubbed the 'mad monk' by fellow students, plays the harpsichord brilliantly in the common room or holds wildly unorthodox religious services in a portion of the basement he has rigged out as a chapel. Wagner, amplified, roars from the apartment of two teachers. A handful of students try on a Black Mass for size."

Bensalem is far from typical. But when "the farthest-out college in the U. S. today" is part of an ostensibly Catholic university, we ought to ask some questions about the role of Church authority in restraining what is to be taught, and what conduct permitted, in Catholic universities. In this way we can view the Catholic university in context with the overall authority problem in the Church.

Purpose of the Catholic University

The first thing to be considered here is the purpose of the Catholic university itself. In this chapter, the term university will be used to include undergraduate as well as graduate schools. In its *Declaration on Christian Education*, the Second Vatican Council said that, in Catholic schools of higher learning, the Church

> seeks in a systematic way to have individual branches of knowledge studied according to their own proper principles and methods, and with due freedom of scientific investigation. She intends thereby to promote an ever deeper understanding of these fields, and as a result of extremely precise evaluation of modern problems and inquiries, to have it seen more profoundly how faith and reason give harmonious witness to the unity of all truth. The Church pursues such a goal after the manner of her most illustrious teachers, especially St. Thomas Aquinas. The hoped-for result is that the Christian mind may achieve, as it were, a public, persistent, and universal presence in the whole enterprise of advancing higher culture, and that the students of these institutions may become men truly outstanding in learning, ready to shoulder society's heavier burdens and to witness the faith to the world.[2]

Referring to this passage in a 1969 address to the Congress of Delegates of Catholic Universities, Pope Paul said, "This means that in addition to the functions of teaching and research carried out, as at every University, the Catholic University, while respecting the legitimate autonomy of earthly values and the specific laws of scientific research, is distinguished as an intellectual community 'in which Catholicism is present and active.'" (Declaration of the General Assembly of the International Federation of Catholic Universities, Congo-Kinshasa, 10–16, September 1968)[3]

"Intellect and its values for the personal life and social body," wrote the Reverend Leo R. Ward, C.S.C., "are the goal of the university. The good of disciplined intellects is the end, and in the Catholic university the good of intellects disciplined as Catholic."[4] John Henry

Cardinal Newman described the purpose of the university, in general, in comparable terms. The university, he said,

> maps out the territory of the intellect, and sees that the boundaries of each province are religiously respected, and that there is neither encroachment nor surrender on any side. It acts as umpire between truth and truth, and, taking into account the nature and importance of each, assigns to all their due order of precedence. It maintains no one department of thought exclusively, however ample and noble; and it sacrifices none. It is deferential and loyal, according to their respective weight, to the claims of literature, of physical research, of history, of metaphysics, of theological science. It is impartial towards them all, and promotes each in its own place and for its own object.[5]

The purpose of the university, in general, then, is intellectual. But we are dealing, as Newman was, not with universities in the abstract, but with the Catholic university in its special relation to the authority of the Church. Newman admitted that the university is an incomplete world if considered in isolation from the truths of religion and particularly from the Catholic Church. The Catholic university, said Newman, "is ancillary certainly, and of necessity, to the Catholic Church. . . . It is ministrative to the Catholic Church, first, because truth of any kind can but minister to truth; and next, still more, because nature ever will pay homage to grace, and reason cannot but illustrate and defend Revelation; and thirdly, because the Church has a sovereign authority, and when she speaks ex cathedra, must be obeyed." While this ministration to the Church is "the remote end of a university," its "immediate end (with which alone we have here to do) is to secure the due disposition, according to one sovereign order, and the cultivation in that order, of all the provinces and methods of thought which the human intellect has created."[6]

The Catholic university, then, exists to serve the Church as well as the intellect. "The Christian school," said Pope Pius XII in an address referring to schools at every level, "will justify its existence in so far as its teachers—clerics or laymen, religious or secular—succeed in forming staunch Christians."[7] The ways of achieving this goal will vary from the kindergarten to the university. But we are concerned here with the tendency of Catholic universities to fail in both their intellectual and their religious missions because of the failure to give proper regard to the authority of the Church.

The Issues

In 1968 the Reverend Robert W. Gleason, a Jesuit professor of theology at Fordham, told a theological meeting that ten to thirty percent of the graduates of Catholic colleges and universities are atheists. Father Gleason described this growth of atheism as a comparatively recent development.[8] Corroboration of this tendency could be obtained from the many parents who send their sons and daughters to Catholic colleges only to find them, on their return, unimpressed by moral absolutes, Sunday Mass obligations, and other elements of the Catholic religion. For example, the 1966 graduates of Mundelein College, a Catholic girls' college in Chicago, were found in a post-graduation survey to be "more secular, more cynical and noticeably less pious than they were as freshmen."[9] "Freedom," "participation," and "involvement" had become the central ideas in their lives, said Dr. Norbert J. Hruby, the school's vice-president. "The percentage of students who were anti-clerical (critical of priests and the Church hierarchy) increased from four percent to fourteen percent and the portion of those who considered certain Catholic rituals to border on the superstitious increased from fourteen to twenty-four percent.

"Where as freshmen they once felt that the best single indication of the value of a person was 'whether or not he or she had good habits and avoided sin,' as seniors this concept changed to 'whether or not he or she is devoted to the welfare of others.' The seniors also indicated that they took teachings and practices of the Church on several topics, including obscenity, fasting, abstinence and birth control much less seriously than they did as freshmen."

To some extent this sort of thing has always occurred, frequently as a temporary turning of the young person away from religion. But now it seems to occur more often, in part as a reflection of a general alienation of college students from God but in part also because of something that has happened to Catholic universities. What has happened, at least in this country, is that many of these schools have lost their commitment to the purpose enjoined upon them by the Church.

The University and the Magisterium

There are three issues here. One concerns the duty of the school in its public profession, and of the faculty in its teaching and public utterances, to conform to the magisterium of the Church. Second is the incidental problem of enforcement—whether Church authorities can and should require the university and its personnel to conform to the magisterium. The third issue involves the tendency of some universities, Catholic as well as secular, to abdicate their own authority over their students.

The first issue, whether the Catholic university must submit to the magisterium, is the single most important question in Catholic higher education today. It should be clear that when one accepts Christ as God and the Catholic Church as His Church with power and authority to declare the truth, one undertakes a special duty to the truths of religion. This is true of the Catholic university as it is of the Catholic man or woman. The Catholic university can fairly be said to default in its intellectual mission no less than in its religious one when it permits its teachers to espouse as true what is contrary to the teaching of that Church. For the Catholic university, as an institution, knows, for instance, that the doctrine of original sin is true. If she permits a teacher to espouse a contrary doctrine she is consenting to the propagation of known falsehood. Also there is the element of scandal to be considered.

Influential voices, however, are now raised to challenge these concepts. In 1967 a statement on "The Nature of the Contemporary Catholic University" was issued at Land O'Lakes, Wisconsin, by officials of the leading Catholic universities in the United States, including the presidents of Georgetown University, Fordham University, the University of Notre Dame, Boston College, and St. Louis University. Composed at a meeting sponsored by the North American Region of the International Federation of Catholic Universities, the statement declared:

> To perform its teaching and research functions effectively the Catholic university must have a true autonomy and academic freedom in the face of authority of whatever kind, lay or clerical, external to the academic community itself. . . . There must be no theological or philosophical imperialism;

all scientific and disciplinary methods and methodologies must
be given due honor and respect.[10]

The statement demanded that no intellectual restrictions be placed
on undergraduates. "This means that the intellectual campus of a
Catholic university has no boundaries and no barriers. . . . The
whole world of knowledge and ideas must be open to the student;
there must be no outlawed books or subjects."[11] In the spring of
1969, representatives of leading Catholic universities throughout the
world and members of the Vatican Congregation for Catholic Education met in Rome.[12] According to the statement adopted by the
meeting, the Catholic university "is limited by no other factor than
the truth it pursues. Every limitation imposed on the university
which would clash with this unconditioned attitude for pursuing
truth would be intolerable and contrary to the very nature of the
university." The statement acknowledged that Church authorities "as
such can intervene" but "only in a situation where the truth of the
revealed message is at stake. Within these limitations, this means
complete freedom of research and of teaching must be guaranteed."
The theologian, it said, "in taking his place in the university, must be
able to pursue his discipline in the same manner as other research
scholars. He must be allowed to question, to develop new hypotheses,
to work toward new understandings and formulations, to publish and
defend his views, and to approach the theological sources, including
pronouncements of the teaching Church, with the free and full play
of modern scholarship. His work should normally be reviewed and
evaluated by his scholarly peers as is the case in other disciplines."
In teaching theology in the university, the Rome statement said,
"the theologian must of course present the authentic teaching of the
Church but he may and should form his students to an intelligent
and critical understanding of the faith, prudent account being taken
of the maturity and previous preparation of the students." At the
same time, the theologian "as an individual . . . is bound to accept
the authentic teaching of the Church and to submit to its legitimately exercised authority."

"In a university without statutory relationships with ecclesiastical
or religious superiors," the statement said, "these authorities may
deal with the theologian as an individual member of the Church. If
they can make representation to the institutional authorities, any
juridical intervention in university affairs must be excluded. In other
institutions provision is made for appropriate action by designated

ecclesiastical or religious superiors. In all cases, however, any action taken by ecclesiastical or religious superiors should conform exactly to their authority as established in the university statutes and should be carried out according to those procedures of due process established in the statutes and recognized as general university common law in the geographical region of the particular university."

The Rome statement was not an official pronouncement of the teaching Church and it carried only the authority of the delegates themselves. Essentially, it provided a basis for continued discussion on the issue. It is significant, too, that the Vatican's Congregation for Catholic Education met in plenary session in October 1969 and strongly affirmed the authority of the magisterium, which extends in the Catholic university "not only to the truths of faith, but also to those matters connected with the truths of faith":

> To fulfill [its] mission, a Catholic university must be seen as existing not only in the world, but also in the Catholic community and therefore it is related to those who preside over the Catholic community: the Catholic hierarchy. Obviously, the specific purpose of the Catholic university cannot be realized if those whose proper function it is to be the authentic guardians of the deposit of faith are relegated to a marginal place in its life and activity.

This position of the Congregation for Catholic Education is clearly correct. But, still, it is strongly challenged in many quarters in the United States and elsewhere. According to the Reverend Neil G. McCluskey, S.J., dean-director of the Institute for Studies in Education at the University of Notre Dame: "The Catholic university must arm its professors of theology with the same academic freedom that is accorded its historians, physicists and sociologists. There is no more academic justification for the entry by a local bishop or provincial into the university discipline of theology, than there is for the local mayor or governor to intrude into the field of political science."[13]

Father McCluskey's is one of the most influential voices in American Catholic education today. He is also the most lucid exponent of the view that would endow professors at Catholic colleges with an academic freedom practically unhindered by doctrinal restrictions. Yet his position here cannot be reconciled with the repeated pronouncements of several Popes and with the very nature of the

Catholic university. Father McCluskey explained his theory in detail as follows:

> It is the prerogative and duty of the scholar to put forth the fruits of his scholarship into the academic marketplace to be examined, tested, modified, accepted, or rejected by his peer group. This body alone can appropriately challenge or approve because it has earned authority and competence in the same field of learning. The very justification for the science of theology in the curriculum as an academic discipline is precisely that it is not catechesis and, therefore, not directly subject to the magisterium or teaching authority of the church. On the level of higher learning, the church's official magisterium has only an indirect influence; that is, the teaching church speaks authoritatively to the consciences of its members in the academic community, just as it does to the consciences of its members holding elective office in political society. Its influence in both spheres is indirect, not direct. The teaching office of the bishop is charismatic and hence his authority is always exercised outside the formal structure of the university.

"Advance and development of theological thought," continued Father McCluskey, "can never take place unless responsible theologians are able to present the results of their investigations with the same liberty as responsible scholars in other fields." The Catholic university is not "the church writ small, nor is it a church nor even the teaching arm of the church."

It is true that the Catholic university is not the Church or simply "the teaching arm of the Church." But it is also true, as Pope Pius IX noted in his 1929 encyclical on the Christian education of youth, that "every Christian child or youth has a strict right to instruction in harmony with the teaching of the Church, the pillar and ground of truth." Quoting the doctrine defined by the First Vatican Council, Pius XI said, "Not only is it impossible for faith and reason to be at variance with each other, they are on the contrary of mutual help. . . . The Church therefore, far from hindering the pursuit of the arts and sciences, fosters and promotes them in many ways. . . . Nor does she prevent sciences, each in its own sphere, from making use of principles and methods of their own. Only while acknowledging the freedom due to them, she takes every precaution to prevent them from falling into error by opposition to divine doctrine, or from overstepping their proper limits, and thus invading and disturbing the domain of faith."[14] Pius XI went on to describe this standard as "an inviolable norm of a just freedom in things didactic, or for rightly understood liberty in teaching; *it should be observed therefore in whatever instruction is imparted to others.*" (Emphasis added)

We are concerned at this point with the obligation of the Catholic university, as an institution, and of its faculty and administrators as individuals, to conform their teaching and statements to the magisterium of the Church. Father McCluskey and the delegates of the International Federation of Catholic Universities would agree that the individual Catholic teacher or administrator is bound in conscience to follow the teaching of the Church, just as all Catholics are so bound. But their view would not concede that the Catholic university, as an institution, has the duty to prevent academic contradictions of the teachings of the Church. The governing principle, instead, would be academic freedom. The argument is also made in this respect that the Catholic university in America cannot be governed by the rules that apply in the Latin countries of Europe and South America.[15] However, the submission of the Catholic university, as an institution, to the teaching Church, is not an accident of culture. Rather it is grounded in the basic duty of the university toward truth and in the nature of the magisterium of the Church. Pope Paul VI made this plain in a letter signed in his name by his Secretary of State, Amleto Cardinal Cicognani, to commemorate University Day in 1968:

> The hallmarks of a Catholic university, of its teaching staff and of its alumni must therefore be its commitment to academic endeavour and its loyalty to Jesus Christ's teaching and to that of his Church. These are the marks by which it must be known to all those who come to it, and be accepted as such whole-heartedly by them as being the guiding principles of its instruction and of its educational system. Where, because of peculiar circumstances, with due respect for the spiritual attitudes of its own teaching staff and of its pupils, a Catholic university does allow those to enroll who may be undergoing a spiritual crisis or disorientation, it must take care, with full regard for the spiritual freedom and sincerity of the individual, to ensure that a climate or mentality is not created which might go counter to its own basic purpose, or might compromise its academic role within the Church or its educative function in relation to youth.

As a "working of the Church in the field of culture," the University should demonstrate in all its cadres—teaching staff, students and collaborators—the essential characteristic of love for the Church, of sympathy with her problems and of involvement in her mission of salvation, by absorbing her spirit and *following her teaching and her directives.* (Emphasis added)[16]

It is significant here that the Pope does not define the role of the Catholic university in terms of a never-ending search for truth. Rather, the Catholic university must also preserve and transmit the truth. The Second Vatican Council emphasized the importance of "due freedom of scientific investigation" in the Catholic university. And in its *Pastoral Constitution on the Church in the Modern World,* the Council said, "In order that such persons may fulfill their proper function, let it be recognized that all the faithful, clerical and lay, possess a lawful freedom of inquiry and of thought, and the freedom to express their minds humbly and courageously about those matters in which they enjoy competence."[17] This freedom of expression applies to the Catholic university as well as to other spheres of Catholic life. However, this freedom is not license. As Pope Paul has pointed out, the Catholic university is working and acting in the name of the Church and therefore must be guided by the magisterium of the Church. The Church, he said,

is well aware that you are acting and working in her name, and that you are carrying out an irreplaceable function for her. It follows that you are closely linked up with her magisterium, in a perfect communion of spirit, heart and will, in the same service of the one people of God, where it is for each one to carry out his own mission, according as the Lord willed, in his unfathomable wisdom, for his Church. (Cf. "Lumen Gentium," n. 12 and 13, and "Dei Verbum," 8 and 10.)

Today, as yesterday, the magisterium remains the authentic guarantee of your inspiration, in freely accepted fidelity to the living tradition received from the Apostles.

Does not your fruitful experience, moreover, bear witness to this? The denominational character of a Catholic University, far from being an obstacle to the scientific value of studies, can and must be a help for the pedagogy of these studies, in the case of both teacher and student, both actuated by a disinterested pursuit of truth, in accordance with the admirable programme of St. Augustine, which inspired so many generations of searchers.[18]

Academic Freedom

A fair test of the Catholicity of a university is whether it systematically presents the teachings of the Church to its students, whether it makes available to its students a firm grounding in scholastic philosophy and whether it permits the infallible or authentic teachings of the Church to be contradicted in the classroom. This contradiction, moreover, can take the form of suspended judgment as well as outright denial. Every university has an express or implicit creed, whether Catholic, Jewish, agnostic, or whatever. It is illusory to expect any university to be neutral on philosophical and especially religious questions. It is therefore unsound to say that a Catholic university is somehow less of a university for being Catholic. But it is true that the Catholic university, unlike its secular counterpart, inherently rejects the relativist approach. It undertakes not only to search for truth, but to affirm and teach that truth which it knows. This duty is of course violated by the teacher who denies, for example, the truth of the Resurrection. But it is also violated by a teacher who equivocates on the factual reality of the Resurrection or presents it primarily in a symbolic sense. And it is violated, too, by the teacher who presents a half-truth, who, for example, presents the theories of Father Teilhard de Chardin without exposing the serious errors in Teilhard's thought and without informing the students that the Sacred Congregation of the Holy Office issued a monitum in 1962, which is still in effect, warning "all Ordinaries as well as the superiors of Religious institutes, rectors of seminaries and presidents of universities, effectively to protect the minds, particularly of the youth, against the dangers presented by the works of Fr. Teilhard de Chardin and of his followers." In other ways, too, a teacher can mislead by indirection.

It is no easy task for the college to prevent these abuses. Any effort to police the classroom could easily infringe upon the proper autonomy of the teacher. Here, as in other areas, there is a seeming conflict of legitimate claims. The teacher and scholar must have the freedom necessary to pursue his academic inquiries and speculations. There is a strong general interst in favor of insulating the teacher from reprisals and intimidation. As the Supreme Court of the United States observed in 1967:

Our Nation is deeply committed to safeguarding academic freedom, which is of transcendent value to all of us and not merely to the teachers concerned. That freedom is therefore a special concern of the First Amendment, which does not tolerate laws that cast a pall of orthodoxy over the classroom.[19]

But whatever the limits imposed by the Constitution on the federal and state governments in defense of academic freedom, a distinction is clearly appropriate with respect to church-related schools and colleges. Even as to public institutions, academic freedom is not absolutely immune to restriction. With the church-related college, some further limitation is clearly required by the nature of the institution. This is especially so in the fields of philosophy and theology, where a conflict with the authentic or infallibly defined teachings of the Church is foreseeable.

If a university is to have an authentic Catholic identity, it should not permit the public contradiction by its faculty or administrators of the infallible or authentic teachings of the Church. Nor does this impinge upon legitimate free inquiry. While inquiry and criticism are desirable within their proper limits, it is no disservice to the truth to regard contradictions of the given truth as simply intellectually unacceptable. Jean Cardinal Daniélou described this inherent limitation on speculation in the field of theology:

There exists an authority to which I have the right to accord unconditional trust. . . .
This is the act of faith, the act of faith which is perfectly justified from the strict point of view of the intelligence, once it is proved that Christ is a witness who is not only a human but also a divine authority.
In the field of faith we have a datum which has been laid down once for all: Christ was conceived by the Virgin Mary, he rose from the dead, he ascended to the right hand of the Father, and he is present amongst us in the Eucharist. This is the datum. Clearly, we shall never come to exhaustive knowledge about it, and theology is consequently no less than "faith in search of understanding," to use the celebrated formula. Its effort will go on forever, because Jesus has greater depth than the whole of the universe and we shall never get to the end of it: we can only advance in understanding what Jesus is. Therefore theological research has something unlimited about it, provided that it stays within its proper object, and continues

to be controlled by that object. The moment it departs from that object it is like a scientific hypothesis which misses the realities of physics and is useless.

And this is where the great dialogue constituting thought inside the Church has its origin. It is a dialogue between authority and enquiry. Questioning has its part to play in it, for it challenges one theory or another in order to progress in understanding of the dialogue, with perpetual reference to the basic datum. But authority's duty is to keep the deposit intact, and to keep research from getting away from its object and being lost in unreality.[20]

The teaching of heresy, therefore, is the teaching of known falsehood. Father William G. Most, president of the Mariological Society of America, recently declared that academic freedom demands that the practitioner use the "true method of his field of knowledge" and that Catholics who ignore the magisterium in their theological pursuits ignore that method. A Catholic theologian, said Father Most, who refuses to accept the magisterium of the Church as the basis for seeking truth is not practicing academic freedom but is a "quack in his field." The task here of the Catholic university is so to apply academic freedom that it will not shelter espousals by teachers or university administrators in the classroom or any public forum, of that which is known by the university as an institution to be untrue, i.e., that which contradicts revelation, or that which contradicts the authentic teaching of the Church.

One answer to this problem may be to require that no priest, religious, or Catholic layman be allowed to teach in a Catholic school at any level if he does not accept the doctrinal teachings summarized in Pope Paul's *Credo*, in the sense in which the Pope intends them, and if he does not accept the authentic teachings of the Church, including *Humanae Vitae*. The *Credo* is a reliable compendium of doctrine. Acceptance or rejection of *Humanae Vitae* and other authentic teachings is a symbolic criterion of one's overall loyalty to the Church itself.

If this test were applied to every Catholic college and university in the country, it would go a long way toward restoring those institutions to their proper position. Although a Catholic university should prefer Catholics in its hiring policies, there will be occasions where it will be desirable to engage a non-Catholic teacher for his competence in a certain area. This would be particularly true in technical, graduate, and professional fields. But with these exceptions, and with special emphasis on courses in theology and philosophy, it is not too much for a Catholic school to ask her teachers that they accept the doctrine upon which she is founded, or at least that they not openly contradict it. Nor should we be concerned here only with those truths that have been solemnly and infallibly defined. Rather, the duty of the Catholic university is to adhere to all the authentic teachings of the Church, whether they are infallibly defined or not. Pope Pius XII made this plain in an address to the faculty and students of the Roman Athenaeum Angelicum:

> You must give diligent and ready assent to the ordinances and decrees of the sacred Magisterium which relate to truths divinely revealed, since the one Catholic Church, the Spouse of Christ, is the faithful guardian and infallible interpreter of the deposit of these truths. But you must receive in a spirit of obedience and of humility those teachings also which deal with questions that relate to things natural and human. For those who profess the Catholic religion, and especially theologians and philosophers, ought—as is right—to hold these teachings in the highest esteem, since matters of this lower order are proposed because they are connected and joined with the truths of Christian faith and the supernatural end of man.[21]

Enforcement by Church Authority

Surely, then, the Catholic university and its faculty are in conscience required to be submissive to the magisterium. But this conclusion does not answer the further question of whether and to what extent the bishops should impose sanctions to enforce that obligation. One view would deny the right of the ecclesiastical authorities to intervene directly in university affairs and would restrict those authorities to an indirect role of making essentially precatory appeals to the consciences of members of the university community. As Father McCluskey described the report adopted by the delegates from Catholic universities at their meeting in Rome in 1969, "if a bishop feels that certain theologizing activity on a given campus is harmful, he then has the right and duty to inform the man, to inform the administration and, if called for, even to warn the faithful that, in his considered judgment, the institution itself has departed from orthodox teaching. This, however, is the limit of his competence. According to the document, any *juridical* intervention in university affairs by ecclesiastical authority must be excluded." (Emphasis in original)[22] On the other hand, it can properly be said that this view could lead to the frustration of the purpose of the Catholic university. Those institutions, if such a view were to prevail, could be permanently diverted from their purpose by recalcitrant administrators and teachers who could use them to undermine the teachings of the Church and the Church would have no practical recourse. The absurdity of this was explained by Cardinal Newman:

> If the Catholic faith is true, a university can not exist externally to the Catholic pale, for it can not teach universal knowledge if it does not teach Catholic theology. This is certain; but still, though it had ever so many theological chairs, that would not suffice to make it a Catholic University; for theology would be included in its teaching only as a branch of knowledge, only as one out of many constituent portions, however important a one, of what I have called philosophy. Hence a direct and active jurisdiction of the Church over it and in it is necessary lest it should become the rival of the Church with the community at large in those theological matters which to the Church are exclusively committed—acting as the representative of the intellect, as the Church is the representative of the religious principle.
>
> . . . And in like manner, it is no sufficient security for the Catholicity of a university, even that the whole of Catholic theology should be professed in it, unless the Church breathes her own pure and unearthly spirit into it, and fashions and moulds its organization, and watches over its teaching, and knits together its pupils and superintends its action.
>
> Nor is this all: such institutions may become hostile to revealed truth in consequence of the circumstances of their teaching as well as of their end. They are employed in the pursuit of liberal knowledge, and liberal knowledge has a special tendency, not necessary or rightful, but a tendency in fact, when cultivated by beings such as we are, to impress us with a mere philosophical theory of life and conduct, in the place of Revelation.[23]

Cardinal Newman's approach is manifestly correct, today as in his own time. However, it is not the purpose of this chapter to define the particular powers of the bishops over the Catholic university. Canon law provides that ordinaries have the right and duty to watch that in Catholic schools within their territory nothing is taught contrary to faith or good morals. This right and duty of vigilance as to faith and morals applies to schools at all levels.[24] We are entitled to hope that the bishops wil give consideration to the possibility of their direct intervention where they conclude that such intervention is warranted by Canon Law and by the particular situation within their jurisdiction. But each case has to be determined by the bishop concerned and it is not our purpose to do other than suggest that the bishops give the matter their serious consideration. Rather, we are more concerned here to appeal to the administrations and faculties of Catholic universities to recognize their duty toward the magisterium. Of course, the distinction between research and teaching is important here. Of its nature the freedom to do research is far less encumbered than is the freedom to teach, to publish, and to speak. It is only when utterance is given to erroneous opinions that danger is presented to others. With regard to those utterances, there surely is no basis for an uncritical application of the secular principles of academic freedom in this area.

Nor is it tenable to distinguish between the seminary and the university so as to concede the power of the Church to enforce her magisterium in the former but not in the latter. The Sacred Congregation for Catholic Education rejected this distinction in its reply to the report of the 1969 meeting in Rome of delegates from the world's leading Catholic universities.[25] As long as the university is conducted under the auspices of the Church, the competence of the magisterium to intervene to correct erroneous teaching is no less clear than it is with regard to the seminary. For the truth is indivisible and it must be upheld in all the institutions connected with the Church.

Are the Universities Really Catholic?

The foregoing discussion may be only of theoretical interest as it relates to some of the leading Catholic universities in America. A number of Catholic universities have deliberately undertaken to secularize themselves in order to qualify for government aid. The legal aspects of this will be discussed in the next chapter. We note the tendency here because if a university has been withdrawn from Church control over its administration, it may also be immune to

Church intervention to prevent violations of the magisterium in its classrooms.

It should be remembered, of course, that Catholic colleges are laboring under a fiscal disadvantage compared with state institutions and their more richly endowed private competitors. Catholic colleges are in financial trouble almost everywhere. For the most part, this can be attributed to the rising costs of operation. Those costs reduce the number of students and this reduction in turn increases the per capita cost of running the college for the students who do attend. Without rehearsing what was said in the previous chapter, the enactment on the college level of some variant of a generous tuition tax credit, supplemented by a GI Bill-type grant for parents who make insufficient income to benefit from a tax credit, should be a priority objective of those who would save Catholic higher education. The remarks in this chapter are not intended to minimize the financial crisis. Some Catholic colleges are closing and many are declining in enrollment. But we are concerned here essentially with defects that all the money in the world will not cure. What is required instead is a redirection of purpose and will.

However, the deficiencies we discuss here are not entirely unrelated to the financial problems. To some unmeasured extent the decline in enrollments in some Catholic colleges can be attributed to a growing feeling that Catholic colleges are really not different enough to make it worth while to pay the higher cost. If secular colleges look more attractive to Catholic parents than they have in the past, one reason is simply the failure of Catholic colleges to provide a Catholic education. This is obviously not true of all Catholic colleges and perhaps not even of a majority. But the disturbing trend is sufficiently evident to warrant concern.

There are many colleges which began with a strong religious commitment, yet today have lost their religious identification in all but a thinly symbolic way. The list would include Harvard, Columbia, Amherst, the University of Chicago, the University of Southern California, and others.[26] Early in 1967, Webster College, a school for girls conducted by the Sisters of Loretto in St. Louis, declared itself wholly secular. Webster's president, Sister Jacqueline Grennan is now married and is the president of Hunter College in New York. "The very nature of higher education," she declared, "is opposed to juridical control by the Church." Following Webster's lead, prominent Catholic colleges, including the University of Notre Dame, Fordham, and a dozen or more others, have shifted to secular control. The question, of course, is whether this process will bring in its train the sort of secularization which occurred at Harvard, Amherst, and other schools which began under denominational auspices. The indications are abundant that it will. "Putting it very bluntly," said the Reverend Leo McLaughlin, S.J., then president of Fordham University, "one reason that the changes are being made in the structure of the boards of trustees is money. . . . It seems to me that in the financial order many Catholic institutions have already passed the point of no return. These colleges simply cannot continue to exist without state aid. In the not too distant future . . . the choice offered to Catholic institutions is going to be quite clear: changes will have to be made within the structure of the Catholic institutions which will make them eligible for federal and state aid or many of them will have to close their doors."[27] Speaking in 1967, the Reverend Theodore M. Hesburgh, C.S.C., president of the University of Notre Dame, described the new governance of Notre Dame by a lay-dominated board of trustees. Noting that the new form was approved by the Vatican, Father Hesburgh said, "the University of Notre Dame is a civil, non-profit, educational corporation, chartered by and operating under the civil law of the State of Indiana, totally directed by this largely lay Board of Trustees. To describe this as 'juridic control by the Church' would be simply untrue. Our University might more properly be called a secular institution, but I would prefer not to thus characterize it, because of the contemporary implications of secularism and secularization which would simply not apply in a professedly Catholic university."[28] The University's form of governance, Father Hesburgh maintained, "places it as an institution under civil, not canon law." Therefore, the Church exercises no juridical control over the members of the administration and faculty in "their university functions."

At this point we face a problem of definition. If a university is Catholic, its duty, as an institution, to submit to the magisterium is clear. This is no less clear of its administrators and faculty in the performance of their official functions and in their public utterances. But if a university does not commit itself to adhere to the magisterium and if it has so altered its corporate structure as to be immune to the juridical control of Church authorities, it ought not to call itself Catholic. For such a university to claim to be Catholic in anything but a sentimental sense, is to work a deception on its students, their parents, and the public. This is true no matter how earnestly the administrators may profess the Catholicity of their schools. Merely calling a university Catholic or suffusing the campus with a Catholic presence will not make it so if there is lacking the essential hallmark of fidelity to the teachings of the Church. While giving those secularizing administrators all due credit for their good intentions, we cannot ignore the inherent unreality of their position.

The leaders of the secularized Catholic universities have squandered a heritage that was not theirs to diminish. In some cases, at least, they have done so, not under the pressure of events, but apparently out of a desire to conform and to be accepted by the secular society and its government. Perhaps we should heed Father Robert I. Gannon, S.J., former president of Fordham University, who recently attacked the administrators and faculties of Catholic colleges who

> would rather be modern than right; would go to any lengths to avoid the stigma of conservatism. In the eyes of such educators a university must be a place where obvious error has a right to equal time. That is why they would maintain that a Catholic university is a contradiction in terms. It is our handicap to know from revelation that some things are false. As for college, they would consider it a blur between high school and research or a job; a place for elementary specialization. That would mean of course the death of the Ratio Studiorum— in fact of any organized pursuit of the Liberal Arts.

"If the sad day ever comes," Father Gannon concluded, "when the tendency to secularize our campuses not only appears but starts to move toward realization, then indeed the time will have come to auction them for industrial parks and send the money to the foreign missions."[29]

The first issue, then, involving the Catholic university and the teaching Church, is the extent to which that university is subject to the magisterium. That she is so subject is clear, not only from the pronouncements of the Popes and Councils, but also from the nature of the university and of the Church as the guardian of truth.

The second issue is that of enforcement. The local ordinary may have the right and duty to intervene in a particular Catholic university to preserve the orthodoxy of its teaching. We are not venturing a conclusion here on this matter of intervention. Rather, whatever action the bishops decide is warranted, Catholic parents are entitled to draw their own conclusions. For theirs is the primary right to educate. They have neither the duty nor the right to commit their children to universities that will not unequivocally adhere to the teaching authority of the Church and will not commit themselves to offer to their students a competent foundation in scholastic philosophy. If a school will not do so, its Catholic pretense is no more than that.

The University's Authority Over Its Students

The third issue here concerns the failure of some Catholic universities to exercise their own authority over their students. This occurs in several ways. One involves curriculum content. The Catholic university should require all its students to take theology and philosophy courses of sufficient number and content to ensure that the students will be afforded a solid and precise knowledge of the history and teachings of the Church and a competent foundation in scholastic philosophy. Regrettably, this duty is not always fulfilled. The College of the Holy Cross, in Worcester, Massachusetts, for example, has abolished its required "core" curriculum, under which all students had been required to take seventeen courses in such subjects as theology, philosophy, English, history, modern languages, and natural science.[30] "As a result of abolishment of the 'core,'" the college explained to its alumni, "students now will be required only to take courses in their major fields. The major department may also ask its students to take courses in other areas. As an example, the History Department might require its majors to take certain courses in modern languages and in the social sciences such as economics, sociology and political science." Henceforth, therefore, a student can go through four years at Holy Cross without taking any theology or philosophy courses at all. This is not necessarily an unmixed evil, in view of the recent orientation of theology and philosophy at Holy Cross. But the change does obliterate the Jesuit method of integrated study—the Ratio Studiorum—that has proven its worth over four centuries. To this extent it is fair to say that the college has ceased to be Jesuit, except in the sense that some Jesuits hold office there. Also, in the sense in which the Second Vatican Council used the term, it has ceased in effect to be a Catholic college.

Other examples abound of this failure of Catholic schools to ensure that their students will receive a systematic exposure to the teachings of the Church. This is not to imply that students should be deprived of the opportunity to examine other traditions and creeds. But a balance must be sought, with primary emphasis on the duty of the university to present the known truths of the Faith in an orderly and complete way.

Another matter in which some Catholic universities have abdicated their own authority is student discipline. Parents are entitled to expect that the Catholic university will provide institutional encouragement and spiritual aids for the student to advance in virtue and personal loyalty to Christ and the Church. Here we find at once the most striking and the most unnecessary default of the Catholic university. Consider, for example, the widespread tendency to turn the government of dormitories over to the students and the allowance of parietal hours or dormitory visiting privileges between the sexes. The anarchy resulting from student rule in some dormitories is obviously a violation of the rights of those students who desire a place congenial to orderly living and study and whose parents are paying a high price for that purpose. But it also, for some students at least, presents serious occasions of sin which they are unprepared to handle.

In other respects, too, administrators of some Catholic universities have abdicated their duty to promote the spiritual welfare of their students. Some Catholic universities have permitted pornographic films or literature on the campus. Some have tolerated drinking and pot smoking in dormitories. Many have drained the theology and philosophy curricula of their former commitment to molding better Catholics so that the best the student can hope for there is a neutral survey course if not an outright subversion of the teaching authority of the Church. Practically all have abolished compulsory Mass, thereby withdrawing from the students a strong inducement to the development of regular devotional habits. Overall, many have offered too little in the way of institutional encouragement to their students to keep the Ten Commandments and develop religious virtues.

In all this, of course, it is generally forgotten that the college and the students are not the only parties involved. The parents, who pay the bills and who will stand before God to answer for the custody of their children, have an interest here. Parents can hardly be faulted for their dismay when Catholic colleges allow their sons and daughters a latitude of personal conduct which would be unthinkable if those young people were still in their own homes.

And the parents are hardly, if ever, consulted on the rules which could lead to the moral corruption of their children. It would be a rare Catholic college that would emphasize in its promotional bulletin that the students would be under practically no moral restraint. Yet that is too often the fact. Surely a little candor is in order. In the proper order of things, the Catholic boarding college should stand *in loco parentis*, taking the place of the parents to a reasonable degree, where the students' moral conduct is concerned. A balance can be achieved here without going to extremes. But too many schools have taken the easy road and relinquished that responsibility.

In a way, the failure of some Catholic colleges to supervise the conduct of their students is a corollary of their efforts to secularize and to emulate their Ivy League counterparts. The unapologetic reinforcement of student morality is a critical difference between an authentically Catholic university and its secular counterpart. It should not be surprising, then, that this difference is one of the first to be erased in the pursuit of acceptance by the secular world.

The further question arises of the response that Catholic universities should make in the face of student turmoil. This is a problem faced by all universities, secular and religious. Certainly the high school graduate of today is not as submissive to authority, whether civil or religious, as was his older brother or father. The college, therefore, has a more difficult product to work with. But, without dwelling on this issue here, it bears mentioning that effective action has been taken on many campuses. The president of St. Bonaventure University drew a standing ovation from more than fifteen hundred students and visiting parents when he announced he was banning the Students for a Democratic Society from the campus because the SDS is "opposed to all that our Republic and our Church and this institution stands for."[31]

Another constructive approach was taken by J. Donald Phillips, president of Hillsdale College, a non-Catholic institution in Michigan. He wrote to all incoming students, advising them that the administration intends to run the school. Not only did Dr. Phillips announce that students who disrupt the campus would be expelled or suspended, but that the same sanctions would be applied to those who "advocate" disruption.[32] This is the crucial point. It is easy for a college administrator to expel those who actually disrupt the school, though too few even do that. But to exclude the agitator, before his words have borne fruit in violence, demands a willingness to stand athwart the reigning absolutes of a free speech construed to the point of license. Sometimes the students who disrupt the school are mere dupes. Sometimes they are not. In both cases, they should be appropriately punished. But some college administrators seem to have forgotten Abraham Lincoln's lament: "Must I shoot a simple-minded soldier boy who deserts, while I must not touch a hair of a wily agitator who induces him to desert? . . . I think that . . . to silence the agitator and save the boy is not only Constitutional but withal a great mercy."[33] Nothing effective will be done to prevent violence and disruption on the campus until subversive organizations such as the SDS, the Black Panthers, and similar groups, as well as serious individual advocates of disruption are wholly excluded from the life of the university as they should be excluded, for the good of the country, from the society as a whole. Similarly, nothing effective will be done to prevent the theological alienation of Catholic college students until the advocates of disloyalty to the authority of the Church are excluded from teaching roles. To an encouraging degree, the effort is being made to prevent violence. We are entitled to hope that a similar effort will be made to prevent the theological and philosophical subversion of the students.

Parents' Alternatives

In their evasion of the teaching authority of the Church and in their abdication of their own authority over their students, some leading Catholic universities in America have relinquished their basic claim to the allegiance of Catholic parents. Yet there is a residual attraction which draws many parents to those schools under the expectation that their children will receive a systematic exposure to the faith and to sound philosophy, will not be actively taught contrary to her doctrine, and will benefit from institutional encouragements to virtue. For too many schools, this implicit expectation is based upon a sham and a fraud.

Something, then, clearly must be done. The first thing is for the faculties and administrators of Catholic universities to awaken to their responsibilities and insist that their schools live up to their Catholic profession or at least refrain from representing themselves as what they are not.

The second recourse is for the bishops to consider their own responsibilities, insofar as their authority has not been frustrated by the corporate secularization of universities which still describe themselves as Catholic. Generalizations cannot be made here. In each case, the ordinary's capacity to act will depend on the juridical structure of the university in question and upon the circumstances of the case, as determined in his own prudent judgment.

However, we must be frank. Most bishops are unlikely to intervene to improve the Catholic universities. At least we are impelled to this conclusion from the performance of the bishops as a national body with respect to the Catholic University of America. In April 1969 a faculty board of inquiry at Catholic University exonerated twenty-one faculty members who had publicly dissented from Pope Paul's encyclical *Humanae Vitae*.[34] Since then the school has continued to tolerate those who openly reject the teaching authority of the Pope on birth control, celibacy, and other issues. *The Standard and Times*, official newspaper of the Archdiocese of Philadelphia, editorialized on March 5, 1970, that "Confidence in the Church will be further eroded, we believe, if the Catholic University of America retains on its faculty not only those who defy Papal teaching but also those who resign from a freely chosen life commitment to the priesthood." Monsignor Eugene Kevane, shortly after he was ousted as dean of the School of Education at Catholic University, attacked "inhibiting philosophisms" which have made it difficult for the school to function "as the Church intends." Monsignor Kevane blamed a climate of "British Empiricism and American Pragmatism" for the pressure that has led to the interpretation of the school's purpose and objective "in terms of philosophical positivism," that has shifted theology from its central position at the University and that has substituted "exclusively" the methods of research proper to empirical sciences. "This has made it increasingly difficult," Monsignor Kevane continued, "for Christian Philosophy to function on this campus as the Church intends and for theology to maintain either its authentic nature or its central position within the institution." If no effective action has been taken by the bishops with regard to the Catholic University of America, it would be optimistic to expect it in the foreseeable future with regard to Catholic universities in general.

In the present confused state of Catholic higher education in America, the concerned parent is faced with a difficult decision. However, there are some things that parents can do. It would hasten a solution if parents would stop supporting Catholic colleges of dubious regularity. In 1969 Donald Barr, headmaster of Dalton School in New York City, wrote:

> On the day that parents stop paying tuition for noneducation, on the day they stop handing out allowances for strike funds and narcotics and reeking apartments, the student revolutions—impatient with reason, violent against restraint, a holiday from self-control—will wither away, and the real learning that must precede intelligent social change will begin.[35]

While Mr. Barr was referring to student disruptions, similar considerations apply to the disruption of orthodoxy through the failure of Catholic universities to adhere to the teachings of the Church. Here, too, the most effective weapon parents have is their tuition money.

Unless parents are confident, after thorough investigation, that the Catholic boarding college they are considering is sound doctrinally and morally, they should keep their children home. Send them to tolerable Catholic colleges at home or, if there is any doubt about the soundness of those Catholic colleges, send them to local public or nonsectarian private colleges.

Sooner or later, sound Catholic colleges will begin to emerge. Thomas Aquinas College opened in 1970 at San Rafael, California, and it may provide a model for Catholic colleges that desire to preserve their identity and survive. One observer described it in these terms:

> 1. Concentrated, in-depth study of all students in the fields of philosophy, mathematics, languages and experimental science.
> 2. Seminars limited to 20 students discussing the great literary and historical classics of all time.
> 3. Tutorial classes in which the teacher will direct searching student question-and-answer sessions.
> 4. Judaeo-Christian ethics combined with a no-nonsense attitude toward campus violence and anarchy.
> 5. Students who look and act like scholars instead of like refugees from some surrealistic version of a hobo jungle.
> 6. Short shrift for the kind of "academic freedom" which does away with any and all rules under the guise of "free inquiry."[36]

But until authentic colleges arise in sufficient numbers to handle the demand, parents ought to shun those schools which, upon investigation, they believe to involve a significant risk to their children. As with elementary and secondary schools, it would be better to expose a student to error in a frankly hostile setting than to expose him to half-truths presented in a Catholic setting that belies the secular reality of the institution.

There is a continuing need, however, for Catholic laymen and laywomen soundly educated in the faith and dedicated to it. Hopefully, the enactment of a tuition tax credit or similar plan will enable parents to establish and support real Catholic colleges to meet this demand. But, in the absence of reliable Catholic colleges, this need can be filled by part-time college-level schools of Catholic theology and scholastic philosophy. These would be similar to the schools of religion that are springing up on the elementary and secondary levels to offset the absence of reliable Catholic schools. These special schools of theology and philosophy would be a loyal part of Catholic higher education, though not within the hierarchical chain of command. They would be analogous to the Newman Clubs, which were designed to strengthen the knowledge and faith of Catholic students at avowedly secular colleges. Also, competently prepared reading lists should be made available to all Catholic students in Catholic or non-Catholic colleges. Of course, it is up to the parents to ensure that their children get, through these special schools or in some other way, the religious education formerly available in Catholic colleges. This entire process will contribute, incidentally, to greater parental responsibility and lay involvement in Catholic higher education.

During the past century, the Catholic Church in America raised a system of education, from elementary to graduate schools which, while not perfect, served the Church and the nation well. Within the past decade and more, however, the patrimony of this system has been squandered by those to whose care it was entrusted. Motivated partly by an inferiority complex and partly by their desire for easy government money, the administrators of the leading Catholic universities have imitated their secular counterparts at the very time when those secular schools were demonstrating their philosophical bankruptcy and their disciplinary futility. If the abdication of their function is to be reversed, Catholic universities will have to commit themselves anew to the teaching authority of the Church. But they will also have to free themselves from their dependence on government aid. This latter task demands a willingness to forego academic luxuries and to resist the lure of perpetual expansion. But it also requires that the Church in America as a whole reconsider its relation to the state. For the surrender of its independence by the Catholic university in exchange for public aid has followed the pattern of the Church as a whole in this country. In exchange for patronage she has held her tongue. It is fitting, then, that we next examine some principles and problems connected with Church-State relations.

XI.

CHURCH AND STATE

In Fremont, California, in 1969, Steven Minyen was sent home from Washington High School and told to return with his parents for a discussion with the principal. His offense: he talked about God to his fellow students in the school yard during lunch hour. Presumably, Steven would have gained the approbation, not condemnation, of the public school authorities if he had discussed some authorized topic, such as the contraceptive efficacy of the pill as compared to the intrauterine loop, which topic is standard fare in eighth-grade sex education courses. After vociferous public protests, the Alameda county counsel ruled that Steven could not be suspended for talking about religion in the school yard, since "the students are free to listen or not, to come and go as they wish." But, said the attorney, Steven could not talk about religion in the classroom.[1] Presumably, he could not do so even if the classroom discussion infringed on matters of vital religious concern to him.

The society which tolerates this sort of thing is hardly the same one that called on the protection of God four times in its own birth certificate, the Declaration of Independence. But it is a society which is capable of worse than muzzling Steven Minyen in a classroom. In 1938 Walter Lippmann said, "The decay of decency in the modern age, the rebellion against law and good faith, the treatment of human beings as things, as mere instruments of power and ambition, is without a doubt the consequence of the decay of the belief in man as something more than an animal animated by highly conditioned reflexes and chemical reactions. For unless man is something more than that, he has no rights that anyone is bound to respect, and there are no limitations upon his conduct, which he is bound to obey."[2] "This is the forgotten foundation of democracy," Lippmann concluded.

The Bishops' Default

The pre-eminent fruit of the "decay of decency" in America is the general tolerance of abortion. In Chapter II we discussed this development and the fact that only the Catholic Church can provide the leadership necessary to reverse the anti-life trend. To do so, the Church in America must be true to herself internally. There must be a due respect for the authority of the Church before she can hope to recall the civil authority from its dangerous course. But the Church in this country must develop a coherent principle to govern her own relations, as a Church, to that civil society.

The response of the American bishops to the abortion movement has been ambivalent. On the state level, many individual bishops and state conferences have fought effectively and well. While their cause has been largely a losing one, they should be credited with whatever success has been achieved in curbing the abortion drive. But on the national level, the bishops have been less effective. At their April 1970 national meeting in San Francisco, the bishops issued a standard deprecation of abortion.[3] This was in the face of the adoption by sixteen states of easy abortion, the striking down by courts of laws in several jurisdictions prohibiting abortion where it is not necessary to save the life of the mother, and the clear commitment of the Nixon Administration to the use of abortion as a weapon in its drive to control population growth. Yet the only thing new in the bishops' statement was their commitment to remove the social stigma surrounding out-of-wedlock pregnancies and "to provide counseling and understanding to the woman who faces a difficult pregnancy." Let us not minimize the importance of removing the economic and psychological causes that move some women to kill their children. It is not enough to be against abortion. One should also extend a hand to the troubled mother of the unborn child. Social programs, counseling, and financial support are all essential here. But the problem requires dual action. When a house is on fire, we do not immediately start to rebuild it with fireproof materials. First, we put out the fire. So it is with abortion. We must plan ways to alleviate the underlying social and moral problems that engender abortion. But we must also take effective moral and political action to prevent the killing of innocent children here and now regardless of their mothers' underlying distress.

It is encouraging, however, that the bishops, at their November 1970 meeting flatly described abortion as murder, directed Catholic hospitals not to allow their facilities to be used by anyone, Catholic or non-Catholic, for the performance of an abortion, and reminded Catholic doctors and nurses that they are morally bound not to take part in an abortion even if the law of the state permits it. This stiffening of attitude is welcome. But the bishops have not yet asserted that Catholic legislators and members of the executive branch, both state and federal, are bound in conscience to oppose liberalization of abortion laws. Nor have the bishops mounted a serious campaign to improve state and federal laws so as to protect the right to live. Without a serious legislative effort, and without a clear declaration of the duties of Catholic officials, the bishops' efforts are doomed to futility. Merely to bind Catholic doctors and nurses in conscience will not arrest the abortion trend. Yet it is within the power of the bishops to mount a campaign that will reverse that trend. What appears to be lacking is the will to do so.

Nineteen seventy was the year that saw the United States Catholic Conference, acting for the bishops, mobilize Catholic support for the welfare reform bill which would provide a guaranteed family income[4] for the unionization of grape workers by Cesar Chavez's United Farm Workers' Organizing Committee[5] and for the Genocide Convention, among other public causes. Needless to say, a Catholic might fairly conclude that the welfare reform bill is fiscally and socially undesirable, that Cesar Chavez ought not to have been supported without some showing that the grape workers actually desired unionization, and that the Genocide Convention exposes American citizens unwisely to the risk of criminal trial before international tribunals for such offenses as causing mental or emotional harm to a member of a minority group. On the other hand, a Catholic might well conclude, for example, that social justice demands the enactment of the welfare reform bill. The point is that, whatever their merits, these are debatable issues on which Catholics might fairly disagree. With abortion, however, there can be no debate for a Catholic. Abortion is evil, morally and socially. Also, it involves innocent life itself. It would be appropriate, therefore, for the bishops to address themselves to the abortion matter with far more intensity than they have evidenced on other, and less important, issues. For the abortion question is more important, for instance, than the issue of racial discrimination. The bishops have been diligent in promoting the cause of racial justice, sometimes by campaigning for measures of doubtful value. Both abortion and racial discrimination are evil, but abortion is the taking of innocent life itself. Nor can we forget that the abortion movement threatens pre-eminently the lives of children of minority groups. Yet the national bishops have been less energetic in defense of the child in the womb than they have been on racial matters and other issues, including their pursuit of government subsidies for parochial schools.

The bishops' stand toward abortion signals their posture toward the entire anti-life society. Their failure, as a national body, to defend the poor and defenseless child in the womb with effective legislative action, justifies the inference that the bishops, as a national body, have come to terms with the anti-life society and with the political leadership that condones or promotes it. Far from declaring serious war against the anti-life features of American society, the bishops have kept their opposition on a gentlemanly level that will ensure that no one, apart from children in the womb, will be hurt by the whole controversy. At the same time the bishops have strengthened their ties to the national administration in Washington. Interestingly, at their April 1970 meeting the bishops praised the Nixon Administration for its efforts to develop "workable relations" with the government of Communist China[6] and, perhaps more significantly, formally endorsed Preisdent Nixon's creation of a Panel on Non-Public Education to explore ways to resolve the problems of private elementary and secondary schools.[7]

There are two reasons, one practical and one philosophical, for the disinclination of the bishops to oppose effectively the secularization and the anti-life tendency of American society. The practical reason is money—the willingness of the leaders of the Church in America to modulate their views in exchange for government support of parochial schools. The philosophical reason is the general acceptance by the Church in America of a theory of pluralism that rationalizes this modulation.

The Pursuit of Government Aid

Of these two reasons, the more important is the financial. Catholic schools at all levels are in serious financial straits. To remedy this plight, the bishops have actively sought government support. They have urged and obtained that support in forms, including direct government grants, which require the aided schools to secularize as the price of the aid. Regrettably, the bishops have not energetically advocated alternate forms of aid, such as the tuition tax credit, which would relieve the financial pressures on the Catholic schools without secularizing government controls. The inference is justified, too, that the urgency with which the bishops have sought government aid has incidentally entailed a softening of the stands they should be expected to take against policies advocated by that government. But to place in context the Church's readiness to accept restrictions in exchange for government aid, we should first examine the original intention of the framers of the United States Constitution on religious matters and how that intention has been frustrated in recent years.

The Agnostic Establishment

The signers of the Declaration of Independence in 1776 affirmed the existence of God in four separate places in that instrument. They announced that the colonies were assuming "the separate and equal station to which the laws of nature and of nature's God entitle them." This manner of referrring to "nature" and "nature's God" was in common use by the deists of that time, who believed in a God but did not concede that He exercised a providential, continuing concern for human affairs. But the three other references to God in the Declaration were clearly theistic, in their affirmation of God and His providence:

We hold these truths to be self-evident: that all men are created equal; that they are endowed, by their Creator, with certain unalienable rights; that among these are life, liberty, and the pursuit of happiness.

We, therefore, the representatives of the UNITED STATES OF AMERICA, in General Congress assembled, appealing to the Supreme Judge of the world for the rectitude of our intentions, do . . . solemnly publish and declare, That these United Colonies are, and of right ought to be, FREE and INDEPENDENT STATES. . . .

And for the support of this Declaration, with a firm reliance on the protection of DIVINE PROVIDENCE, we mutually

pledge to each other our lives, our fortunes, and our sacred
honour. (Emphasis in original)[8]

The Constitution, unlike the Declaration of Independence, was a
blueprint rather than a proclamation. The Constitution, drafted in
1787 and approved the following year, was concerned with the
distribution and limitation of governmental powers among the
states and the newly created federal government. Understandably,
it made no reference to God, but the attitude of the people of the
United States toward religion may be seen in the First Amendment,
which was part of the Bill of Rights submitted by the First Congress to the states and approved in 1791.

The two clauses of the First Amendment that deal with religion
read: "Congress shall make no law respecting an establishment of
religion, or prohibiting the free exercise thereof." These provisions
have since been made applicable, by judicial decisions, to state and
local governments. The establishment clause of the First Amendment was designed to ensure government neutrality among theistic
creeds, that is, among religions that acknowledge a belief in God.
But government neutrality was not required as between theistic religions, on the one hand, and nontheistic creeds that do not profess
a belief in God. There is evidence, indeed, that the First Amendment was intended to permit government encouragement of Christian sects, as distinguished from Judaism and other non-Christian
creeds, so long as neutrality was maintained by government toward
all Christian sects. Mr. Justice Joseph Story, who served on the
Supreme Court of the United States from 1811 to 1845 and who
was, incidentally, a leading Unitarian, described the historical meaning of the First Amendment:

> Probably at the time of the adoption of the constitution, and
> of the first amendment to it . . . the general if not the uni-
> versal sentiment in America was, that Christianity ought to
> receive encouragement from the state so far as was not incom-
> patible with the private rights of conscience and the freedom
> of religious worship. An attempt to level all religions, and to
> make it a matter of state policy to hold all in utter indifference,
> would have created universal disapprobation, if not universal in-
> dignation.
> But the duty of supporting religion, and especially the Chris-
> tian religion, is very different from the right to force the con-
> sciences of other men or to punish them for worshipping God

in the manner which they believe their accountability to him requires. . . . The rights of conscience are indeed, beyond the just reach of any human power. They are given by God, and cannot be encroached upon by human authority without a criminal disobedience of the precepts of natural as well as of revealed religion.

The real object of the amendment was not to countenance, much less to advance, Mahometanism, or Judaism, or infidelity, by prostrating Christianity; but to exclude all rivalry among Christian sects, and to prevent any national ecclesiastical establishment which should give to a hierarchy the exclusive patronage of the national government.[9]

It is clear, in any event, that government, pursuant to the establishment clause, could generate an atmosphere of public hospitality toward theistic religions in general so long as no official impartiality was shown toward any particular creed. Logically, nontheistic beliefs were not considered to be religions under the establishment clause of the First Amendment. Otherwise, an affirmation by government that there is a God would be a governmental preference, through the assertion of the essential truth of theism, of a combination of religious sects—i.e., those that believe in God—to the disparagement of those other religions which do not profess such a belief. On the contrary, rather than regarding theism and nontheism as merely variant religious sects within a broadly defined category of "religion," the establishment clause regarded theism as the common denominator of all religions and nontheism it considered not to be a religion at all. Government itself could profess a belief in God and, so long as a practical neutrality was maintained among the theistic sects, the neutrality command of the establishment clause would not be breached.

Under the free exercise clause, however, prohibiting an infringement of the free exercise of religion, it is clear that "religion" was always construed to include nontheistic beliefs. Thus, a Jew or a Mohammedan would be protected in the free exercise of his own non-Christian theistic belief, but so would an atheist or agnostic be protected from compulsion in the exercise of his nontheistic creed. The free exercise clause is of high importance. But the basic alteration of the status of religion under the Constitution has come about through the Supreme Court's interpretation of the establishment clause of the First Amendment.

The determinative question here is the definition of religion for purposes of the establishment clause. Beginning in 1961,[10] the Supreme Court of the United States has defined "religion" to include both theistic and nontheistic beliefs. Speaking for the Court in the 1961 case of Torcaso v. Watkins, Justice Hugo Black wrote, "Among religions in this country which do not teach what would commonly be considered a belief in the existence of God are Buddhism, Taoism, Ethical Culture, Secular Humanism and others."[11] Since then, the Court has applied the basic establishment clause rule of neutrality to this new definition of religion.[12] Thus, government is now required to maintain neutrality not only among theistic religions but also as between the two great classes of religion, the theistic and the nontheistic.

But, as the Supreme Court's rulings in the past decade indicate, this neutrality is practically impossible of achievement. In the school prayer cases in 1962 and 1963, for example, the Supreme Court enjoined upon government a perpetual suspension of judgment on the very question of whether God exists. In the first decision[13] the Court invalidated the recitation in public schools of the state-composed regents' prayer, and in the second ruling[14] the court forbade the recitation of the Lord's Prayer and devotional reading of the Bible in public schools. In neither case was any child compelled to participate in the exercise. In his seventy-four-page concurring opinion in the 1963 case, Justice William Brennan strained to demonstrate that the decision did not foreshadow further extreme rulings. He argued that the ruling did not require such things as the erasure of God's name from our coinage, the repeal of the national motto, etc. But the basic rationale of the decision was epitomized in his comment on the words "under God" in the pledge of allegiance: "The reference to divinity in the revised Pledge of Allegiance, for example, may merely recognize the historical fact that our nation was believed to have been founded 'under God.'" The pledge, in Justice Brennan's view, is merely one of "the various patriotic exercises and activities used in the public schools and elsewhere which, whatever may have been their origins, no longer have a religious purpose or meaning."[15] In short, the words "under God" can remain in the pledge only if they are not meant to be believed, if they are a mere historical commemoration of the fact that the founders, deprived of the insight of the ruling justices, actually believed that this nation was "under God." It is clear, too, that the suspension of judgment on the question of whether God exists involves a governmental preference of agnosticism, the belief that the existence of God is unknown or unknow-able.

The establishment of agnosticism as the national religion has an impact on parochial schools that receive government aid. It is a settled principle that the recipient of a public subsidy will be bound by constitutional restrictions which bind the subsidizing govern-ment, at least where the subsidy involves substantial government supervision over the use of the grant.[16] The principle is that there is no such thing as a free lunch.

This principle is applicable to private schools receiving govern-ment subsidies. For instance, Roman Catholic schools in Brooklyn and elsewhere were allowed to participate in Operation Head Start only after they took the crucifixes off the classroom walls and eliminated sectarian and even moral instruction from the school day; it was only at the intercession of Sargent Shriver that the nuns were allowed to teach in their habits in their own schools. As Monsignor Eugene J. Molloy, superintendent of schools of the Diocese of Brooklyn, explained in a letter to the editor of the New York *Times* on July 8, 1965, the diocesan school system "has opened the doors of its nonpublic schools to this national effort. It has freely and gladly welcomed to its classrooms children of all faiths. With reluctance born of conviction that religious values are important in the welfare of the community, it has stripped those classrooms of religious symbols. It has formally pledged that, in order to cooperate with the community effort to meet an urgent need, no religious, much less sectarian, values or doctrines will be taught in this program." It is true that in Operation Head Start, unlike the ordinary case of public aid to religious schools, public school children came onto the parochial school premises to receive the special preschool instruction provided by the program. But this distinction has no enduring significance. For the courts are likely to hold, if they follow the school prayer decisions, that parochial schools receiving direct and substantial public aid are instrumental-ities of the state to the extent that they cannot prefer their own parishioners in their admission policies and therefore must open their doors to the community at large. At this point, the differences between public and parochial schools will be accidental.

The false neutrality between theism and nontheism has serious consequences for higher education as well. In the 1966 case of Horace Mann League *v.* Board of Public Works,[17] the highest court of Maryland held unconstitutional grants by the state legislature to three colleges because the schools were too religious in their orientation. At Notre Dame College, the court emphasized, "each class in the new science building would open with a prayer." The grant to St. Joseph College was invalid because its science building would contain "crucifixes, 'maybe' statues, and 'very likely' water-fonts." Western Maryland's difficulty was that "the image of the college in the community is strongly Methodist." A fourth grant to Hood College, however, was sustained because, despite its loose affiliation with the United Church of Christ, the college had become sufficiently sterilized of its former religious atmosphere. The Supreme Court declined to review the Horace Mann decision on its merits, but the lesson is clear from this and comparable examples. As state and federal subsidies to private schools increase, those schools at every level will be secularized. The conversion of Catholic colleges to secular control in order to qualify for government aid is a prime example of the impact of this principle on Catholic colleges that pursue government grants. But it is a principle that applies at all levels of education. Even the textbooks that can be provided to parochial school pupils under a 1968 ruling of the Supreme Court have to be "secular books" "approved by the public school authorities."[18]

In this textbook case, the court stressed that the "financial benefit" it allowed "is to parents and children, not to schools." This allowance of aid to the child and his parents may inferentially support the constitutionality of such indirect forms of aid as the tuition tax credit, tuition grant and voucher, discussed in Chapter IX. But, despite the allowance of textbooks and bus rides for parochial school children, the secularizing impact of the Supreme Court's school prayer decisions is unmistakable in many federal and state programs which now provide aid directly to Catholic schools.

When we speak of secularizing controls of course, we are not talking about the government regulations to which all schools are properly subject whether they receive public aid or not. Certain building, sanitary, curriculum, and certification requirements are in this category. But the secularizing controls go beyond these administrative requirements. Rather, they operate to prevent the school from achieving the very purpose for which it exists. They tend to minimize any difference in curriculum and atmosphere between the public and the Catholic school.

There was ample reason, therefore, for Catholics and other supporters of church-related schools to support the school prayer amendment,[19] introduced in Congress in 1962 and continually thereafter, to amend the Constitution to undo the school prayer decisions and their secularizing mandate. Yet it was the withholding of support by Catholic leaders that played a crucial role in defeating the amendment in 1964. When the Senate Judiciary Committee held hearings in 1962, four Catholic spokesmen, including the representative of Francis Cardinal Spellman of New York, supported the amendment and no Catholic leader opposed it. Two years later, however, when the House Judiciary Committee held its hearings, there were nine Catholics in favor of the amendment (but no representative of the hierarchy, with the exception of Bishop Fulton J. Sheen, whose testimony was coupled in press accounts with that of Governor George Wallace, who appeared the same day in favor of the amendment). But in those 1964 hearings, there were seventeen Catholic witnesses opposed, including spokesmen for many Catholic periodicals, the lay director of the Legal Department of the National Catholic Welfare Conference, and a couple of lawyer-priests, including the Reverend Robert F. Drinan, S.J., dean of Boston College Law School, who was elected to Congress from Massachusetts in November 1970.

The rise in Catholic opposition to the amendment was apparently due in part to an unfounded fear that a prayer amendment would unsettle the existing interpretations of the First Amendment which tend to favor the constitutionality of some forms of federal aid to church-related schools. Also, the opposition might well have stemmed from a reluctance to antagonize some non-Catholic groups whose support might be necessary to procure the enactment of a major program of federal aid.[20] Since then, the Church has received federal aid for its schools, under the Elementary and Secondary Education Act of 1965 and other enactments. But that aid has not solved the problems of those schools. They are still financially hard-pressed. And the acceptance of government grants to parochial schools has made the government and the Church partners in the overall educational enterprise. Also, the extension of aid directly from government to school, instead of through the parents under a tuition tax credit or similar device, increases the identity of interest between the federal officialdom and the clerical bureaucracy which manages the parochial schools on a national level. It should not be surprising, then, if Church criticism of government on other issues is muted. The conclusion is justified that the Church would act more forcefully on abortion and other primary issues if she were not subtly indebted to the government of which she is a patronage client.

It would serve the interest of the Church and of the nation as well if the bishops would insist that the pattern of public aid to parochial schools be changed from the direct subsidy given to the school to the more sensible technique of a tuition tax credit, tuition grant or voucher. This would put the control of education where it belongs, with the parents rather than with the educational bureaucracies of church or state. At the same time, the national bishops ought to insist more forcefully that the extension of government aid, whether to the parents or to the schools, gives no warrant to the public authorities to drain those schools of their religious significance. In educating their children parents are conferring a benefit upon the state as well as upon the children. They are entitled to reasonable state support in this endeavor and the state has no right to deny them such support if they prefer their children to have a religious education. As the Supreme Court of the United States noted in the landmark Everson case in 1947:

On the other hand, other language of the amendment commands that New Jersey cannot hamper its citizens in the free exercise of their own religion. Consequently, it cannot exclude individual Catholics, Lutherans, Mohammedans, Baptists, Jews, Methodists, Non-believers, Presbyterians, or the members of any other faith, *because of their faith or lack of it*, from receiving the benefit of public welfare legislation.[21] (Emphasis in original)

This equality of treatment is a plain dictate of the free exercise clause of the First Amendment. It ought to prevail over what Justice Potter Stewart has aptly termed the Supreme Court's "insensitive and sterile construction of the Establishment Clause."[22] One way to enforce this principle of equality would be to support an amendment to the United States Constitution to reverse the secularistic postulates of the school prayer decisions.

A Misdirected Pluralism

The philosophical reason for the bishops' ineffective response to the secularization of American society involves the question of pluralism. Until Vatican II, the most widely held Catholic position on church-state relations maintained, in the words of Monsignor John A. Ryan, former director of the Social Action Department of the National Catholic Welfare Conference, that

the State should officially recognize the Catholic religion as the religion of the commonwealth; accordingly it should invite the blessing and the ceremonial participation of the Church for certain important public functions, as the opening of legislative sessions, the erection of public buildings, etc., and delegate its officials to attend certain of the more important festival celebrations of the Church; it should recognize and sanction the laws of the Church, and the religious as well as the other rights of the Church's members.[23]

This position found some support in statements by Pius XI, Pius XII, and especially Leo XIII. This "confessional state," however, could be fully achieved only in the "completely Catholic state," that is, "a political community that is exclusively, or almost exclusively, made up of Catholics."[24] In this state, non-Catholics would not be compelled to join the Church and non-Catholic worship would be permitted in such a way "as to be an occasion neither of scandal nor of perversion to the faithful."[25] This ideal of the confessional state was said to be the thesis, as distinguished from the hypothesis, a less desirable situation the Church would tolerate so long as she could not bring about the thesis in a given country.[26]

The theoretical goal of the confessional state embarrassed some American Catholics and caused some non-Catholics to discount the Church's professions of faith in the American system. The acceptance by Catholics of the traditional position implied to some that Catholics would endure the constitutional guarantees of religious freedom only until they were strong enough to overturn them and make the Catholic Church the official established American Church.

Father John Courtney Murray, S.J., who died in 1967, provided the rationale by which a successful challenge was finally made to the basic assumption of the traditional theory.[27] What Father Murray did was to reject the notion of the confessional state as the ideal thesis to be sought by Catholics as an ultimate goal. Rather, he said, the confessional state was merely a hypothesis, a temporary expedient that could be justified only in certain countries at certain times. To replace the confessional state as the thesis and unchanging ideal, Father Murray proposed three "transtemporal" and "controlling" principles:

> (a) The first principle is that of the freedom of the Church. The formula has two senses . . . as the spiritual power—her freedom to teach, rule and sanctify, with all that these powers imply as necessary for their free exercise. And . . . as the Christian people—their freedom to hearken to the doctrine of the Church, obey her laws. . . .
>
> (b) The second principle is that of the necessary harmony between the two laws, [i.e., religious and secular] whereby the life of man is governed, and between the whole complex of social institutions and the exigencies of the Christian conscience. . . .
>
> (c) The third principle is that of the necessary cooperation of the Church and state—a cooperation that is ordered and bilateral.[28]

These principles, freedom of the Church, harmony and cooperation were derived by Father Murray from divine positive law. Though capable of varied applications in different times and places, they were asserted by him as unchanging in principle.

Father Murray laid great stress on the free exercise of religion, emphasizing particularly the primary importance of freedom of conscience. There is a close parallel here between his approach and the original intent of the First Amendment to the United States Constitution. It is significant, too, that Father Murray was the main architect of Vatican II's Declaration on Religious Freedom. For the Declaration placed, among "the values proper to the human spirit . . . in the first place, the free exercise of religion in society."[29] The Declaration's harmony with the free exercise clause of the First Amendment is further seen in its dictum, "that all men are to be immune from coercion on the part of individuals or of social groups and of any human power, in such wise that in matters religious no one is to be forced to act in a manner contrary to his own beliefs. Nor is anyone to be restrained from acting in accordance with his own beliefs, whether privately or publicly, whether alone or in association with others, within due limits."[30] While this right is not absolute, it cannot be regarded as a temporary expedient. Rather, it "has its foundation in the very dignity of the human person as this dignity is known through the revealed Word of God and by reason itself."[31]

While Vatican II clearly recognized the right of every person to the free exercise of religion, it was less clear on the question of establishment of religion. The Declaration on Religious Freedom apparently demoted the confessional state to the level of a hypothesis, saying that a legal preference of "one religious body" would be authorized if it were required "in view of peculiar circumstances obtaining among certain peoples" and provided that the free exercise of religion were adequately protected.[32] On December 9, 1965, two days after the Declaration was adopted, Pope Paul VI acknowledged "the renunciation by the Church of a condition of legal privilege in society. The Church does not make, as a matter of right or of divine law, the claim that she should be established as the 'religion of the state.' Her claim is freedom, nothing more."[33] The Pope here was rephrasing the statement of the Declaration that "the Freedom of the Church is the fundamental principle in what concerns the relations between the Church and governments and the whole civil order."[34] This, in turn, is simply a restatement of Father Murray's first "controlling" principle.

While the Declaration on Religious Freedom exalted the free exercise of religion and demoted the confessional state to the level of a hypothesis to be justified in peculiar circumstances rather than a thesis to be sought as an unchanging ideal, it left undetermined the important issue of the duty of the state to worship God. The Declaration did say that "it leaves untouched traditional Catholic doctrine on the moral duty of men and societies toward the true religion and toward the one Church of Christ."[35] But the meaning of that duty was not spelled out by the Council.

This is the crucial issue in the United States—the capacity and duty of the state to recognize and affirm the existence of God. As we have noted above, the Supreme Court has required that government maintain neutrality toward all religions and as between theistic and nontheistic religions. This corresponds closely to the position taken by Father Murray. While affirming the sovereignty of God over American society, Father Murray distinguished society from the state and he limited the state to secular functions. Under the Constitution, in his opinion, "the area of state—that is, legal—concern was limited to the pursuit of certain enumerated secular purposes (to say that the purposes are secular is not to deny that many of them are also moral; so for instance the establishment of justice and peace, the promotion of the general welfare, etc.). Thus made autonomous in its own sphere, government was denied all competence in the field of religion. In this field freedom was to be the rule and method; government was powerless to legislate respecting an establishment of religion and likewise powerless to prohibit the free exercise of religion. Its single office was to take legal or judicial steps necessary on given occasions to make effective the general guarantee of freedom."[36]

The state, in the Murray view, was secularized, desanctified, incapable of elevation by grace and incompetent to recognize God. He regarded the state as a secular and functional "set of institutions." And, of course, he regarded the "confessional state," with its governmental preference of Catholicism, as inapplicable to the United States. But Father Murray carefully distinguished the "lay" state, "such as the American which makes no absolutistic claims and does not oppose religion," from the "laic" state, "such as the late nineteenth-century French state which asserted the state's competence in religion."[37] In the American system, according to Father Murray, the state and government, as distinguished from society, are to be separate from the Church and neutral on all matters of religion. The Church's only influence on public affairs would be through the "indirect power" exerted by its citizens who would seek to infuse Catholic moral principles into law and public policy. Through this action of individual Catholics in behalf of public morality, Father Murray believed that a working relationship between Church and State would be created, pursuant to the "unchanging" principles of freedom of the Church, harmony and cooperation. It is in this context that we should understand Father Murray's stress on the "pluralist" character of American society and on the need for "consensus": "By pluralism here I mean the coexistence within the one political community of groups who hold incompatible views with regard to religious questions. . . . Pluralism therefore implies disagreement and dissension within the community. But it also implies a community within which there must be agreement and consensus."[38]

Father Murray believed the "indirect power" of the Church, working on the consciences of the faithful, would be a real force moving them to translate their beliefs into individual public action. Unfortunately, there is an evident reluctance on the part of some Catholics to carry the teachings of the Church into public life. When Governor John A. Burns of Hawaii refused to veto that state's permissive abortion law, he said he would not allow his Catholic beliefs to influence his actions as a public official.[39] Father Murray would hardly approve such reluctance. But we may fairly wonder whether the reluctance of some to apply the teachings of the Church in public life is not an unintended by-product of his rigid distinction between society and the state and his emphasis on the secular character of the latter. Some Catholics tend to slide from the proposition that the Church has no right to impose its beliefs on others to the indefensible position that Catholics should hesitate to advance even positions which are amply justified on secular grounds, when those positions happen to coincide with the teaching of the Church. It is feared that their advancement will be criticized by the opposition as an illicit intrusion of religion into the affairs of the state. It is reasonable to ask whether this timidity is not bred from a mating of the lay state and Father Murray's "consensus." The general need for consensus is clear. But consensus of itself is not the primary end. Also, if we would preserve religious liberty, we must reach a point where we are prepared at all costs to resist the prevailing consensus. While he did not regard consensus as an absolute, it is fair to say that Father Murray did give it a prominence which opened the door to overemphasis.

While the National Conference of Catholic Bishops has strongly protested the expansion of federal birth control programs, the character of the bishops' response lends credence to the assessment by Democratic Congressman Paul Rogers, of Florida, that the bishops "just want to be on the record against the bill. I see no efforts to really strongly oppose the legislation."[40] Abortion, of course, is the ultimately indispensable technique of the population control and family planning movements. If the bishops will not oppose abortion, with moral and political power as well as words, all the fancy parochial school buildings and language laboratories in the world will count for nothing. Unfortunately, however, the present tendency is for the Church in America to renounce its duty in exchange for a modus vivendi with the secular state from which it draws its patronage in the form of money and acceptance.

The Remedies

In the foregoing discussion, we have seen that the reason for the American Church's default in confronting the anti-life society is twofold—both practical and philosophical. It is financial pressure on the one hand, and the influence of a misdirected pluralism on the other. But, as the reason for the default is both practical and philosophical, so are the remedies.

Practical Forms of Aid

On the practical level, there are several steps that can be taken by the nation's bishops to preserve the independence of the Church and to reverse the anti-life trend. For one thing, no measure would more enhance the Church's freedom, and her capacity to oppose evil, than a clear insistence by the bishops, as a national body, that:

1. The parents of children in church-related schools are entitled to public aid for the service they render the state in educating their children;
2. That such aid must be limited to forms that will not compromise the independence and religious character of those schools.

The most desirable form of such aid would be a tuition tax credit supplemented by a GI Bill type grant to parents who make insufficient income to benefit from the tax credit. The tax credit should apply to tuition paid to academically qualified private schools, whether church-related or not. If the law were to provide for a tax credit, up to $400, for tuition paid, the taxpayer would figure his federal income tax payable and would then subtract $400, or whatever lesser amount he paid for tuition, from his tax payable. Where parents make insufficient income to benefit from a tax credit, a GI Bill type grant up to $400 should be made to those parents for tuition paid. The program would thus open the doors of private and other church-related schools to the poor. This grant could be accomplished at little administrative expense. The taxpayer on his federal income-tax form would note the tuition he has paid during the year and his reimbursement could be made without creating any new governmental bureaucracy. If he paid $400 tuition and his total tax owed were $50, he would pay no tax and the revenue service would "refund" to him $350.

The schools would benefit from such a program through charging tuition or raising existing tuition to take advantage of the tax credit. The tax credit program would not entail significant government controls over the schools because, unlike direct government grants to the schools, the tuition money the schools would receive would never have been government money. Even the GI Bill type grants to the parents would not entail substantial control over the schools to whom the parents had paid tuition. As with the GI Bill for military veterans, the government's control would be limited to ascertaining that the school is qualified by objective academic criteria.[41] Senator Abraham Ribicoff from Connecticut and others have proposed a tax credit for college tuition and expenses.[42] His plan would ensure diversity and strength in college education and it should be enacted. But it is urgent, too, that a similar concept be applied to primary and secondary levels of education.

An alternative to the tuition tax credit/GI Bill at the elementary and secondary levels would be a straight tuition grant. This measure, sometimes called the GI Bill for Junior, has been widely proposed, particularly at the federal level. It would involve a direct government grant to parents to be used to pay tuition at any private school, whether church-related or not. It would be similar in its effects to the tuition tax credit plan outlined above, and would not entail an undue risk of government control of the schools at which the parents choose to spend their tuition grant. The tuition tax credit, however, could be administered more simply.

A third alternative, similar to the straight tuition grant, would be the voucher system, as proposed by economist Milton Friedman and others. Here the state would issue a tuition voucher redeemable at any qualified elementary or secondary school, public, private, or parochial. The voucher would be in the amount of the state's per capita expenditure on public-school education. The voucher system could bring a greater volume of aid to parochial schools, since it would be keyed to the relatively high cost per pupil of educating a child in the public schools. However, the public school system in the United States is basically financed at the state and local levels. Unlike the tuition tax credit or GI Bill tuition grant, which could more feasibly be enacted at the federal level, the introduction of a voucher system would more appropriately require separate legislative action in each state.

Any of these plans, the combined tuition tax credit/GI Bill, the straight GI Bill type grant or the voucher system would promote a desirable competition between the public and private school systems. It would guarantee parental freedom of choice to parents of all races and all creeds and it would extend that freedom to lower-income parents who today have no alternative to the public schools. Also, it would further the course of sound, orthodox teaching in Catholic schools, since parents would have the means to initiate private schools where parish schools fail to teach authentic doctrine.

It is not unrealistic to hope that one of these programs can be enacted. The recent trend is strongly in favor of government aid to church-related and other private schools at both the federal and state levels. In 1965 Congress provided large-scale support to those schools in the Elementary and Secondary Education Act. Since 1968 at least six states have extended substantial cash aid directly to parochial schools. At least twenty-seven states offer services free of charge to private schools—mostly bussing, but also including aid such as textbooks, hot lunches, and health care. A dozen states have formally approved "dual enrollment," enabling parochial schools to cut expenses by sending pupils to public schools part time for some subjects. Hawaii offers a small tax credit to families with school-age children.[43]

Clearly the main motive for this growing aid is economic. Parochial schools provide a substantial saving to the taxpayers, who are thereby relieved of the cost of educating parochial school students in the public schools. In 1969 it was calculated that the forty-two thousand students in the Catholic schools of the two dioceses of New York and Brooklyn alone represented a saving to the taxpayer of over $500 million, since in New York City and the surrounding suburbs the average per pupil figure for public education is at least $1250.[44] For education is less expensive in church-affiliated schools than in public schools. In the spring of 1969 the entire Catholic school system of Helena, Montana, was closed. More than three hundred elementary and six hundred high school students went into Helena's public school system, an enrollment jump of fifteen percent. In Helena the public high school per pupil costs are $639 per year and elementary per pupil costs $553. Per pupil costs in the Catholic schools were $442 for high school and $154 for elementary schools.[45] Comparative cost figures from other places are similar in their effect. Surely the most profitable course for the taxpayer is to extend some relief to the parents of parochial students, who have to pay full taxes for the public schools they do not use. Failing a public assumption of part of the cost of educating parochial school children, the taxpayers will pick up the entire bill when those children are forced into the public schools.

Similar considerations apply to Church-related colleges. There has never been a more opportune time for the bishops to advance the basic right of parents over the education of their children at every level and to break the pattern of public aid which neutralizes Catholic schools while ostensibly supporting them.

To Defend the Child in the Womb

A second practical step that could be taken by the bishops would be to toughen their stand against abortion. The Catholic Church alone can provide the leadership to reverse the growing hostility of American law toward innocent life. No human being is more innocent and helpless than the child in the womb. If the Church, the natural protector of the defenseless, will not rally fiercely to his aid, there is little hope that his life will be protected by anyone else. Because of the rapidity with which abortion is becoming an accepted part of American life, the situation requires more from the bishops than jeremiads. We are entitled, instead, to expect that the bishops, as a national body, will consider doing the following:

1. *Formally repudiate the theory advanced by some that Catholics should cooperate in repealing laws forbidding abortion.* The most prominent advocate of this view is Jesuit Father now Congressman, Robert F. Drinan. He bases his argument on the erroneous assumption that repeal of all prohibitions against abortion would reduce the total number of abortions. But even if it would, Father Drinan's position is still indefensible. Instead of resisting the killing of innocent children he would have the Church sit down with those who would authorize abortion so as to work out more efficient ways to process the slaughter. The bishops should specify that no Catholic may in good conscience maintain this position, since it involves an active cooperation with the intrinsic evil of abortion. This repudiation of the Drinan position is important, for the growing acceptance of his erroneous view has contributed to the fragmentation of the hitherto solid Catholic front against abortion.[46]

2. *Declare that no Catholic legislator or member of the executive branch, on both the federal and state levels, may in good conscience support or vote for relaxation of abortion laws.*

This ought not to include judges as a general rule, since courts generally do not consider abortion from a policy standpoint. When a judge rules that a certain law is void or unenforceable because of conflict with an overriding statutory or constitutional standard, he is usually not articulating his own view as to the wisdom or morality of abortion as such. There may be exceptions, but the judge in his function is to be distinguished from the legislator or governor who urges or votes for repeal of prohibitions against abortion on the ground that the prohibition is undesirable as a matter of policy or wisdom. Excommunication or other appropriate sanctions should be applied to Catholic legislators and members of the executive branch who do urge or support repeal of abortion prohibitions. Canon Law provides a penalty of excommunication, or deposition for a cleric, for those who procure an abortion, not excepting the mother.[47] It is worth considering whether a public official who urges that abortion be freely permitted, and who acts in his official capacity so as to make that permission a fact, is not himself an instigator of abortion within the meaning of those canons under which certain cooperators in a crime incur guilt for it.[48]

3. *Declare that no Catholic may in good conscience vote for any legislator or member of the executive branch who supports or votes for a relaxation of the abortion laws.* This should apply to such officials and legislators regardless of their stand on such issues as aid to parochial schools. Abortion is the crucial question in determining the future of America. It is time that Catholics acted in concert to shape that future by political retaliation against those who would jeopardize it by their votes.

4. *Declare that all Catholic legislators and members of the executive branch are bound in conscience to work for and enforce effective prohibitions against abortion in all states.* It is no longer adequate for a legislator to refrain from voting for the destruction of children in the womb. Rather, there is an affirmative duty to support the right to live by seeking effective protections for it.

5. *Declare that Catholic businessmen are bound in conscience to withdraw advertising, where it is within their power and right to do so, from publications that support abortion.* The adverse posture of much of the mass media has been a real obstacle blocking a restoration of respect for life. While maintaining due respect for contractual obligations, there is no reason why Catholics should voluntarily subsidize the promoters of anti-life policies.

6. *Declare that all Catholics are bound in conscience to support an amendment to make the United States Constitution's guarantees of due process of law and the equal protection of the laws applicable to the unborn child.* This could be done by inserting "from the moment of conception" into the relevant clauses of the Fifth and Fourteenth Amendments. For example, "No person, *from the moment of conception,* shall be . . . deprived of life, liberty or property, without due process of law." And, "nor shall any State deprive any person, *from the moment of conception,* of life, liberty or property, without due process of law; nor deny to any person, *from the moment of conception,* within its jurisdiction the equal protection of the laws." Under any proper construction, the Constitution already gives this protection to the child in the womb. But it ought to be made specific for two reasons: First, to prevent any possible misconstruction that would permit the child in the womb, unlike his elder brethren, to be killed for the convenience of others. Second, and more important, to serve an educational purpose through the campaign for amendment to carry the issue clearly to the American people and to force them to a choice. Unlike the citizens of Nazi Germany, the American people have the political capacity to stop the slaughter of the innocents. Whether they will summon the conviction and energy to do so is a doubtful question. But clearly it is the duty of the American bishops to remind the people of the injustice they condone and of their capacity to root it out. A campaign of education in support of this constitutional amendment would awaken many people to the realities of which they are presently unaware. But perhaps the American people, having the choice, will refuse to act. In that case, the responsibility will at least rest where it properly belongs and the Church will not be to blame. For if the bishops ignore the opportunity to educate the people and to change our law to protect innocent life, then those bishops will be implicated in the outcome.

Unfortunately, there is no indication at this writing that the bishops, as a national body, will take any of these proposed actions. It is clear, instead, that the burden of promoting effective respect for life will rest upon the laity. Lacking effective leadership from the bishops, Catholic laymen can still take significant action themselves. Every legislator and governor who supports abortion should be opposed by a candidate who is willing and able to challenge him directly on this issue. If the candidates of the established political parties will not do it without equivocation, independent candidates should be placed on the ballot under the name of the Right-to-Life Party, or some other suitable name, to seek the defeat of every incumbent or aspirant who will not commit himself to oppose abortion. State election laws provide various means to qualify independent candidates for election to state legislatures, governorships, and the United States Congress. In fact, if the means prove available, and if both the Republican and Democratic candidates favor abortion, consideration might well be given to running a candidate for president on the single issue of support for the right of innocent children to live. Secondly, the amendment to the United States Constitution discussed above should be promoted. Every candidate for the state legislature and for Congress should be opposed if he will not commit himself unambiguously to support such an amendment.

A New Pluralism

These, then, are two practical approaches that could be taken by the bishops—to preserve the independence of Church-related schools and to protect the lives of innocent children. But decisive action on the practical level is unlikely to have a lasting impact unless it is accompanied by a reorientation of view by the bishops on the philosophical plane. The most important thing that could be done by the bishops here would be to free themselves of the disabling concept of pluralism espoused by Father John Courtney Murray. This would not involve a diminution of Father Murray's personal stature or a disparagement of his contributions in other respects to theology, philosophy, and jurisprudence. All it would involve would be a realization that the Murray theory of the wholly secular state has not worked in America. Instead, it has facilitated the growth of a public policy hostile in major respects to religious and moral values and to the independence of the Church.

To repudiate Father Murray's notion of the secular state would not imply that the bishops favor the establishment of the Catholic Church as the official church of the United States. Rather, there is a middle ground which would be consistent with the American system as conceived by its founders and which would promote that freedom of the Church, harmony and cooperation which Father Murray primarily sought. Under this middle approach, government would prefer theistic religion and would encourage theistic religious organizations. Government would be required, under the establishment clause of the First Amendment, to maintain neutrality in its support of religion. It would have to treat all theistic denominations equally but it would not have to bestow its favors equally on nontheistic groups as well. The free exercise of religion of all, including nontheists, would be protected by the free-exercise clause of the First Amendment as presently construed. This free exercise, moreover, would include the right of nontheists to propagandize and promote their religions publicly.

This middle ground would seem to be consistent with Catholic teaching. It would differ from the old confessional-state concept in that the government would prefer theism in general rather than Catholicism in particular. But it would not require a renunciation in principle of the theory that, in a Catholic society, the Catholic Church could be the official Church where such is dictated by circumstances. The Church in America would be free to set about her task of converting America in a condition of free competition among religions.

The affirmation of a government power to prefer theism would recognize that as between theism and nontheism government cannot be neutral without preferring the agnosticism which is itself a form of nontheistic religion. It would put a stop to the establishment of secularism as the national religion. And it would preserve an authentic dualism between Church and state. An attitude of impartial hospitality on the part of the state toward all theistic sects, with protection for the free exercise of religion of all would stop the erosion of Church independence under the pressure of a subsidizing secular state. And it would, coincidentally, advance the freedom of the Church, harmony and cooperation which Father Murray primarily sought to promote.

XII.

CONCLUSION

We see with amazement how many sane and honest citizens, even wise and respected teachers and responsible public men, cannot find in themselves the energy to defend and revive intelligently a patrimony of civilization won by immense sacrifices and available to the enjoyment of all; the energy to save society, and especially future generations, from the consequences of useless and ruinous material and moral destruction.[1]

The paralysis to which the Pope refers is an affliction of the spirit. It crosses national and sectarian lines. It has paved the way for the dominance of the anti-life mentality. And it has undermined the respect for authority which is essential to the cohesion of both the religious and secular orders. The growing disrespect for authority is only one aspect of the general crisis of the spirit. And the authority problem in the Church is a smaller part of it still. But the revolt against authority in the Church is of critical importance. Her internal disarray has impeded the Church from giving to the world the leadership she alone can provide in the face of the rising anti-life tendencies. Also, any efforts to rekindle respect for authority in society at large will be in vain unless that respect is renewed within the Church as well.

In this brief chapter, in the nature of a postscript, there is no need to summarize what has been said before. Instead, it will be helpful here to emphasize three final points.

The first point is that, in seeking to promote respect for authority in the Church, we must be careful to maintain our balance. On the one hand we should avoid the fearful and defensive attitude that would confuse former customs with the authentic teaching or tradition of the Church. "Some Catholics," said Cardinal Daniélou, "assume a too anxious attitude, every time there is a discussion of some exegetical problem or some formulation of the faith, and they regard it as an immediate threat to the substance of what they believe."[2] The Church is not so fragile that she must close the door to every speculative current of thought. Instead, there is a broad area for legitimate discussion and opinion. It is the task of the teaching Church to mark the boundaries of that area. And we can safely rely on her to do so. Of course, on the other hand, we must not be counted among the elite who excuse themselves from the discipline of the Church. The Reverend Philip Hughes, in discussing the appearance of prideful "elite" groups of Christians in the first two centuries after Christ, remarked on the recurrent appearance, throughout the entire history of the Church, of "Catholics who propose to explain Catholicism by synthesis with the intellectual life of the time, Catholics who look back from the difficulties of the moment to the happy time of a far-off golden age of primitive faith, Catholics who turn from an official teaching that does not encourage their personal likings to an alleged private inspiration that sets them apart from the ordinary discipline."[3] At this time particularly, the influence of such recalcitrants can impede the Church's performance of her mission.

The second point in this chapter is that the upholding of orthodoxy in the Church requires more than argument or learning. Rather, an interior redirection is of first importance. "The Church needs to put the Council into practice," Paul VI has said. But each person, according to the Pope, "must begin the work of reforming and purifying the Church by reforming and purifying himself; he must strive to conform himself to the Gospel before requiring others to do so; he should search his own heart before questioning others."[4] The Popes and the Councils have shown the way for the Church. We can do our part if we follow them to the best of our ability; if we learn the case for her teachings and present that case to others; and, especially, if we pray.

Finally, for the third point here, we should be optimistic about the Church. Of course, we know she will survive for all time. But we also can be sure that she will stand firm against the degenerate forces of anti-life. Malcolm Muggeridge once explained, "Why I Am Not a Catholic," as owing to his belief that "the Roman Catholic Church as an institution seems to me fated to join the Gadarene slide on which our civilization is clearly set. . . . Through the hightide of scientific utopianism the Roman Church held splendidly aloof; now that this utopianism is discredited and at its last gasp, suddenly and inexplicably the Church is under increasing pressure to come forward as its half-hearted and faltering champion."

The Catholic Church, concluded Muggeridge, "will be carried stage by stage, as the Protestant Churches have been, to relinquish all its positions. Married priests, lipstick nuns, permissive marriage, sanctified adultery, divorce and abortion, Catholic schools and colleges producing the same yahoos as non-Catholic ones—it will all happen, is happening."[5]

Superficially, the Church seems to be faltering. And the rebellion against her authority is real. But she herself is steady. Under the guidance of the Pope and the bishops teaching in communion with him, she will surely preserve the faith. But she will do more. She will confirm the prediction of Archbishop John Murphy of Cardiff, Wales, that only the Church will stand against the world of "1984":

> It is the Church which fights for the unborn child, for the rights of parents to educate their children, for the dignity of the marriage contract, for the dignity of the individual being. And in some secular humanistic future, when the only sin will be pain, the only evil ill health; when childbearing will be looked upon as a disease, and terminal illnesses will not be tolerated, when it is just possible that the free, human beings will be forbidden to have a child, or a smoke, or a drink, save by prescription of the National Health; in that cold, clinical future, you will search in vain for the rebels save in the ranks of the Catholic Church.

The Church will resist effectively only when, through a regeneration of faith and obedience, its members close ranks behind the Pope and the authentic teaching authority of the Church. But she will do more than resist. The Church will show the way to restore a civil society respectful of the person and of life itself. And this leadership of the Church, in restoring morality to the civil order, will be in keeping with the opening words of the *Dogmatic Constitution on the Church:* "Christ is the Light of nations."[6]

APPENDIX

Proclaimed by the Holy Father
at the Closing
of the Year of Faith, June 30, 1968

VENERABLE BROTHERS
AND BELOVED SONS,

With this solemn liturgy We end the celebration of the nineteenth centenary of the martyrdom of the holy Apostles Peter and Paul, and thus close the Year of Faith. We dedicated it to the commemoration of the holy Apostles in order that We might give witness to Our steadfast will to be faithful to the Deposit of the faith[1] which they transmitted to Us, and that We might strengthen Our desire to live by it in the historical circumstances in which the Church finds herself in her pilgrimage in the midst of the world.

We feel it Our duty to give public thanks to all who responded to Our invitation by bestowing on the Year of Faith a splendid completeness through the deepening of their personal adhesion to the Word of God, through the renewal in various communities of the profession of faith, and through the testimony of a Christian life. To Our Brothers in the Episcopate especially; and to all the faithful of the Holy Catholic Church We express Our appreciation and We grant Our blessing.

Likewise We deem that We must fulfill the mandate entrusted by Christ to Peter, whose successor We are, the last in merit; namely, to confirm Our brothers in the faith.[2] With the awareness, certainly, of Our human weakness, yet with all the strength impressed on Our spirit by such a command, We shall accordingly make a profession of faith, pronounce a creed which, without being strictly speaking a dogmatic definition, repeats in substance, with some developments called for by the spiritual condition of our time, the creed of Nicaea, the creed of the immortal Tradition of the Holy Church of God.

In making this profession, We are aware of the disquiet which agitates certain modern quarters with regard to the faith. They do not escape the influence of a world being profoundly changed, in which so many certainties are being disputed or discussed. We see even Catholics allowing themselves to be seized by a kind of passion for change and novelty. The Church, most assuredly, has always the duty to carry on the effort to study more deeply and to present in a manner ever better adapted to successive generations the unfathomable mysteries of God, rich for all in fruits of salvation. But at the same time the greatest care must be taken, while fulfilling the indispensable duty of research, to do no injury to the teachings of Christian doctrine. For that would be to give rise, as is unfortunately seen in these days, to disturbance and perplexity in many faithful souls.

It is important in this respect to recall that, beyond scientifically verified phenomena, the intellect which God has given us reaches that which is, and not merely the subjective expression of the structures and development of consciousness; and, on the other hand, that the task of interpretation—of hermeneutics—is to try to understand and extricate, while respecting the word expressed, the sense conveyed by a text, and not to re-create, in some fashion, this sense in accordance with arbitrary hypotheses.

But above all, We place Our unshakable confidence in the Holy Spirit, the soul of the Church, and in theological faith upon which rests the life of the Mystical Body. We know that souls await the word of the Vicar of Christ, and We respond to that expectation with the instructions which We regularly give. But today We are given an opportunity to make a more solemn utterance.

On this day which is chosen to close the Year of Faith, on this Feast of the Blessed Apostles Peter and Paul, We have wished to offer to the Living God the homage of a profession of faith. And as once at Caesarea Philippi the Apostle Peter spoke on behalf of the Twelve to make a true confession, beyond human opinions, of Christ as Son of the Living God, so today his humble Successor, Pastor of the Universal Church, raises his voice to give, on behalf of all the People of God, a firm witness to the divine Truth entrusted to the Church to be announced to all nations.

We have wished Our profession of faith to be to a high degree complete and explicit, in order that it may respond in a fitting way to the need of light felt by so many faithful souls, and by all those in the world, to whatever spiritual family they belong, who are in search of the Truth.

To the glory of God Most Holy and of Our Lord Jesus Christ, trusting in the aid of the Blessed Virgin Mary and of the Holy Apostles Peter and Paul, for the profit and edification of the Church, in the name of all the Pastors and all the faithful, We now pronounce this profession of faith, in full spiritual communion with you all, beloved Brothers and Sons.

PROFESSION OF FAITH

We believe in one only God, Father, Son and Holy Spirit, Creator of things visible such as this world in which our transient life passes, of things invisible such as the pure spirits which are also called angels,[3] and Creator in each man of his spiritual and immortal soul.

We believe that this only God is absolutely one in His infinitely holy essence as also in all His perfections, in His omnipotence, His infinite knowledge, His providence, His will and His love. He is He Who Is, as He revealed to Moses[4]; and He is Love, as the Apostle John teaches us[5]: so that these two names, Being and Love, express ineffably the same divine Reality of Him Who has wished to make Himself known to us, and Who "dwelling in light inaccessible,"[6] is in Himself above every name, above every thing and above every created intellect. God alone can give us right and full knowledge of this Reality by revealing Himself as Father, Son and Holy Spirit, in Whose Eternal Life we are by grace called to share, here below in the obscurity of faith and after death in eternal light. The mutual bonds which eternally constitute the Three Persons, Who are each one and the same Divine Being, are the blessed inmost life of God Thrice Holy, infinitely beyond all that we can conceive in human measure.[7] We give thanks, however, to the Divine Goodness that very many believers can testify with us before men to the Unity of God, even though they know not the Mystery of the Most Holy Trinity.

THE FATHER

We believe then in the Father who eternally begets the Son, in the Son, the Word of God, who is eternally begotten, in the Holy Spirit, the uncreated Person who proceeds from the Father and the Son as their eternal Love. Thus in the Three Divine Persons, *coaeternae sibi et coaequales*,[8] the life and beatitude of God perfectly One superabound and are consummated in the supreme excellence and glory proper to uncreated Being, and always, "there should be venerated Unity in the Trinity and Trinity in the Unity."[9]

THE SON

We believe in Our Lord Jesus Christ, Who is the Son of God. He is the Eternal Word, born of the Father before time began, and one in substance with the Father, *homoousios to Patri*,[10] and through Him all things were made. He was incarnate of the Virgin Mary by the power of the Holy Spirit, and was made man: equal therefore to the Father according to His divinity, and inferior to the Father according to His humanity,[11] and Himself one, not by some impossible confusion of His natures, but by the unity of His person.[12]

He dwelt among us, full of grace and truth. He proclaimed and established the Kingdom of God and made us know in Himself the Father. He gave us His new commandment to love one another as He loved us. He taught us the way of the Beatitudes of the Gospel: poverty in spirit, meekness, suffering borne with patience, thirst after justice, mercy, purity of heart, will for peace, persecution suffered for justice's sake. Under Pontius Pilate He suffered, the Lamb of God bearing on Himself the sins of the world, and He died for us on the Cross, saving us by His redeeming Blood. He was buried, and, of His own power, rose the third day, raising us by His Resurrection to that sharing in the divine life which is the life of grace. He ascended to heaven, and He will come again, this time in glory, to judge the living and the dead: each according to his merits—those who have responded to the Love and Pity of God going to eternal life, those who have refused them to the end going to the fire that is not extinguished.

And His kingdom will have no end.

THE HOLY SPIRIT

We believe in the Holy Spirit, Who is Lord, and Giver of life, Who is adored and glorified together with the Father and the Son. He spoke to us by the Prophets; He was sent by Christ after his Resurrection and His Ascension to the Father; He illuminates, vivifies, protects and guides the Church; He purifies the Church's members if they do not shun His grace. His action, which penetrates to the inmost of the soul, enables man to respond to the call of Jesus: Be perfect as your Heavenly Father is perfect (Mt. 5:48).

MARY, EVER VIRGIN

We believe that Mary is the Mother, who remained ever a Virgin, of the Incarnate Word, our God and Saviour Jesus Christ,[13] and that by reason of this singular election, she was, in consideration of the merits of her Son, redeemed in a more eminent manner,[14] preserved from all stain of original sin[15] and filled with the gift of grace more than all other creatures.[16]

Joined by a close indissoluble bond to the Mysteries of the Incarnation and Redemption,[17] the Blessed Virgin, the Immaculate, was at the end of her earthly life raised body and soul to heavenly glory[18] and likened to her risen Son in anticipation of the future lot of all the just; and We believe that the Blessed Mother of God, the New Eve, Mother of the Church,[19] continues in Heaven her maternal role with regard to Christ's members, cooperating with the birth and growth of divine life in the souls of the redeemed.[20]

ORIGINAL SIN

We believe that in Adam all have sinned, which means that the original offence committed by him caused human nature, common to all men, to fall to a state in which it bears the consequences of that offence, and which is not the state in which it was at first in our first parents, established as they were in holiness and justice, and in which man knew neither evil nor death. It is human nature so fallen, stripped of the grace that clothed it, injured in its own natural powers and subjected to the dominion of death, that is transmitted to all men, and it is in this sense that every man is born in sin. We therefore hold, with the Council of Trent, that original sin is transmitted with human nature, "not by imitation, but by propagation" and that it is thus "proper to everyone."[21]

We believe that Our Lord Jesus Christ, by the Sacrifice of the Cross, redeemed us from original sin and all the personal sins committed by each one of us, so that, in accordance with the word of the Apostle, "where sin abounded, grace did more abound."[22]

BAPTISM

We believe in one Baptism instituted by Our Lord Jesus Christ for the remission of sins. Baptism should be administered even to little children who have not yet been able to be guilty of any personal sin, in order that, though born deprived of supernatural grace, they may be reborn "of water and the Holy Spirit" to the divine life in Christ Jesus.[23]

THE CHURCH

We believe in one, holy, catholic, and apostolic Church, built by Jesus Christ on that rock which is Peter. She is the Mystical Body of Christ; at the same time a visible society instituted with hierarchical organs, and a spiritual community; the Church on earth, the pilgrim People of God here below, and the Church filled with heavenly blessings; the germ and the first fruits of the Kingdom of God, through which the work and the sufferings of Redemption are continued throughout human history, and which looks for its perfect accomplishment beyond time in glory.[24] In the course of time, the Lord Jesus forms His Church by means of the Sacraments emanating from His Plenitude.[25] By these she makes her members participants in the Mystery of the Death and Resurrection of Christ, in the grace of the Holy Spirit who gives her life and movement.[26] She is therefore holy, though she has sinners in her bosom, because she herself has no other life but that of grace: it is by living by her life that her members are sanctified; it is by removing themselves from her life that they fall into sins and disorders that prevent the radiation of her sanctity. This is why she suffers and does penance for these offences, of which she has the power to heal her children through the Blood of Christ and the Gift of the Holy Spirit.

Heiress of the divine promises and daughter of Abraham according to the Spirit, through that Israel whose Scriptures she lovingly guards, and whose Patriarchs and Prophets she venerates; founded upon the Apostles and handing on from century to century their ever-living word and their powers as Pastors in the Successor of Peter and the Bishops in communion with him; perpetually assisted by the Holy Spirit, she has the charge of guarding, teaching, explaining and spreading the Truth which God revealed in a then veiled manner by the Prophets, and fully by the Lord Jesus. We believe all that is contained in the Word of God written or handed down, and that the Church proposes for belief as divinely revealed, whether by a solemn judgment or by the ordinary and universal magisterium.[27] We believe in the infallibility enjoyed by the Successor of Peter when he teaches ex cathedra as Pastor and Teacher of all the faithful,[28] and which is assured also to the Episcopal Body when it exercises with him the supreme magisterium.[29]

We believe that the Church founded by Jesus Christ and for which He prayed is indefectibly one in faith, worship and the bond of hierarchical communion. In the bosom of this Church, the rich variety of liturgical rites and the legitimate diversity of theological and spiritual heritages and special disciplines, far from injuring her unity, make it more manifest.[30]

Recognizing also the existence, outside the organism of the Church of Christ, of numerous elements of truth and sanctification which belong to her as her own and tend to Catholic unity,[31] and believing in the action of the Holy Spirit who stirs up in the heart of the disciples of Christ love of this unity,[32] We entertain the hope that the Christians who are not yet in the full communion of the one only Church will one day be reunited in one Flock with the one only Shepherd.

We believe that the Church is necessary for salvation, because Christ, who is the sole Mediator and Way of salvation, renders Himself present for us in His Body which is the Church.[33] But the divine Design of salvation embraces all men; and those who without fault on their part do not know the Gospel of Christ and His Church, but seek God sincerely, and under the influence of grace endeavour to do His will as recognized through the promptings of their conscience, they in a number known only to God, can obtain salvation.[34]

THE MASS

We believe that the Mass, celebrated by the priest representing the person of Christ by virtue of the power received through the

Sacrament of Orders, and offered by him in the name of Christ
and the members of His Mystical Body, is the Sacrifice of Calvary
rendered sacramentally present on our altars. We believe that as
the bread and wine consecrated by the Lord at the Last Supper
were changed into His Body and His Blood which were to be
offered for us on the Cross, likewise the bread and wine consecrated
by the priest are changed into the body and Blood of Christ
enthroned gloriously in Heaven, and We believe that the mysterious
presence of the Lord, under what continues to appear to our senses
as before, is a true, real and substantial presence.[35]

THE EUCHARIST

Christ cannot be thus present in this Sacrament except by the
change into His Body of the reality itself of the bread and the
change into His Blood of the reality itself of the wine, leaving
unchanged only the properties of the bread and wine which our
senses perceive. This mysterious change is very appropriately called
by the Church transubstantiation. Every theological explanation
which seeks some understanding of this mystery must, in order to be
in accord with Catholic faith, maintain that in the reality itself, in-
dependently of our mind, the bread and wine have ceased to exist
after the Consecration, so that it is the adorable Body and Blood
of the Lord Jesus that from then on are really before us under
the sacramental species of bread and wine,[36] as the Lord willed
it, in order to give Himself to us as food and to associate us with
the unity of His Mystical Body.[37]

The unique and indivisible existence of the Lord glorious in
Heaven is not multiplied, but is rendered present by the Sacrament
in the many places on earth where Mass is celebrated. And this
existence remains present, after the Sacrifice, in the Blessed Sacrament which is, in the tabernacle, the living heart of each of our
churches. And it is our very sweet duty to honour and adore in
the Blessed Host which our eyes see, the Incarnate Word Whom
they cannot see, and Who, without leaving Heaven, is made present
before us.

GOD'S KINGDOM NOT OF THIS WORLD

We confess that the Kingdom of God begun here below in
the Church of Christ is not of this world whose form is passing,

and that its proper growth cannot be confounded with the progress of civilization, of science or of human technology, but that it consists in an ever more profound knowledge of the unfathomable riches of Christ, an ever stronger hope in eternal blessings, an ever more ardent response to the Love of God, and an ever more generous bestowal of grace and holiness among men. But it is this same love which induces the Church to concern herself constantly about the true temporal welfare of men. Without ceasing to recall to her children that they have not here a lasting dwelling, she also urges them to contribute, each according to his vocation and his means to the welfare of their earthly city, to promote justice, peace and brotherhood among men, to give their aid freely to their brothers, especially to the poorest and most unfortunate. The deep solicitude of the Church, the Spouse of Christ, for the needs of men, for their joys and hopes, their griefs and efforts, is therefore nothing other than her great desire to be present to them, in order to illuminate them with the light of Christ and to gather them all in Him, their only Saviour. This solicitude can never mean that the Church conform herself to the things of this world, or that she lessen the ardour of her expectation of her Lord and of the eternal Kingdom.

ETERNAL LIFE

We believe in the life eternal. We believe that the souls of all those who die in the grace of Christ, whether they must still be purified in Purgatory, or whether from the moment they leave their bodies Jesus takes them to Paradise as He did for the Good Thief, are the People of God in the eternity beyond death, which will be finally conquered on the day of the Resurrection when these souls will be reunited with their bodies.

We believe that the multitude of those gathering around Jesus and Mary in Paradise forms the Church of Heaven, where in eternal beatitude they see God as He is,[38] and where they also, in different degrees, are associated with the holy Angels in the divine rule exercised by Christ in glory, interceding for us and helping our weakness by their brotherly care.[39]

We believe in the communion of all the faithful of Christ, those who are pilgrims on earth, the dead who are attaining purification, and the blessed in Heaven, all together forming one Church and We believe that in this communion the merciful love of God and of His Saints is ever listening to our prayers, as Jesus told us: Ask and you will receive.[40] Thus it is with faith and in hope that We look forward to the resurrection of the dead, and the life of the world to come.

Blessed be God Thrice Holy. Amen.

From the Vatican Basilica, 30th June 1968.

PAULUS PP. VI

NOTES

I. *Disorder in the Ranks*

1. South Bend, Ind., *Tribune*, July 31, 1969, p. 68, col. 2
2. New York *Times*, Oct. 20, 1966, p. 65, col. 3
3. New York *Times*, Aug. 11, 1969, p. 33, col. 2
4. See column of Bishop William L. Adrian, *The Wanderer*, Aug. 18, 1969, p. 2, col. 1
5. *Our Sunday Visitor*, Nov. 2, 1969, p. 14, col. 3
6. New York *Times*, Aug. 11, 1969, p. 33, col. 2
7. The Rev. Daniel Lyons, S.J., *Twin Circle*, Sept. 7, 1969, p. 4, col. 1
8. See *Twin Circle*, Nov. 2, 1969, p. 4, col. 1
9. *Our Sunday Visitor*, Apr. 19, 1970, p. 1, col. 3
10. Daniélou, "Faith Eternal and Man Today," *Franciscan Herald*, 1970, 206.
11. See Maritain, *The Peasant of the Garonne* (1968)
12. New York *Times*, Sept. 3, 1969, p. 11, col. 1
13. New York *Times*, Mar. 5, 1970, p. 67, col. 4
14. *The Wanderer*, Jan. 22, 1970, p. 8, col. 1
15. *Our Sunday Visitor* (Fort Wayne-South Bend edition), May 24, 1970, p. 1, col. 4
16. *Our Sunday Visitor* (Fort Wayne-South Bend edition), June 7, 1970, p. 3, col. 5
17. New York *Times*, Sept. 7, 1969, p. 1, col. 1
18. *L'Osservatore Romano*, English language edition, Oct. 30, 1969, p. 1, col. 1
19. Statement by Dr. Albert C. Outler of Southern Methodist University, *The Tablet*, Jan. 9, 1964, p. 15, col. 1
20. See Morley, "Time and Time Again," *Franciscan View*, April/Spring/1969, 28
21. New York *Times*, Nov. 9, 1969, p. 12E, col. 1
22. New York *Times*, Nov. 9, 1969, p. 12E, col. 1
23. *The Wanderer*, July 30, 1964
24. *The Long Island Catholic*, July 10, 1969, p. 11, col. 3
25. Newman, *The Arians of the Fourth Century* (1871), 465
26. *Acta Apostolicae Sedis* 58 (1966), 659; *The Wanderer*, Oct. 20, 1966, p. 1, col. 5
27. Daniélou, "Faith Eternal and Man Today," *Franciscan Herald*, 1970, 206.

II. *The Anti-Life Society*

1. Boston *Globe*, May 19, p. 1, col. 3; London *Daily Telegraph*, May 18, 1970
2. The photograph is available from the Catholic Central Union of America, 3835 Westminster Place, St. Louis, Mo. 63108
3. New York *Times*, Feb. 7, 1971, p. 70, col. 3
4. *U.S. News & World Report*, June 8, 1970, 83
5. *Twin Circle*, June 14, 1970, p. 6, col. 2
6. Washington, D.C., *Star*, May 3, 1970, p. A26, col. 1
7. New York *Times*, June 1, 1970, p. 1, col. 2
8. New York *Times*, Feb. 9, 1970, p. 14, col. 4
9. New York *Times*, Mar. 17, 1970, p. 23, col. 3
10. New York *Times*, June 1, 1970, p. 1, col. 2
11. *Medical-Moral Newsletter*, Apr. 1967
12. New York *Times*, Mar. 14, 1968, p. 20, col. 3
13. New York *Times*, July 13, 1970, p. 1, col. 3
14. *The Wanderer*, Dec. 11, 1969, p. 2, col. 5
15. New York *Times*, Oct. 22, 1969, p. 5, col. 4
16. New York *Times*, Mar. 20, 1970, p. 4, col. 4
17. New York *Times*, Aug. 9, 1970, p. 31, col. 1
18. New York *Times*, Apr. 8, 1970, p. 1, col. 2
19. *Summa Theologica*, I–II, Q. 96, Art. 2
20. New York *Times*, Jan. 9, 1967
21. See Levine, "Sexual Sensationalism and the First Amendment," *New York State Bar Journal*, Apr. 1970, 193
22. See H.R. 15554 (91st Cong., 2d Sess.)
23. *L'Osservatore Romano*, English language edition, Oct. 9, 1969, p. 1, col. 1
24. *L'Osservatore Romano*, English language edition, Oct. 9, 1969, p. 1, col. 1
25. New York *Times*, Dec. 10, 1969
26. *L'Osservatore Romano*, English language edition, Oct. 9, 1969, p. 1, col. 1; New York *Times*, Oct. 9, 1969, p. 1, col. 1
27. *The Wanderer*, May 16, 1963, p. 4, col. 3
28. *The Wanderer*, Sept. 18, 1969, p. 1, col. 2
29. *L'Osservatore Romano*, English language edition, Sept. 18, 1969, p. 1, col. 2
30. Pope Pius XII, "Address to the Women of Italian Catholic Action," Oct. 26, 1941; *Major Addresses of Pope Pius XII* (the Rev. Vincent A. Yzermans, ed.) (1961), 46
31. New York *Times*, Mar. 1, 1970, p. 71, col. 6
32. *Newsweek*, June 15, 1970, 111
33. New York *News*, Mar. 17, 1969, p. 37, col. 6
34. *The Wanderer*, May 1, 1969, p. 7, col. 1

35. *U.S. News & World Report*, Sept. 15, 1969, p. 10, col. 1
36. New York *Times*, Mar. 5, 1970, p. 1, col. 7; New York *Times*, Mar. 24, 1970, p. 8, col. 1; South Bend, Ind., *Tribune*, June 10, 1970, p. 2, col. 6
37. New York *Times*, June 10, 1970, p. 27, col. 2
38. Guitton, *The Pope Speaks* (1967), 275
39. South Bend, Ind., *Tribune*, Dec. 11, 1969, p. 6, col. 1
40. *Twin Circle*, Apr. 20, 1969, p. 4, col. 1
41. *The Wanderer*, Sept. 19, 1968, p. 10, col. 1
42. *The Wanderer*, Sept. 19, 1968, p. 10, col. 1
43. *Young India*, Mar. 12, 1925; quoted in Fischer, *The Essential Gandhi* (1962), 241
44. *Young India*, Apr. 2, 1925; quoted in *The Wanderer*, Oct. 3, 1968, p. 1, col. 1
45. *Young India*, Sept. 16, 1926; quoted in *The Wanderer*, Oct. 3, 1968, p. 1, col. 1
46. *Harijan*, Oct. 3, 1936; quoted in *The Wanderer*, Oct. 3, 1968, p. 1, col. 1
47. *Harijan*, May 5, 1946; quoted in *The Wanderer*, Oct. 31, 1968, p. 1, col. 1
48. Curran, *Contemporary Problems in Moral Theology* (1970), 144, 146
49. See Rice, *The Vanishing Right to Live* (1969), 126
50. Griswold *v.* Connecticut, 381 U.S. 479 (1965)
51. New York *Times*, Nov. 25, 1969, p. 19, col. 1
52. Column of Paul Scott, *The Wanderer*, Jan. 22, 1970, p. 2, col. 5
53. *The Wanderer*, Feb. 26, 1970, p. 11, col. 5
54. *Twin Circle*, Jan. 25, 1970; see U. S. Public Law 91–572 (1970)
55. Chicago *Sun Times*, Tuesday, Mar. 3, 1970, p. 17, col. 1
56. *Cong. Rec.*, Feb. 24, 1970, S.2278
57. S.3746 (91st Cong., 2d Sess.)
58. *U.S. News & World Report*, Feb. 23, 1970, 68, 71
59. Chicago *Tribune*, July 19, 1969, Sec. 1, p. 5, col. 2
60. Church League of America, *News and Views*, May 1969, p. 13
61. *L'Osservatore Romano*, English language edition, Aug. 22, 1968, p. 3, col. 1

III. *Humanae Vitae*

1. New York *Times*, Apr. 23, 1967, p. E8, col. 4
2. *The Critic*, Dec. 1966–Jan. 1967, 24
3. Ford and Lynch, "Contraception: A Matter of Practical Doubt?" *Homiletic & Pastoral Review*, Apr. 1968, 563, 569
4. See Kirk, "Paul VI and the Power That Withholds," *The Critic*, Dec. 1968–Jan. 1969, 42, 44
5. *The Wanderer*, Oct. 30, 1969, p. 1, col. 3

6. Father John C. Ford, S.J., of Weston College, has translated this sentence as follows: "Likewise every act that intends to *impede procreation* must be repudiated, whether that act is intended as an end to be attained or as a means to be used, and whether it is done in anticipation of marital intercourse, or during it, or while it is having its natural consequences." [Letter from the Rev. John C. Ford, S.J., to Charles E. Rice, June 19, 1970] The original Latin text reads: "Item quivis respuendus est actus, qui, cum coniugale commercium vel praevidetur vel efficitur vel ad suos naturales exitus ducit, id tamquam finem obtinendum aut viam adhibendam intendat, *ut procreatio impediatur*." [Acta Apostolicae Sedis 60 (1968) 490] [Emphasis added]
7. Costanzo, "Papal Magisterium and 'Humanae Vitae,'" *Thought*, Autumn 1969, 377, 395
8. *The Wanderer*, Jan. 23 1969, p. 4, col. 4
9. New York *Times*, Aug. 11, 1968, p. 32, col. 1
10. New York *Times*, July 30, 1968, p. 1, col. 6
11. *Medical-Moral Newsletter*, Sept. 1968, 2
12. New York *Times*, Dec. 30, 1968, p. 20, col. 7
13. New York *Times*, July 31, 1968, p. 1, col. 1
14. New York *Times*, Aug. 2, 1968, p. 1, col. 2
15. J. M. Kelly, quoted by Msgr. Rudolph C. Bandas, *The Wanderer*, Aug. 22, 1968, p. 3, col. 1
16. The New York *Times*, July 31, 1969, p. 1, col. 1
17. See discussion in Milhaven, "The Grounds of the Opposition to Humanae Vitae," *Thought*, Autumn 1969, 342, 345
18. *L'Osservatore Romano*, English language edition, Sept. 19, 1968, p. 1, col. 1
19. *L'Osservatore Romano*, English language edition, Sept. 19, 1968, p. 1, col. 1
20. New York *Times*, Nov. 16, 1968, p. 1, col. 3
21. *Twin Circle*, Dec. 1, 1968, p. 4, col. 2
22. See Wattenberg, "The Nonsense Explosion," *The New Republic*, Apr. 4 and 11, 1970, 18; New York *Times*, June 29, 1967, p. 3, col. 1; *U.S. News & World Report*, Apr. 17, 1967, 48; New York *Times*, Feb. 26, 1968, p. 1, col. 2; *U.S. News & World Report*, Mar. 11, 1968, 57
23. *World Almanac*, 1970, 72
24. Food and Agriculture Organization of the United Nations, *The State of Food and Agriculture*, 1969, 1, 2, 5
25. Philadelphia *Inquirer*, Oct. 11, 1969
26. New York *Times*, Mar. 29, 1970, p. 62, col. 3
27. New York *Times*, Mar. 15, 1970, p. E10, col. 1
28. Chicago *Tribune*, Feb. 2, 1970, sec. 1, p. 16, col. 1
29. See discussion by Barbara Ward, *Long Island Catholic*, June 26, 1969, p. 10, col. 3
30. *L'Osservatore Romano*, English language edition, July 3, 1969, p. 3
31. Fleming, "Confrontation in Washington: The Cardinal vs. the Dissenters." New York *Times* Magazine, Nov. 24, 1968, 54

32. *L'Osservatore Romano*, English language edition, Sept. 26, 1968,
    p. 4, col. 3
33. *McCall's*, Oct. 1967, 137; Guitton, *The Pope Speaks* (1967), 275
34. Ford and Lynch, "Contraception: A Matter of Practical Doubt?"
    Homiletic & Pastoral Review, Apr. 1968, 563, 572
35. Reed, "Natural Law, Theology, and the Church," *Theological
    Studies*, Mar. 1965, 40, 56–57
36. *The Long Island Catholic*, Dec. 29, 1966, p. 10, col. 3
37. *The Wanderer*, Feb. 20, 1969, p. 4, col. 1
38. *Humanae Vitae*, No. 4
39. Noonan, *Contraception* (1965), xix
40. Costanzo, "Papal Magisterium and 'Humanae Vitae,'" *Thought*,
    Autumn 1969, 377, 394, 396, 398
41. *Dogmatic Constitution on the Church*, No. 25

IV. *Authority*

1. Benson, *Lord of the World* (1907), 129–30
2. *L'Osservatore Romano*, English language edition, Jan. 23, 1969,
   p. 1, col. 1
3. *The Observer Review* (London), Jan. 1, 1967
4. Second Vatican Council, *Dogmatic Constitution on the Church*,
   No. 22
5. Second Vatican Council, *Decree on the Bishops' Pastoral Office
   in the Church*, No. 2
6. *L'Osservatore Romano*, English language edition, Dec. 18, 1969,
   p. 1, col. 3
7. Pope Paul VI, General Audience, Dec. 10, 1969; *L'Osservatore
   Romano*, English language edition, Dec. 18, 1969, p. 1, col. 3
8. *Dogmatic Canons and Decrees* (Devin-Adair, 1912), 249, 250,
   256–57
9. Daniélou, "Authority in the Church," *Franciscan View*, Apr./Spring/
   1969, 33, 35
10. *L'Osservatore Romano*, English language edition, Aug. 28, 1969,
    p. 5, col. 2
11. Galatians 2:11
12. *Summa Theologica*, II–III, Q. 33, Art. 4
13. *Summa Theologica*, III. Q. 72, Art. 11
14. *Summa Theologica*, Suppl., Q. 40, Art. 6
15. *Summa Theologica*, Suppl., Q. 40, Art. 6
16. *Summa Theologica*, Suppl., Q. 40, Art. 6
17. Colossians, 4:17
18. *Summa Theologica*, II–II, Q. 33, Art. 4
19. Second Vatican Council, *Dogmatic Constitution on the Church*,
    No. 22
20. *The Wanderer*, Oct. 16, 1969, p. 1, col. 1
21. *Twin Circle*, Nov. 9, 1969, p. 3, col. 3

22. *L'Osservatore Romano*, English language edition, Oct. 16, 1969, p. 1, col. 1; *U.S. News & World Report*, Nov. 3, 1969, 43
23. Second Vatican Council, *Dogmatic Constitution on the Church*, No. 25
24. Second Vatican Council, *Dogmatic Constitution on the Church*, No. 25
25. Second Vatican Council, *Dogmatic Constitution on the Church*, No. 25
26. *L'Osservatore Romano*, Aug. 8, 1968; see Costanzo, "Papal Magisterium and 'Humanae Vitae,'" *Thought*, Autumn 1969, 377, 410–11
27. The Rev. Sabbas J. Kilian, O.F.M., "The Question of Authority in Humanae Vitae," *Thought*, Autumn 1969, 327, 336
28. Second Vatican Council, *Dogmatic Constitution on the Church*, No. 25
29. Newman, *Letter to His Grace the Duke of Norfolk* (1875), 118
30. Von Hildebrand, "Belief and Obedience: The Critical Difference," *Triumph*, March 1970, 11
31. Second Vatican Council, *Dogmatic Constitution on the Church*, No. 25
32. *The Wanderer*, Oct. 2, 1969, p. 4, col. 2
33. Second Vatican Council, *Dogmatic Constitution on the Church*, No. 25
34. Murray, *We Hold These Truths* (1960), 329–30
35. See Costanzo, "Papal Magisterium and 'Humanae Vitae,'" *Thought*, Autumn 1969, 377, 388–91; Reed, "Natural Law, Theology and the Church," *Theological Studies*, Mar. 1965, 40, 47
36. Second Vatican Council, *Declaration on Religious Freedom*, No. 14
37. Pope Pius XII, Radio Address, Mar. 23, 1952
38. Pope Pius XII, *Allocution Magnificate Dominum*, Nov. 2, 1954
39. Patrick Cardinal O'Boyle, "Instruction on the Catholic Conscience," Oct. 9, 1968; *Catholic Standard*, Oct. 10, 1968
40. Second Vatican Council, *Dogmatic Constitution on the Church*, No. 25
41. Second Vatican Council, *Dogmatic Constitution on the Church*, No. 25
42. *Summa Theologica*, I, Q. 79, Art. 13
43. Newman, *Letter to His Grace the Duke of Norfolk* (1875), 137
44. Newman, *Letter to His Grace the Duke of Norfolk* (1875), 135–36
45. *L'Osservatore Romano*, English language edition, Feb. 13, 1969, p. 1, col. 1
46. *L'Osservatore Romano*, English language edition, Feb. 20, 1969, p. 1, col. 1
47. *L'Osservatore Romano*, English language edition, Feb. 20, 1969, p. 1, col. 1
48. *L'Osservatore Romano*, English language edition, Feb. 20, 1969, p. 1, col. 1
49. *Documentation*, Nov.–Dec. 1968, 19
50. *Summa Theologica*, I–II, Q. 19, Art. 6

51. Second Vatican Council, *Pastoral Constitution on the Church in the Modern World*, Nos. 50 and 51
52. O'Boyle, "Instruction on the Catholic Conscience," Oct. 9, 1968; *Catholic Standard*, Oct. 10, 1968
53. Second Vatican Council, *Declaration on Religious Freedom*, No. 2
54. Second Vatican Council, *Declaration on Religious Freedom*, No. 1
55. O'Boyle, "Instruction on the Catholic Conscience," Oct. 9, 1968; *Catholic Standard*, Oct. 10, 1968
56. *L'Osservatore Romano*, English language edition, May 2, 1968, p. 1, col. 1
57. *L'Osservatore Romano*, English language edition, Aug. 22, 1968, p. 1, col. 1
58. Newman, *The Idea of a University* (Image ed., 1959), 360
59. *L'Osservatore Romano*, Apr. 5, 1969; *The Pope Speaks*, Vol. 14, 15
60. New York *Times*, Dec. 29, 1969, p. 30, col. 1
61. *The Wanderer*, Feb. 12, 1970, p. 1, col. 5
62. Patrick Cardinal O'Boyle, "Instruction on the Catholic Conscience," Oct. 9, 1968; *Catholic Standard*, Oct. 10, 1968

V. Discordant Ideas

1. *The Wanderer*, Feb. 13, 1969, p. 1, col. 3
2. *The Ram*, Fordham University, Apr. 11, 1968, 2
3. Fletcher, *Situation Ethics: The New Morality* (Westminster Press, 1966), 26, 31, 125, 133
4. See *Our Sunday Visitor*, July 24, 1966, p. 7, col. 1
5. See *U.S. News & World Report*, Nov. 27, 1967, 67
6. *Our Sunday Visitor*, July 24, 1966, p. 7, col. 1
7. "'The Arrangement' at College," *Life*, May 31, 1968, 56–60
8. *U.S. News & World Report*, Mar. 2, 1970, 56
9. New York *Times*, Nov. 8, 1969, p. 1, col. 3
10. *U.S. News & World Report*, Aug. 25, 1969, 32
11. Hefner, "The Playboy Philosophy," *Playboy*, July 1963, 49–50
12. *National Catholic Reporter*, Dec. 13, 1967, p. 8, col. 3
13. Wertham, *A Sign for Cain* (1966), 159; Rice, *The Vanishing Right to Live* (1969), 62
14. See Paul Ramsey, *Deeds & Rules of Christian Ethics* (1967)
15. *Guide for Living* (Selected Addresses and Letters of Pope Pius XII) (Quinlan, ed.) (1958), 211, et. seq.
16. *Guide for Living* (Selected Addresses and Letters of Pope Pius XII) (Quinlan, ed.) (1958), 215, et. seq.
17. Davis, *Moral and Pastoral Theology* (1958), Vol. I, 204; Connell, *Outlines of Moral Theology* (1953), 51; Rickaby, *Moral Philosophy* (1905), 33–34
18. Davis, *Moral and Pastoral Theology* (1958), Vol. I, 91
19. *The Wanderer*, Dec. 22, 1966

20. Champlin, *Don't You Really Love Me?* (1968), 127
21. Champlin, *Don't You Really Love Me?* (1968), 135–36
22. The Wanderer, Nov. 28, 1968, p. 10, col. 3
23. John C. Bennett, *Christianity and Our World* (1943), 1
24. Georgia Harkness, *The Modern Rival of the Christian Faith* (1952), 16
25. Henlee H. Barnette, *The New Theology and Morality* (1967), 73–74
26. Hughes, *A Popular History of the Catholic Church* (1947), 258
27. Smith, *The Teaching of the Catholic Church* (1962), Vol. I, 3
28. Freemantle, *Papal Encyclicals in Their Historical Context* (1956), 196
29. New Catholic Encyclopedia (1967), Vol. IX, 995
30. Cotter, *The Encyclical Humani Generis, with a Commentary* (1952), 79; see Denzinger, *The Sources of Catholic Dogma* (Deferrari, trans.) (1957), No. 2079
31. Cotter, *The Encyclical Humani Generis, with a Commentary* (1952), 55

VI. *The Clergy and Religious*

1. New York *Times*, Mar. 10, 1970, p. 20, col. 3
2. *L'Osservatore Romano*, English language edition, May 29, 1969, p. 6, col. 1
3. New York *Times*, Apr. 16, 1969, p. 17, col. 1
4. *L'Osservatore Romano*, English language edition, May 29, 1969, p. 6, col. 1
5. *L'Osservatore Romano*, English language edition, May 29, 1969, p. 6, col. 1
6. *L'Osservatore Romano*, English language edition, July 3, 1969, 3
7. *L'Osservatore Romano*, English language edition, Dec. 26, 1969, p. 1, col. 1
8. *L'Osservatore Romano*, English language edition, Dec. 25, 1969, p. 1, col. 1
9. *The Wanderer*, July 24, 1969, p. 10, col. 6
10. Chicago *Tribune*, June 2, 1970, Sec. 1, p. 14, col. 1; *Twin Circle*, June 21, 1970, p. 1, col. 5
11. New York *Times*, Oct. 5, 1967, p. 41, col. 4
12. South Bend, Ind., *Tribune*, Sept. 5, 1969, p. 48, col. 1
13. *Franciscan Herald*, Dec. 1969, 354
14. New York *Times*, June 27, 1970, p. 16, col. 3
15. *Franciscan Herald*, Aug. 1969, 225
16. *L'Osservatore Romano*, English language edition, Feb. 27, 1969, p. 1, col. 1
17. *The Wanderer*, May 15, 1969
18. L'Heureux, "The New American Jesuits," *Atlantic*, Nov. 1969, 59, 64
19. New York *Times*, Nov. 13, 1969, p. 14, col. 1

20. New York *Times*, May 12, 1970, p. 3, col. 5; *The Wanderer*, Feb. 12, 1970, p. 1, col. 6
21. *Twin Circle*, Feb. 22, 1970, p. 12, col. 1
22. *The Wanderer*, Apr. 16, 1970, p. 1, col. 6
23. South Bend, Ind., *Tribune*, May 10, 1970, p. 18, col. 1
24. *The Critic*, Dec. 1967, Jan. 1968
25. New York *Times*, Feb. 10, 1970, p. 1, col. 3; *Catholic Currents*, Apr. 15, 1970, 1
26. *Our Sunday Visitor*, Apr. 12, 1970, p. 11, col. 1
27. The Official Catholic Directory (1970); Catholic Almanac (1970), 530
28. *Twin Circle*, Mar. 1, 1970, p. 4, col. 1
29. New York *Times*, May 17, 1970, p. E15, col. 6
30. *Twin Circle*, Mar. 1, 1970, p. 4, col. 1
31. See the "Instruction on the Renewal of Religious Formation," issued by the Sacred Congregation for Religious and for Secular Institutes, *L'Osservatore Romano*, English language edition, Feb. 13, 1969, p. 6, col. 1; see also, New York *Times*, Aug. 19, 1970, p. 2, col. 3
32. *The Wanderer*, Oct. 2, 1969, p. 1, col. 1
33. *L'Osservatore Romano*, Nov. 23, 1969; *The Pope Speaks*, Vol. 14 (1970), 365
34. Epistle of St. Paul to the Romans 16:17–18

VII. *Ecumenism*

1. *L'Osservatore Romano*, English language edition, Sept. 25, 1969, p. 2, col. 2
2. Second Vatican Council, *Decree on Ecumenism*, No. 1
3. Pope Paul VI, General audience, Jan. 21, 1970
4. Second Vatican Council, *Dogmatic Constitution on the Church*, No. 25
5. *L'Osservatore Romano*, English language edition, Jan. 30, 1969, p. 1, col. 1
6. Second Vatican Council, *Decree on Ecumenism*, No. 4
7. Second Vatican Council, *Decree on Ecumenism*, No. 3
8. Second Vatican Council, *Decree on Ecumenism*, No. 4
9. Second Vatican Council, *Decree on Ecumenism*, No. 3
10. Second Vatican Council, *Dogmatic Constitution on the Church*, No. 42
11. Pope Paul VI, *L'Osservatore Romano*, English language edition, Jan. 30, 1969, p. 1, col. 1
12. Miller & Wright, editors, *Ecumenical Dialogue at Harvard* (1964), 63–64
13. Dulles, S.J., "Dogma as an Ecumenical Problem," *The Catholic Mind*, May 1969, 15, 25
14. For a detailed refutation of Father Dulles' position, see David

Fitch, S.J., and Joseph S. Brusher, S.J., "Two Views of Avery Dulles, S.J.," *Triumph*, July 1970, 24

15. *L'Osservatore Romano*, English language edition, Jan. 30, 1969, p. 1, col. 1
16. Second Vatican Council, *Decree on Ecumenism*, Nos. 4 and 6, n. 27 and n. 33
17. *Acta Apostolicae Sedis* 54 (1962), 792; see Second Vatican Council, *Decree on Ecumenism*, No. 4, No. 6; *The Documents of Vatican II* (Walter M. Abbott, S.J., general ed.) (1966), 349
18. *Triumph*, June 1967, 4
19. *L'Osservatore Romano*, English language edition, Jan. 30, 1969, p. 1, col. 1
20. New York *Times*, July 14, 1969, p. 15, col. 1
21. New York *Times*, July 27, 1969, p. E9, col. 1
22. *L'Osservatore Romano*, English language edition, Jan. 30, 1969, p. 1, col. 1
23. Second Vatican Council, *Declaration on the Relationship of the Church to Non-Christian Religions*, No. 1
24. Second Vatican Council, *Declaration on the Relationship of the Church to Non-Christian Religions*, No. 2
25. Second Vatican Council, *Pastoral Constitution on the Church in the Modern World*, No. 21
26. South Bend, Ind., *Tribune*, Oct. 17, 1969, p. 5, col. 1; see Brown, *The Protest of a Troubled Protestant* (1969)
27. Brown, "A Protestant Case for Co-Belligerency," *Triumph*, Sept. 1969, 24, 25
28. *Triumph*, Mar. 1967, 4
29. *L'Osservatore Romano*, May 23–24, 1966; *The Pope Speaks*, Vol. 11 (1966), 328
30. Hearing, "Communist Exploitation of Religion," Subcommittee on Internal Security, United States Senate, May 6, 1966
31. Second Vatican Council, *Decree on Ecumenism*, No. 4; see note 25 in No. 4
32. Second Vatican Council, *Constitution on the Sacred Liturgy*, No. 9
33. *The Wanderer*, Jan. 1, 1970, p. 1, col. 1
34. Pius XI, *Encyclical Rerum Ecclesiae*, Feb. 28, 1926
35. *L'Osservatore Romano*, English language edition, June 19, 1969, p. 3, col. 1
36. Second Vatican Council, *Decree on Ecumenism*, No. 4

VIII. *The Liturgy*

1. Claridge, *Margaret Clitherow* (1966), 19
2. Claridge, *Margaret Clitherow* (1966), 19
3. *National Catholic Reporter*, May 29, 1968, p. 4, col. 1
4. *National Catholic Reporter*, Aug. 13, 1969, p. 3, col. 6

5. Second Vatican Council, *Constitution on the Sacred Liturgy*, No. 2
6. Second Vatican Council, *Constitution on the Sacred Liturgy*, No. 14
7. Second Vatican Council, *Decree on the Bishops' Pastoral Office in the Church*, No. 30
8. *L'Osservatore Romano*, English language edition, May 8, 1969, p. 1, col. 1
9. *L'Osservatore Romano*, English language edition, May 22, 1969, p. 8, col. 1
10. *L'Osservatore Romano*, English language edition, Nov. 13, 1969, p. 7, col. 1
11. *Triumph*, Dec. 1969, 22B
12. Second Vatican Council, *Constitution on the Sacred Liturgy*, No. 50
13. *L'Osservatore Romano*, Nov. 20, 1969; *The Pope Speaks*, Vol. 14 (1970), 326
14. Second Vatican Council, *Constitution on the Sacred Liturgy*, No. 36
15. *L'Osservatore Romano*, Nov. 27, 1969; *The Pope Speaks*, Vol. 14 (1970), 329
16. *Triumph*, May 1970, 10
17. *The Wanderer*, July 30, 1970, p. 1, col. 4
18. Second Vatican Council, *Constitution on the Sacred Liturgy*, No. 14
19. Second Vatican Council, *Constitution on the Sacred Liturgy*, No. 22
20. Von Hildebrand, "Belief and Obedience: The Critical Difference," *Triumph*, Mar. 1970, 11
21. *Catholic Currents*, July 15, 1970, p. 2, col. 2; see *L'Osservatore Romano*, English language edition, May 28, 1970
22. See Potter, "The Liturgy Club," *Triumph*, May 1968, 10
23. *Twin Circle*, June 21, 1970
24. *Twin Circle*, Aug. 30, 1970, p. 7, col. 1
25. *Catholic Currents*, Feb. 2, 1970, p. 2, col. 1
26. *New York Times*, Oct. 11, 1969, p. 30, col. 3
27. *New Book Review*, Oct. 1969, 10–11
28. *Triumph*, June 1970, 11
29. The address of the Laymen's Commission on the English Liturgy is 5224 Easton Drive, North Springfield, Va. 22151
30. D. E. Moran, C.S.S.R., "Has the New Liturgy Killed Personal Piety?" Ligourian Pamphlets, 1966, 3–4
31. *L'Osservatore Romano*, English language edition, Feb. 20, 1969, p. 3, col. 1
32. *New York Times*, Dec. 25, 1969, p. 41, col. 1
33. *The Wanderer*, Jan. 15, 1970, p. 1, col. 4
34. See *Twin Circle*, Nov. 30, 1969, p. 6, col. 1
35. Derrick, "Pavane for a Dead Liturgy," *Triumph*, Dec. 1969, 16, 17
36. *The Wanderer*, May 22, 1969, p. 1, col. 6
37. *L'Osservatore Romano*, Aug. 21, 1969; *The Pope Speaks*, Vol. 14 (1969), 206
38. *L'Osservatore Romano*, Aug. 21, 1969; *The Pope Speaks*, Vol. 14 (1969), 208

IX. *Elementary and High Schools*

1. *Barron's*, Sept. 11, 1967
2. *The Wanderer*, Jan. 15, 1970, p. 8, col. 1
3. "Are the Catholic Schools Dying?" *Look*, Oct. 21, 1969, 105
4. New York *Times*, Sept. 4, 1969, p. 48, col. 1
5. New York *Times*, Mar. 25, 1968, p. 47, col. 1
6. New York *Times*, Sept. 8, 1969, p. 41, col. 6
7. See *The Wanderer*, Sept. 25, 1969, p. 1, col. 4; detailed reports can be obtained from the Cardinal Mindszenty Foundation, Box 11321, St. Louis, Mo., 63105; National Federation of Laymen, Inc., Box 56058, Chicago, Ill. 60656; St. Michael Associates, Box 421, Station A, Flushing, N.Y. 11358; Catholics United for the Faith, 1291 North Avenue, New Rochelle, N.Y.; and Credo, Box 9093, Houston, Tex. 77011.
8. *L'Osservatore Romano*, English language edition, Dec. 12, 1968, p. 3, col. 1
9. *Our Sunday Visitor*, July 26, 1970, p. 1, col. 3
10. *Our Sunday Visitor*, July 26, 1970, p. 1, col. 3
11. *Our Sunday Visitor*, July 26, 1970, p. 1, col. 3
12. *National Catholic Reporter*, Aug. 21, 1968, p. 1, col. 3
13. *National Catholic Reporter*, Aug. 21, 1968, p. 1, col. 3
14. *National Catholic Reporter*, Aug. 21, 1968, p. 1, col. 3
15. Second Vatican Council, *Decree on the Bishops' Pastoral Office in the Church*, No. 13
16. Second Vatican Council, *Decree on the Bishops' Pastoral Office in the Church*, No. 14
17. The following are doctrinally sound, attractive, and interesting catechism texts available to the schools and to individual parents:
    For grade school:
    Way, Truth and Life Series by the Daughters of St. Paul, 50 St. Paul Avenue, Jamaica Plain, Boston, Mass.
    Faith of Our Fathers Series, by Msgr. Rudolph G. Bandas, E. M. Lohmann Co., Sibley Street, St. Paul, Minn. 55101
    St. Joseph New Baltimore Catechism, Christ and Country Books, Box 1107, Rockford, Ill. 61105
    The Father McGuire New Catechism Series, Msgr. Michael A. McGuire, Church of St. Frances of Rome, Moore Plaza & E. 236th Street, Bronx, N.Y. 10466
    For high school:
    Faith of Our Fathers Series, by Msgr. Bandas
    Way, Truth and Life Series, by the Daughters of St. Paul
    The Faith Explained by Leo Trese, Fides Publishers, Notre Dame, Ind. 46556
18. *Twin Circle*, July 7, 1968, p. 1, col. 5

19. *Catholic Currents*, Dec. 24, 1969, p. 8, col. 1
20. *Seedbed of Faith—or Unbelief?* The Wanderer Press (1969), 22
21. *The Wanderer*, Sept. 18, 1969, p. 10, col. 6; *Twin Circle*, Sept. 14, 1969, p. 2, col. 5
22. *Our Sunday Visitor*, July 26, 1970, p. 1, col. 3
23. *Our Sunday Visitor*, July 26, 1970, p. 1, col. 3
24. Letter from Dr. Rhoda Lorand to Mrs. A. G. Weiner, 2108 Lyon Avenue, Belmont, Calif. 94002, July 20, 1968
25. Statement of the Hon. John Rarick, Cong. Rec., Feb. 7, 1969, E965
26. For an analysis of these bibliographies and of the New York Archdiocese sex education program see *Sex Education Program of the New York Archdiocese: An Evaluation*, available from Catholics United for the Faith, Inc., 1291 North Avenue, New Rochelle, N.Y. 10804
27. Diocese of Rochester, *Sex Education and Family Life* (2d ed.), 2
28. See Engel *v.* Vitale, 370 U.S. 421, 431 (1962)
29. *Guide for Living, Selected Addresses and Letters of Pope Pius XII* (Quinlan, ed.) (1959), 56
30. Second Vatican Council, *Declaration on Christian Education*, No. 1
31. *Declaration on Christian Education of Vatican Council II*, Commentary by the Rt. Rev. Mark J. Hurley (Paulist Press, 1966), 88–89
32. *Sex Education*, Catholics United for the Faith, 9 Rockwood Road, Plandome, N.Y. (1969), 6
33. Statement of the Hon. John R. Rarick, Cong. Rec., Feb. 7, 1969, E965
34. Statement of the Hon. John Rarick, Cong. Rec., Feb. 7, 1969, E965
35. *Human Events*, Feb. 6, 1969
36. For example, Parents for Orthodoxy in Parochial Education, Box 277, Lagunitas, Calif. 94938; Church League of America, 422 North Prospect Street, Wheaton, Ill. 60187
37. See Bandas, "Crisis in the Teaching of Religion," *The Wanderer*, Mar. 20, 1969, p. 2, col. 4
38. *The Wanderer*, May 14, 1970, p. 1, col. 6
39. Second Vatican Council, *Declaration on Christian Education*, No. 6
40. Second Vatican Council, *Declaration on Christian Education*, No. 6
41. Second Vatican Council, *Declaration on Christian Education*, No. 8

X. *The Catholic University*

1. "Bensalem," *Look*, May 19, 1970, 29
2. Second Vatican Council, *Declaration on Christian Education*, No. 10
3. *L'Osservatore Romano*, English language edition, May 8, 1969, p. 4, col. 1

4. Ward, *Blueprint for a Catholic University* (1949), 176
5. Newman, *The Idea of a University* (Image ed., 1959), 415, 416
6. Newman, *The Idea of a University* (Image ed., 1959), 416
7. Address of Pope Pius XII to the Third General Assembly of the International Office of Catholic Teaching, Sept. 14, 1958; *The Pope Speaks*, Vol. 5, 337, 339
8. *Long Island Catholic*, Aug. 8, 1968, p. 17, col. 5
9. *The Wanderer*, Mar. 30, 1967
10. Grisez, *Academic Freedom and Catholic Faith*, NCEA Bulletin, Nov. 1967, 15, 17
11. New York *Times*, July 30, 1967; Triumph, Sept. 1967, 37
12. See McCluskey, ed., *The Catholic University: A Modern Appraisal* (1970), 1–28, 346–365
13. McCluskey, *Catholic Education Faces Its Future* (1969), 253–54
14. Pope Pius XI, *Christian Education of Youth*, quoting Conc. Vat., Sess. 3, cap. 4
15. See McCluskey, "Rome Replies (Act II)." *America*, March 28, 1970, 330
16. *L'Osservatore Romano*, English language edition, Apr. 4, 1968, p. 5, col. 1
17. Second Vatican Council, *Pastoral Constitution on the Church in the Modern World*, No. 62
18. Address by Pope Paul VI to the Congress of Delegates of Catholic Universities, *L'Osservatore Romano*, English language edition, May 8, 1969, p. 4, col. 1
19. Keyishian *v.* Board of Regents of New York, 385 U.S. 589, 603 (1967)
20. *L'Osservatore Romano*, English language edition, Nov. 20, 1969, p. 11, col. 1
21. *L'Osservatore Romano*, Jan. 15, 1958; *The Pope Speaks*, Vol. 5, (1958) 91, 92–93
22. McCluskey, "Rome Replies (Act II)," *America*, Mar. 28, 1970, 330–32
23. Newman, *The Idea of a University* (Image ed., 1959), 222–24
24. Code of Canon Law, Canon 1381; Bouscaren, Ellis, and Korth, *Canon Law: A Text and Commentary* (1966), 771–72
25. McCluskey, "Rome Replies (Act II)," *America*, Mar. 28, 1970, 330
26. See *Crossroads*, College of the Holy Cross, Oct. 1969, p. 5, col. 1
27. Address by the Rev. Leo McLaughlin, S.J., to the Fordham University Alumni Federation, Jan. 24, 1967
28. Address by the Rev. Theodore M. Hesburgh, C.S.C., Dec. 9, 1967
29. *The Jesuit*, Autumn 1969
30. College of the Holy Cross, *Crossroads*, Apr. 1970, p. 1, col. 1
31. *The Wanderer*, May 22, 1969, p. 10, col. 1
32. *U.S. News & World Report*, Sept. 30, 1968
33. Harlow, *The Growth of the United States* (1943), 551–52
34. New York *Times*, Apr. 14, 1969, p. 1, col. 1

35. See column of Alice Widener, Houston *Tribune*, Oct. 30, 1969, p. 4, col. 4
36. Dr. Max Rafferty, Houston *Tribune*, Dec. 11, 1969, p. 5, col. 3

XI. *Church and State*

1. Chicago *Tribune*, Nov. 7, 1969, Sec. 1, p. 24, col. 3
2. New York *Times*, Apr. 2, 1969, p. 46, col. 5
3. New York *Times*, Apr. 24, 1970, p. 16, col. 3
4. *Our Sunday Visitor* (Fort Wayne-South Bend edition), Apr. 26, 1970, p. 1, col. 6
5. *Our Sunday Visitor* (Fort Wayne-South Bend edition), Aug. 9, 1970, p. 1, col. 3
6. New York *Times*, May 10, 1970, p. 4, col. 1
7. *Triumph*, June 1970, 7
8. See Rice, *The Supreme Court and Public Prayer* (1964), 29
9. Story, *Commentaries on the Constitution of the United States* (1891), Secs. 1874, 1876, 1877
10. Torcaso v. Watkins, 367 U.S. 488, (1961)
11. Torcaso v. Watkins, 367 U.S. 488, 495 (1961)
12. Abington School District v. Schempp, 374 U.S. 203 (1963)
13. Engle v. Vitale, 370 U.S. 421 (1962)
14. Abington School District v. Schempp, 374 U.S. 203 (1963)
15. 374 U.S. at 303, 304
16. Burton v. Wilmington Parking Authority, 365 U.S. 715 (1961); Simkins v. Cone Memorial Hospital, 323 F.2d 959 (4th Cir. 1963), certiorari denied, 376 U.S. 938 (1964)
17. Horace Mann League v. Board of Public Works, 220 A.2d 51, 61 (Md., 1966), certiorari denied, 385 U.S. 97 (1966)
18. Board of Education v. Allen, 392 U.S. 236, 243–45 (1968)
19. S.J. Res. 192 (91st Cong., 2d Sess.)
20. See Rice, "Where Are the Clergymen?" *National Review*, Aug. 23, 1969, 833
21. Everson v. Board of Education, 330 U.S. 1, 16 (1947)
22. Sherbert v. Verner, 374 U.S. 398, 414 (1963)
23. Ryan and Boland, *Catholic Principles of Politics* (1940), 316
24. Ryan and Boland, *Catholic Principles of Politics* (1940), 319
25. Ryan and Millar, *The State and the Church* (1922), 35
26. Love, John Courtney Murray: *Contemporary Church-State Theory* (1965), 97
27. See Rice, "We Hold No Truths?" *Triumph*, Sept. 1968, 11
28. Murray, The Problem of State Religion, *Theological Studies*, Vol. XII (1951), 156–57
29. Second Vatican Council, *Declaration on Religious Freedom*, No. 1
30. Second Vatican Council, *Declaration on Religious Freedom*, No. 2
31. Second Vatican Council, *Declaration on Religious Freedom*, No. 2
32. Second Vatican Council, *Declaration on Religious Freedom*, No. 6

33. Murray, *Religious Liberty: An End and a Beginning* (1966), 186
34. Second Vatican Council, *Declaration on Religious Freedom*, No. 13
35. Second Vatican Council, *Declaration on Religious Freedom*, No. 1
36. Murray, *We Hold These Truths* (1960), 66–67
37. See Love, *John Courtney Murray: Contemporary Church-State Theory* (1965), 75
38. Murray, *We Hold These Truths* (1960), X
39. New York *Times*, Feb. 25, 1970, p. 1, col. 6
40. *The Wall Street Journal*, Aug. 14, 1970, p. 6, col. 3
41. See Rice, "Freedom of Choice in Education," *The Wanderer*, April 9, 1970, p. 4, col. 1
42. Cong. Rec., Dec. 5, 1969, S.15845
43. *U.S. News & World Report*, May 4, 1970, 34
44. New York *Times*, Sept. 4, 1969, p. 48, col. 1
45. *U.S. News & World Report*, Sept. 29, 1969, p. 33
46. See *U.S. Catholic/Jubilee*, July 1970, 44
47. Canon 2350, Sec. 1; Bouscaren, Ellis, and Korth, *Canon Law: A Text and Commentary* (1965), 934
48. Bouscaren, Ellis, and Korth, *Canon Law: A Text and Commentary* (1965), 869–71; Della Rocca, *Manual of Canon Law* (1958), 526–35

XII. *Conclusion*

1. Pope Paul VI, *L'Osservatore Romano*, Dec. 22, 1968; *The Pope Speaks*, Vol. 13 (1969), 356, 359
2. *L'Osservatore Romano*, English language edition, May 22, 1969, p. 7, col. 2
3. Hughes, *A Popular History of the Catholic Church* (1953), 10
4. *L'Osservatore Romano*, April 26, 1970; *The Wanderer*, June 11, 1970, p. 10, col. 3
5. *The Wanderer*, Aug. 29, 1968, p. 1, col. 2
6. Second Vatican Council, *Dogmatic Constitution on the Church*, No. 1

APPENDIX

The Credo *of the People of God*

1. Cf. 1 Tim. 6, 20
2. Cf. Lk. 22, 32
3. Cf. *Dz.-Sch.* 3002
4. Cf. Ex. 3, 14
5. Cf. 1 Jn. 4, 8
6. Cf. 1 Tim. 6, 16
7. Cf. *Dz.-Sch.* 804
8. Cf. *Dz.-Sch.* 75
9. Cf. *Dz.-Sch.* 75
10. Cf. *Dz.-Sch.* 150
11. Cf. *Dz.-Sch.* 76
12. Cf. *Ibid.*
13. Cf. *Dz.-Sch.* 251–252
14. Cf. *Lumen Gentium* 53
15. Cf. *Dz.-Sch.* 2803
16. Cf. *Lumen Gentium* 53
17. Cf. *Lumen Gentium* 53, 58, 61
18. Cf. *Dz.-Sch.* 3903
19. Cf. *Lumen Gentium* 53, 56, 61, 63; cf. Paul VI, *Alloc. for the Closing of the Third Session of the Second Vatican Council:* AAS LVI [1964] 1016; cf. *Exhort. Apost. Signum Magnum,* Introd.
20. Cf. *Lumen Gentium* 62; cf. Paul VI, *Exhort. Apost. Signum Magnum,* p. 1, n. 1
21. Cf. *Dz.-Sch.* 1513
22. Cf. Rom. 5, 20
23. Cf. *Dz.-Sch.* 1514
24. Cf. *Lumen Gentium* 8 and 5
25. Cf. *Lumen Gentium* 7, 11
26. Cf. Sacrosanctum Concilium 5, 6; cf. *Lumen Gentium* 7, 12, 50
27. Cf. *Dz.-Sch.* 3011
28. Cf. *Dz.-Sch.* 3074
29. Cf. *Lumen Gentium* 25
30. Cf. *Lumen Gentium* 23; cf. *Orientalium Ecclesiarum* 2, 3, 5, 6
31. Cf. *Lumen Gentium* 8
32. Cf. *Lumen Gentium* 15
33. Cf. *Lumen Gentium* 14
34. Cf. *Lumen Gentium* 16
35. Cf. *Dz.-Sch.* 1651
36. Cf. *Dz.-Sch.* 1642, 1651–54; Paul VI, *Enc. Mysterium Fidei*
37. Cf. *S. Th.,* III, 73, 3
38. Cf. 1 Jn. 3, 2; *Dz.- Sch.* 1000
39. Cf. *Lumen Gentium* 49
40. Cf. Lk. 10, 9–10, Jn. 16, 24